What Global Economic Crisis?

Also by Philip Arestis

INTRODUCING MACROECONOMIC MODELLING: An Econometric Study of the United Kingdom

MONEY, PRICING DISTRIBUTION AND ECONOMIC INTEGRATION

Also by Michelle Baddeley

INVESTMENT: Theories and Analysis

Also by John McCombie

ECONOMIC GROWTH AND THE BALANCE-OF-PAYMENTS CONSTRAINT (*with A. P. Thirlwall*)

MEASURING ECONOMIC GROWTH: An Evaluation and Critique of the Aggregate Production Function (*with Jesus Felipe*)

What Global Economic Crisis?

Edited by

Philip Arestis
Professor of Economics
Levy Economics Institute
USA

Michelle Baddeley
Gonville and Caius College
Cambridge

and

John McCombie
Downing College
Cambridge

First published in hardcover 2001
First published in paperback 2004 by
PALGRAVE MACMILLAN
Houndmills, Basingstoke, Hampshire RG21 6XS and
175 Fifth Avenue, New York, N. Y. 10010
Companies and representatives throughout the world

PALGRAVE MACMILLAN is the global academic imprint of the Palgrave
Macmillan division of St. Martin's Press, LLC and of Palgrave Macmillan Ltd.
Macmillan® is a registered trademark in the United States, United Kingdom
and other countries. Palgrave is a registered trademark in the European
Union and other countries.

ISBN 0–333–80017–6 hardback
ISBN 1–4039–3496–7 paperback

This book is printed on paper suitable for recycling and made from fully
managed and sustained forest sources.

A catalogue record for this book is available from the British Library.

Library of Congress Cataloging-in-Publication Data
What global economic crisis? / edited by Philip Arestis, Michelle Baddeley
and John McCombie.
        p. cm.
    Papers of a conference held at Gonville and Caius College, Cambridge in
Sept. 1999.
    Includes bibliographical references and index.
        ISBN 1–4039–3496–7 (pbk.)
        1. Financial crises–Congresses. 2. International finance–Congresses.
3. Globalization–Congresses. I. Arestis, Philip, 1941– II. Baddeley, Michelle,
1965– III. McCombie, J. S. L., 1940–

HB3722.W49 2004
332'.042–dc22   2003067265

10   9   8   7   6   5   4   3   2   1
13 12 11 10 09 08 07 06 05 04

Printed and bound in Great Britain by
Antony Rowe Ltd, Chippenham and Eastbourne

Contents

List of Tables and Figures

Tables

Figures

Foreword

G. C. Harcourt

I am delighted to write the foreword to this volume, first, because the contributors have written on pressing, important issues which currently face us as economists, and, secondly, because the conference and the volume also celebrate the life (still going strong) and the work of John Cornwall. John has done so much during his 70 years and more to pinpoint how and why our economies malfunction and what may be done to offset this. He was always motivated, first, by the harm which malfunctioning does to those least able to defend themselves, and secondly, by a sustained attempt to offset cynicism, self-serving, and stupidity in policy-making and, it must be said, in the profession too.

The central focus of this volume is on financial crises, past and present, their causes and cures. But there are supporting themes as well. The contributors come to their task from the observations of historical economic episodes; they develop theoretical frameworks to take them in and to suggest new or altered institutions to cope with systemic ill-effects. The policies suggested are humane, practical and effective, given a not unreasonable modicum of political goodwill. In all this, John Cornwall's contributions, in the past and at the conference itself with Wendy, are fundamental.

List of Abbreviations

BCBS	Basle Committee on Banking Supervision
CIS	Community Innovation Survey
DRAM	Dynamic Random Access Memory
ECB	European Central Bank
EMT	efficient market theory
ERM	exchange rate mechanism
ESCB	European System of Central Banks
FDI	foreign direct investment
FTC	Federal Trade Commission
GATT	General Agreement on Tariffs and Trade
GDP	gross domestic product
HICP	Harmonized Index of Consumer Prices
IIF	Institute of International Finance
IMCU	International Money Clearing Unit
IMF	International Monetary Fund
LDC	less developed nations
LOLR	lender-of-last-resort
LPT	liquidity preference theory
MAI	Multilateral Agreement on Investment
MITI	Ministry of International Trade and Industry (Japan)
NICs	newly industrializing countries
OECD	Organization for Economic Cooperation and Development
R&D	research and development
SOEs	state-owned enterprises
TCDC	Technical Cooperation among Developing Countries
TNCs	transnational corporations
TRIMs	trade-related investment measures
TRIPs	trade-related aspects of intellectual property rights
UNCTAD	United Nations Conference on Trade and Development
UNDP	United Nations Development Programme
WTO	World Trade Organization

Notes on the Contributors

Philip Arestis is Director of Research at the Centre for Economic and Public Policy, Department of Land Economy, University of Cambridge, and is Professor of Economics at the Levy Economics Institute, New York. He has taught at a number of universities in the UK. He was a member of the *Economics and Econometrics* RAE panel in 1996, and on the panel for the RAE 2001 (*Economics and Econometrics*). He was also appointed as Quality Assessor for the quality assessment exercise in Economics of the *Scottish Higher Education Funding Council*, the *Welsh Funding Councils* and more recently of the *Higher Education Funding Council in England*. He has been a member of the *Council of the Royal Economic Society* (RES), and the Secretary of the RES Standing Conference of Heads of Department in Economics (CHUDE). His research interests are in the areas of Macroeconomics, Monetary Economics, Applied Econometrics, Political Economy and Applied Political Economy. He has published as sole author or editor, as well as co-author and co-editor, a number of books, ranging from *Introducing Macroeconomic Modelling: An Econometric Study of the United Kingdom* (Macmillan, 1982) to *Money, Pricing Distribution and Economic Integration* (Macmillan, 1997). He has contributed in the form of invited chapters to numerous books and produced research reports for research institutes. He has published widely in academic journals. He has been editor and joint editor, and has served on the editorial board, of a number of journals.

Michelle Baddeley is Deputy Director of the Centre for Economic and Public Policy, Department of Land Economy, University of Cambridge, and Fellow and Director of Studies in Economics at Gonville and Caius College, Cambridge. She graduated with a Bachelor of Arts (Psychology) and Bachelor of Economics from the University of Queensland and a PhD in Economics from Cambridge University. Her recent research has focused on the role of rationality and expectations in theories of investment; Keynes's analysis of rationality; patterns of convergence and persistence in OECD labour markets; methodological approaches in applied econometrics and the economic impacts of tourism. She has published in a number of journals, including *Applied Economics, European Urban and Regional Studies* and the *Journal of Regional Science*. Currently, she is writing a book entitled *Investment: Theories and Analysis* for Macmillan.

John Cornwall is McCulloch Emeritus Professor of Economics at Dalhousie University in Halifax, Canada. His publications include *Growth and Stability in a Mature Economy* (Martin Robertson, 1972), *Modern Capitalism: Its Growth and Transformation* (Martin Robertson, 1977), *The Conditions for Economic Recovery* (Martin Robertson, 1983), *Economic Recovery for Canada: A Policy Framework* (James Lorimer, 1984; with Wendy Maclean), *The Theory of Economic Breakdown* (Blackwell, 1990) and *Economic Breakdown and Recovery* (ME Sharpe, 1994). He is a Fellow of the Royal Society of Canada.

Wendy Cornwall is Professor of Economics at Mount Saint Vincent University, Halifax, Canada and Adjunct Professor at Dalhousie University, Halifax, Canada. Before this, she held an appointment in the Economics Department at Dalhousie. Her publications include *An Economic Recovery for Canada: A Policy Framework* (with John Cornwall; 1984) and *A Model of the Canadian Financial Flow Matrix* (with J. A. Bronx; 1989). She has published a variety of articles on the flow of funds, applied econometrics and economic growth, both in scholarly journals and in books. She is currently writing a book with John Cornwall for Cambridge University Press, entitled *Modelling Capitalist Development*.

Paul Davidson occupies the Holly Chair of Excellence in Political Economy at the University of Tennessee and is the Editor of the *Journal of Post Keynesian Economics*. He has written, co-authored, or edited 18 books including *Post Keynesian Macroeconomic Theory* and *Money and the Real World*. He has published 225 professional journal articles, book chapters, etc.

Rahul Dhumale graduated with honours from Duke University and then earned his MSc in Economics from Oxford University and his PhD from Cambridge University. He has worked as a consultant for the World Bank, the ILO and the IMF. He is presently a Fellow on the Faculty of the Judge Institute at Cambridge University.

John Grieve Smith is a Fellow of Robinson College, Cambridge. After reading economics at Cambridge, he joined the Economic Section of the Cabinet Secretariat (later to move to the Treasury). He served as economic adviser in the British Embassy in Washington and then worked in the Atomic Energy Authority and the Iron and Steel Board, where he was head of the Economics Department. After three years as an under-secretary in the Department of Economic Affairs, he returned to the steel industry and was Director of Planning in British Steel until 1980 when he became an Industrial Management Teaching Fellow at the City University Business School. Since 1982 he has been a Fellow of Robinson College. He is the author of *Full Employment: A Pledge Betrayed* (Macmillan, 1997) and co-editor with Jonathan Michie of *Managing the Global Economy* (Oxford, 1995) and *Global Instability* (Routledge, 1999).

Geoff Harcourt is Emeritus Reader in the History of Economic Thought at the University of Cambridge (1998), Emeritus Fellow of Jesus College, Cambridge (1998) and Professor Emeritus at the University of Adelaide. Harcourt was born in 1931 in Melbourne, Australia and educated at the Universities of Adelaide and Cambridge. He has taught mainly at the Universities of Adelaide and Cambridge. He has published 160 papers in learned journals and/or chapters of books and has authored or co-authored, edited or co-edited 18 books, including *Some Cambridge Controversies in the Theory of Capital* (1972), five volumes of selected essays, and *A 'Second Edition' of the General Theory*, 2 vols (edited with P. A. Riach; 1997). He was made an officer in the General Division of the Order of Australia (A. O.) in 1994 'for services to economic theory and to the history of economic thought' and, in 1996, Distinguished Fellow of the Economic Society of Australia. He is married with four children and two grandchildren.

John McCombie is Director of the Centre for Economic and Public Policy, Department of Land and Economy, University of Cambridge and Fellow in Economics at Downing College, Cambridge. He has previously held positions at the University of Hull and the University of Melbourne. His research interests include the study of the growth disparities between the advanced countries, economic growth and the balance-of-payments constraint, Kaldorian growth models, the economics of Keynes, criticisms of the aggregate production function and economic methodology. He has published in such journals as the *Economic Journal*, *Journal of Post Keynesian Economics*, *Oxford Economic Papers*, the *Manchester School*, and *Urban Studies* and has contributed chapters to a number of books. He is the author (with A. P. Thirlwall) of *Economic Growth and the Balance-of-Payments Constraint*. He is currently writing a book (with Jesus Felipe) entitled *Measuring Economic Growth: An Evaluation and Critique of the Aggregate Production Function*.

Paul Ormerod is the author of the *Death of Economics* (1994) and *Butterfly Economics* (1998). The former has been translated into ten languages, and the latter is due to appear in seven already. He studied economics at Cambridge 1968–71 and took the MPhil in economics at Oxford in 1971–73. He was an economic modeller and forecaster at the National Institute of Economic and Social Research, and from 1982–92 director of economics at the Henley Centre for Forecasting. He is currently a director of Volterra Consulting Ltd. His most recent academic publication is in *Physica A* and is 'Random Matrix Theory and the Failure of Macroeconomic Forecasting'.

Gabriel Palma is currently Lecturer in the Faculty of Economics and Politics, Cambridge University. He has doctorates in both Economics (Oxford) and Politics (Sussex). His main area of research interest (and publication) is the study of the economies of Latin American and East Asian countries and their integration within the World Economy. This entails the study of these economies from the point of view of their economic history, macroeconomics, international trade and international finance. He has also published in the area of history of ideas in Development Economics and Politics, in particular the Latin American Structuralist and Dependency School's contribution to the analysis of development.

Pascal Petit is a CNRS (National Center for Scientific Reseach) Director of Research, working at CEPREMAP in Paris, a research institute affiliated with the French Commissariat du Plan. His research focuses on the issues of structural change, productivity, growth and employment in the OECD countries. He has published books and articles on the nature and consequences of the contemporary technical change (largely centred around the information and communication technologies) and on the role of services in the dynamics of internationalization and economic growth. These include *Slow Growth and the Service Economy* (1986), *The Economics of Industrial Modernization* (with Cristiano Antonelli and Gabriel Tahar, 1992), *L'économie de l'information* (1998) (as editor) and *Technology and the Future of European Employment* (with Luc Soete, 2000).

Malcolm Sawyer is Professor of Economics, University of Leeds and Head of Economics Division: he was formerly Professor of Economics at the University of York. He is managing editor of *International Review of Applied Economics* and managing co-editor of *International Papers in Political Economy*. He is the editor of the series *New Directions in Modern Economics* published by Edward Elgar, and elected member of the Council of the Royal Economic Society. He is the author of nine books, the most recent is *Unemployment, Imperfect Competition and Macroeconomics: Essays in the Post Keynesian Tradition* (Edward Elgar) and he has edited 11 books the most recent is *The Legacy of Michal Kalecki* vols. 1 and 2 (Edward Elgar). He has published nearly 100 articles and chapters, and the most recent include (both with P. Arestis), 'How many cheers for the Tobin financial transactions tax?', *Cambridge Journal of Economics*, vol. 21(6), pp. 753–68 and 'Keynesian policies for the new millennium', *Economic Journal*, vol. 108, pp. 181–95.

Mark Setterfield is Associate Professor of Economics at Trinity College, Hartford, Connecticut, USA. His principle research interests are macro-dynamics and in particular, path dependency in macroeconomics. He is the author of *Rapid Growth and Relative Decline: Modelling Macroeconomic Dynamics with Hysteresis* (Macmillan, 1997), editor of *Growth, Employment and Inflation: Essays in Honour of John Cornwall* (Macmillan, 1999), and has published in such journals as *The Manchester School, Cambridge Journal of Economics, Journal of Post Keynesian Economics* and *European Economic Review*.

Ajit Singh, an Indian economist who graduated from Punjab University and obtained his PhD at the University of California, Berkeley, has been teaching economics at Cambridge University since 1965. He is currently Professor of Economics at the University and Senior Fellow at Queens' College Cambridge. Between 1970 and 1994 he was Director of Studies in Economics at Queens'. He also held, between 1987 and 1994, the Dr. William M. Scholl Visiting Chair in the Department of Economics at the University of Notre Dame in the US. He has been a senior economic adviser to the governments of Mexico and Tanzania and a consultant to various UN developmental organizations, including the World Bank, the ILO, UNCTAD and UNIDO. He is the author of *Takeovers: Their Relevance to the Stockmarket and the Theory of the Firm* and co-author of *Growth, Profitability and Valuation*, both published by Cambridge University Press. He has also published extensively in academic economic journals. His most recent books are the edited volume (with A. Dutt and K. Kim), *The State, Markets and Development* (Edward Elgar, 1994), and the monographs, *Corporate Financial Patterns in Industrialising Countries*, Technical Paper No. 2, World Bank/IFC, Washington, DC, 1995 and (with G. Whittington and V. Saporta), *The Effects of Hyper-Inflation on Accounting Ratios: Financing Corporate Growth in Industrialising Economies*, Technical Paper No. 3, World Bank/IFC, 1997. His essay, 'How do developing country corporations finance their growth?' was awarded a

US$5000 prize and Bronze medal in the Amex Awards Competition, 1994. His new book (co-edited with Candace Howes), *Competitiveness Matters: US Industry, Industrial Policy and Economic Performance* is shortly to be published by University of Michigan Press (Ann Arbor).

M. G. Quibria is Assistant Chief Economist (research) at the Economics and Development Resource Center of the Asian Development Bank in Manila, Philippines. He holds MA and PhD degrees in Economics from Princeton University. Before he joined the Asian Development Bank, he held teaching/research positions at the University of Dhaka; Nuffield College, Oxford; and Boston University. He is the author of numerous books and articles in professional economic journals in the areas of economic development and international trade.

Joy A. Quitazol is currently a macroeconomics consultant at the Economics and Development Resource Center of the Asian Development Bank. She holds an MA in economics and is presently a PhD candidate at the School of Economics, University of the Philippines. Her fields of interests include public finance, economic and financial analysis, project monitoring and evaluation, health policy development issues, competitive business environment profiles, and studies on industry trends and outlook.

1
Introduction: What Global Economic Crisis?

Philip Arestis, Michelle Baddeley and John McCombie

The papers in this book were presented at a conference on Global Financial Crisis, held in Gonville and Caius College, Cambridge, UK, in early September 1999. The idea for the conference (and accompanying book) evolved during the Fifth Post Keynesian Workshop, held in Knoxville, Tennessee, in June 1998. At this workshop a number of us discussed our concern that economics has a reputation for being an excessively esoteric discipline; the opportunities to bridge the gap between economic theorizing and real-world policy-making are becoming increasingly limited. In addition, the increasing factionalism within economics is perhaps stifling important debates on issues of great concern to anyone interested in economic, social and political welfare. Thus, the aims of our conference were to make an important and lasting contribution to the policy debates, without adhering to any one dogmatic tradition. A further and no less important reason for the conference was to present to John Cornwall with his Festschrift.

In selecting a theme for our conference, we wanted to address an issue of great importance to policy-makers and also to enable academic economists to make a meaningful contribution (as well as promoting cooperation amongst academic economists). Examining the global implications of economic crises was an obvious choice. With unprecedented trends towards globalization (in part propelled by rapid developments in information technology), the global repercussions of economic crises are more profound than ever before, particularly for developing countries. Furthering our understanding of the destabilizing effects of financial crises on economic growth, stability and development, and designing institutions to foster effective policy coordination will be of tremendous importance as the pace of globalization accelerates in the twenty-first century.

The volume begins with a theoretical piece by Paul Davidson. This piece can be thought of as setting the theoretical scene for the rest of the book. In *If Markets are Efficient, Why Have There Been so Many International Financial Market Crises since the 1970s?*, Paul Davidson extends Keynes's principle of effective demand to an open economy setting. He develops Keynes's incompatibility thesis (that flexible exchange rates and free international capital mobility are incompatible with full employment and economic growth). He argues that changes in exchange rates reflect speculative positions not changes in trade patterns; thus flexible exchange rates contribute to volatility. Exchange rate fluctuations affect the trade balance, the interest rate and the rate of domestic investment and thus the level of aggregate demand. The resultant uncertainty undermines entrepreneurial confidence, depresses the inducement to invest in projects with irreversible sunk costs (particularly given the prospect of being lumbered with irreversible costly idle capacity). In this way, exchange rate uncertainty depresses global investment, output and employment.

Davidson describes how, on the basis of the efficient markets hypothesis, mainstream neoclassical economists alleged that Keynes's incompatibility thesis was wrong. The resultant orthodox policy prescriptions focus around promoting financial liberalization to ensure an optimal allocation of resources and mainstream economists argue that short-term financial crises are a necessary disciplinary device. Davidson also looks at the historical record. After the Golden Age, financial liberalization was accompanied not only by increasingly fragile global financial markets but also by a series of liquidity crises. In contrast, in periods such as the time of the gold standard, the absence of alternative currencies reduced the speculative element in short-term financial flows. Transparency and discipline alone do not overcome financial market instability but appropriate solutions are elusive. A Tobin tax probably would not solve these problems: the empirical evidence suggests that financial transactions costs increase rather than moderate market volatility. This evidence highlights the need both for central control of exchange rates and for international agreements to place more responsibility for resolving international payments imbalances on the creditor nations.

In contrast to the orthodox view, Keynes's liquidity preference theory suggests that there is no such thing as an efficient equilibrium price; efficient markets are not liquid, liquid markets are not efficient. Vigilant regulation is needed. So Davidson advocates a package of policy prescriptions centred about a profound overhaul of the entire international payments system. Specifically, Davidson suggests the implementation of an international clearing union based around reserve assets, convertibility, fixed exchange rates, overdraft facilities and a trigger mechanism to encourage creditor nations to spend 'excessive' credit balances from current account surpluses.

Fixed exchange rates should be instituted to adapt only in response to permanent increases in efficiency wages with current account surpluses transferred to countries with full employment but current account deficits. Chapter 3 deals with issues raised in Paul Davidson's theoretical contribution. In *Reforming the International Financial Architecture*, M.G. Quibria and Joy Quitazol examine some of the fundamental dilemmas in devising an effective international financial architecture. The inflexibility of the Bretton Woods financial architecture in the face of increasing economic integration and increasing capital mobility was highlighted during the Mexican and Asian financial crises. In response, a myriad of policy proposals has evolved. However, as Quibria and Quitazol observe, the different goals pursued by the policy-designers are incompatible. They argue that 'policy-makers want the benefit of financial market integration; they want exchange rate stability; and they want monetary independence. But unfortunately, they cannot have them all simultaneously' (this volume, p. 37). Quibria and Quitazol proceed to critically assess a number of policy proposals for reform of the international financial architecture and conclude that whilst the ideas are often interesting and innovative they are also often impractical and inconsistent. This necessarily implies that international consensus on effective policy design is likely to be elusive. In response, Quibria and Quitazol advocate a package of proposals based around the fundamental goal of promoting decentralization in crisis management policy. Along with decentralization they suggest a number of simple policy innovations, including the introduction of minimum international standards of financial practice and prudent regulation of capital accounts, the reform of exchange rate regimes, the creation of an orderly debt restructuring framework and the encouragement of private sector credit lines.

John Grieve Smith continues with a similar theme in *An Agenda for a New Bretton Woods*. This chapter highlights the importance of instigating a fundamental review of the 1944 Bretton Woods arrangements in order to tackle financial failures and their consequences. Focusing on the 1997 East Asian crisis, this paper identifies key factors contributing to the instability: there were important weaknesses in domestic financial systems; liberalization reforms encouraged short-term flows of capital

4 What Global Economic Crisis?

and the affected countries suffered a loss of competitive position because their currencies were pegged to the US dollar. A major factor in the East Asian crisis was the herd behaviour of investors: investors focused on choosing the investments and loans most likely to be chosen by other investors and lenders. The resultant instability of capital movements was crucial in the genesis of the East Asian Crisis.

Grieve Smith argues that the inherent instability of global financial markets poses a continuing threat. The problem can only be tackled by re-examining the rules and principles affecting capital flows in order to consider what actions should be taken to encourage and stabilize (particularly long-term) capital flows to and from developing countries. Greater exchange rate stability could be encouraged via a two-tiered system of managed exchange rates: one tier would address regional arrangements *vis-à-vis* core currencies (US dollar, yen and euro) and the second tier would pertain to global exchange rates between these core currencies. Prudential regulation should address issues such as improving information and tightening backing arrangements. Furthermore, fundamental changes to crisis management arrangements are essential if unwarranted deflationary policy prescriptions are to be avoided. Grieve Smith concludes that if governments cooperate more effectively in strengthening international institutions, world trade and investment will be facilitated.

Philip Arestis and Malcolm Sawyer turn their attention to a more regional issue, and ask the question *Will the Euro Bring Economic Crisis to Europe*? The initial introduction of the euro has, against many expectations, been accompanied by a decline in its value (notably *vis-à-vis* the dollar and sterling). It has also been introduced at a time of high levels of unemployment within most of the European Union (EU). The chapter argues that these are serious problems, which are compounded by a number of other difficulties. Most important of these are the policy and institutional arrangements within which the euro is embedded. It is suggested that the economies of the EMU are likely to suffer from the introduction of the euro.

The difficulties just referred to will take a number of forms, but they focus on two rather different aspects that could qualify for the term crisis. First, the euro has been launched with high levels of unemployment (of the order of 10 per cent of the workforce) and with particularly severe disparities in unemployment experience and in standards of living. At the end of 1998, the rate of unemployment was over 20 per cent in Spain, and in double figures in Finland, France, Germany, Ireland and Italy. These high levels of unemployment are likely to continue in the foreseeable future, and the policy arrangements that surround the operation of the euro, notably the objectives of the European Central Bank (ECB) and the workings of the *Stability and Growth Pact*, will have a deflationary bias. These levels of and disparities in unemployment could be termed a crisis. Second, the introduction of the euro and the associated institutional setting could well serve to exacerbate tendencies towards financial crises, including the volatility and subsequent collapse of asset prices and runs on the banking system. There may be some additional forces of instability arising from the relationship between the dollar and the euro as two major global currencies and the current trade imbalances. Further, the operating arrangements of the European System of Central Banks (ESCB) can be seen as inadequate to cope with such financial crises. Three crucial areas of problems are identified. The first emanates from asymmetric shocks; the second from different channels of influence of monetary policy; the third problem arises from the differences in interest rate elasticities of the demand for money in the eleven EMU countries. Yet another area of difficulty arises from the enormous liquidity in the EMU area that may very well spring from the 'dollar overhang' and the removal of all financial controls in the area.

John and Wendy Cornwall turn to another aspect of the problem in hand and analyse the issues of power and conflict in the chapter entitled *Globalization, the Distribution of Power, and Full Employment*. They focus on the contributions of Keynes (1936) and Kalecki (1971) in informing our understanding of the impact of power on the economy. Kalecki argued that full employment capitalism and full political democracy were incompatible in the long run. Keynes argued that prolonged unemployment was a source of power struggles that would contribute to the destruction of capitalism and democracy. Furthermore, Keynes asserted that unemployment is destabilizing whilst Kalecki asserted that it would be consciously used by capitalists to stabilize the system. This paper argues that, by clarifying the determinants and role of power in capitalism, Kalecki and Keynes uncovered features of capitalism that can inform our understanding of the more recent performance of developed capitalist economies.

From examining economic performance during the Golden Age, it seems that Keynes's analysis of the role of full employment in ensuring political stability was apposite. However, for the period following the Golden Age, Kalecki's analysis of the political business cycle seemed to describe the sequence of events more fully: increasing unemployment resulted from increased labour militancy. However, Kalecki's analysis was a short-term one and does not seem to describe the long-term sequence of events in the aftermath of the Second World War. Also, whilst Kalecki focused on capital as the dominant power during all phases of the political cycle, it appears that during the Golden Age a relatively equal distribution of power between capital and labour emerged from processes of consultation, compromise and cooperation. The Cornwalls argue that the lessons for today's experience focus on the noticeable imbalance of power in favour of capital in today's economic environment. Globalization and loose labour market conditions have encouraged labour market flexibility and thus capital and government have condoned current labour market conditions. This power imbalance is likely to be sustained and current high levels of unemployment are likely to persist.

Ajit Singh and Rahul Dhumale's chapter on *Competition Policy, Development, and Developing Countries* addresses the emphasis placed by policy-makers in major developed countries on devising some international agreements and rules on competition policy. Whilst UNCTAD's early objectives focused on developing an international framework to regulate and control the actions of large corporations in order to promote development in the South, today concern focuses on promoting the goals of major corporations from the North. Thus the advanced industrial countries advocate 'level playing fields' in order to allow their corporations easy access to developing countries' markets. However, the firms in developing countries lack the advantages of the corporations from developed countries and an increasing degree of market concentration has developed, favouring the large corporations from developed countries. Singh and Dhumale's chapter sheds some light on the inadequacies of the competition policy approaches adopted in the North and reflected in the WTO's approach. Following an in-depth analysis of competition policy, Singh and Dhumale arrive at an alternative set of policy implications to those proposed by the WTO. They suggest the introduction of national competition policies designed to promote sustained economic growth but in ways that are appropriate to a given country's level of development. Competition policies appropriate to developed countries are likely to be inappropriate in developing countries.

More specifically, Singh and Dhumale argue that, in the analysis of competition policies, emphasis should be placed on dynamic rather than static efficiency considerations. Furthermore, an 'optimal' (rather than maximum) degree of competition and an optimal combination of competition and cooperation should be promoted. Governments and business should cooperate in the coordination of investment decisions. Healthy competition should be recognized as an appropriate criterion for assessing eligibility for state support; similarly, the need for coordination of industrial and competition policies should be recognized. Finally, in response to current surges in mergers and take-overs, Singh and Dhumale recommend the establishment of an international competition authority, which would prevent the restrictive practices of the large and growing multinational corporations.

In *A Brazilian-Style 'Ponzi'* Gabriel Palma shows that the 1999 Brazilian financial crises had many unique features compared with those of, for example, Mexico (1994) and the East Asian economies (1997). Brazil shared many characteristics with the other crisis-affected countries, in particular a rapid move towards deregulation of its international capital markets. However, the traditional explanations of the causes of crises, namely moral hazard and cronyism, seem to be relatively less important in Brazil. A key factor instrumental in precipitating the Brazilian crisis was the high interest rates that the government had, ironically, adopted earlier to defend the economy from external shocks and to avoid the worse excesses that had occurred with other countries' financial liberalization. The high interest rates were successful in checking a potentially massive private credit expansion. However, a consequence was the rapid increase in Brazil's public debt as a share of GDP. A 'catch-22' situation developed. The high interest rates led to foreign borrowing and these required a high interest rate policy to be maintained in order to defend the banking systems' foreign exchange exposures. But this placed the banks' domestic exposures in a precarious position and these required a fall in interest rates. The Brazilian government opted for the first course 'at the cost of bankruptcies on banks' domestic assets exposures – and they opted to foot the bill', as Palma puts it. This led to a blow-out in public debt and 'ponzi' finance took over, leading to the almost inevitable financial crisis.

Pascal Petit examines the role of internationalization in propelling growth. In *Technology and Growth: Between Regionalization and Globalization*, Petit examines the progress of internationalization since the Golden Age. He argues that intangible transactions have enlarged the scope of economic agents. There has been a re-shuffling of the forms of competition and in the process countries have devised new rules and institutions to preside over internationalization. These rules and institutions can be subdivided into three groups relating to the governance of trade flows, technology transfer and access to inter-

national finance. Petit advocates systems for information and knowledge management in order to develop the positive externalities that
promote growth. Petit notes that, where monitoring might be effective,
regional policies may be appropriate but he concludes that structural
regional policies can only have macroeconomic effects if there is some
international agreement about the welfare objectives of these policies.

Paul Ormerod, in the chapter entitled *The Keynesian Micro-
Foundations of the Business Cycle: Some Implications of Globalization*, provides an alternative business cycle model to that presented within Real
Business Cycle theory. Real business cycle models have been widely
criticized for their failure qualitatively to capture cyclical movements
in real-world economic data. Thus Paul Omerod presents a model of
endogenously determined business cycles that embeds Keynes's key
insights about the role of business sentiment in determining the short-
term output growth of heterogeneous, interacting firms. Heterogeneity
is incorporated into the model by allowing firms to be of different size.
Simulations of this model show that it offers a superior empirical
account of US business cycles to that presented within real business
cycle models. In addition, the model implies that, if globalization produces an increase in concentration ratios, the variability of output over
the cycle will increase accordingly.

In the penultimate chapter, entitled *An Historical Perspective on
Speculative Bubbles and Financial Crises: Tulipmania and the South Sea
Bubble*, Michelle Baddeley and John McCombie examine speculative
bubbles. Speculative bubbles play a key role in exacerbating financial
fragility and precipitating financial crises and therefore it is important to
understand the processes that generate speculative bubbles. Michelle
Baddeley and John McCombie begin by reviewing the different
theoretical methodologies used to analyse speculative bubbles. These
analyses are crucially dependent upon assumptions about rationality and
uncertainty. Whilst, theoretically at least, the existence of 'rational'
speculative bubbles is not necessarily inconsistent with the Rational
Expectations (RE) and Efficient Markets hypotheses, speculative bubbles
are probably more meaningfully understood in terms of contagion
effects, herd behaviour and irrational forces.

Michelle Baddeley and John McCombie then examine two historical
examples in order to assess the role of irrational versus rational forces
in propelling speculative bubbles and financial crises. The two cases
chosen are Tulipmania (the seventeenth-century episode when the
price of tulip bulbs rose spectacularly in Holland over a matter of
weeks, only to be followed by an even more spectacular fall); and the

South Sea Bubble that occurred in England in the early eighteenth century. Whilst some analysts, such as Garber, argued that these asset price rises merely reflected changing fundamental values, the evidence seems clear that in neither of these cases can the rapid increases in prices (and the even more sudden price collapses) be represented by changes in fundamentals.

Nonetheless, once it is acknowledged that speculative bubbles in asset prices do represent deviations from fundamental values, the alternative theoretical explanations for speculative bubbles cannot easily be separated using empirical evidence. A number of theoretical approaches can be adopted which will explain the existence of speculative bubbles. However, the approaches differ in the assumptions made about the information set available to a given individual; the degree of belief associated with this information; and the way expectations are formed. The RE approach circumvents these considerations by postulating that investors' information sets are founded on some objective basis and prices will change only in response to news. In practice, bubbles do not collapse because of news but for other less well-defined reasons arising from changes in expectations of the investors themselves. Furthermore, as emphasized in Keynesian analyses, rules of thumb can be optimal decision-making tools under conditions of endemic uncertainty. In these situations the crash may well be determined by intangible factors such as an unpredictable change of sentiment by even a small number of investors. In other words, the decision to hold on to any asset is dictated by a whole host of subjective factors and is likely to very volatile. Michelle Baddeley and John McCombie conclude therefore that it is important to take into account the behaviour of the market in the formation of an individual's expectations because only along these lines can a more complete understanding of speculative bubbles and crashes be found.

This volume concludes with Mark Setterfield's *John Cornwall: A Brief Appreciation*, in recognition of John Cornwall's tremendous contributions to the debates on globalization, development and unemployment. Mark Setterfield emphasizes that, although the object of John Cornwall's inquiry has changed over time, a coherent vision of capitalist macrodynamics emerges throughout his work, in his focus on two grand themes, namely, that demand matters and that institutions matter. These themes emerge in John Cornwall's work on the operation of Say's Law in reverse; the role of institutions in ameliorating conflict and uncertainty; path dependency; and evolutionary Keynesianism.

In his work on 'Say's Law in Reverse', Cornwall emphasizes aggregate demand as the leading element in the determination of the level of economic activity, both in the short run and the long run. Aggregate demand influences the utilization of productive resources at all points in time. In this way, Cornwall reacted against the 1960s doctrine that focused on Harrod's natural rate of growth as being independent of the actual rate of growth. Cornwall argues that the supply-determined nature of long-run growth cannot be taken for granted.

Mark Setterfield then turns to Cornwall's work on the roles of conflict, uncertainty and institutions in determining macroeconomic outcomes. The insight that the price mechanism fails to create a system that is self-regulating about a structurally stable, supply-determined level of economic activity (or growth path) is central to Cornwall's macrodynamic vision. The price mechanism cannot effectively equilibrate the economy because it cannot coordinate expectations in the presence of endemic uncertainty. Animal spirits exert a more crucial influence on behaviour and they involve far more than mere computation and calculation based on price signals. Furthermore, the price mechanism cannot coordinate incompatible aims and interests and hence there is always potential for endemic and pervasive socio-economic conflict in capitalist systems. For this reason, institutions are of crucial importance in structuring economic activity: they provide a basis for action in an uncertain world; they are a source of information regarding the likely future behaviour of others and they regularize relations between parties whose interests are mutually exclusive. In this way, relatively enduring institutions can ameliorate uncertainty and conflict.

Mark Setterfield focuses on a further theme in Cornwall's work: his emphasis on the role of non-equilibrating change arising from path-dependent macrodynamics. Cornwall argues that institutions influence aggregate demand – especially through their impact on the viability of reflationary macroeconomic policies. Similarly, demand influences institutions. In other words, a two-way interaction exists between aggregate demand and institutions. This joint interaction is not mechanically self-equilibrating. Thus Cornwall describes an economy that is continually unfolding, determined by path-dependent processes rather than tending towards a terminal state of rest. When applied to the study of the long run, this 'evolutionary Keynesian' framework describes processes of negative feedback: demand and institutional regimes conducive to successful macroeconomic performance are shown to give way to regimes conducive to inferior performance, and vice versa. Capitalism is, or at least has been to date, subject to fluctuating periods of good and bad macroeconomic performance, and each of these episodes is closely related to the structure and performance of preceding and successive episodes. Finally, Mark Setterfield focuses on the development and application of Cornwall's ideas about evolutionary Keynesianism. Cornwall's macrodynamic vision raises a number of issues that will continue to inspire and challenge economists for some time to come, particularly in explaining the apparently superior economic performance of the USA relative to other OECD countries. Mark Setterfield also highlights three of John Cornwall's defining qualities as an economist: his important and lasting contributions to economics, spanning theory, application and methodology; his preparedness to take economics seriously and to 'to do some good'; and his untiring efforts as an advisor and inspiration to his students.

As a final word, we would very much like to thank all the conference participants and contributors, as well as Meghnad Desai who was kind enough to entertain us as the after-dinner speaker. We are very grateful to Meghnad who came along to Cambridge after a long flight from another engagement abroad. We also wish to express our gratitude to Palgrave, and to Tim Farmiloe in particular, for commissioning the book just before his retirement (and this is a good place to wish him well for the future). We would also like to thank Mark Roberts for the help he gave us looking after the delegates during the days of the conference. We would like to thank Gonville and Caius College, Cambridge, for hosting the conference. In particular, we would like to thank Ed Davey, Wendy Evans, George Jones, Douglas Sharpe, Tony Smith and all their staff for their contributions to the smooth running of the conference and in providing comfortable accommodation and good food. Finally, we would like to thank the British Academy, without whose generous financial support the conference would not have been possible.

2
If Markets are Efficient, Why Have There Been So Many International Financial Market Crises Since the 1970s?

Paul Davidson

Introduction

Until 1973 the post-war international payments system was, in large measure, shaped by Keynes's thesis that flexible exchange rates and free international capital mobility are incompatible with global full employment and rapid economic growth in an era of multilateral free trade (Felix, 1997–8). This resulted in a stable international monetary system that permitted the global economy to experience unparalleled economic growth and prosperity despite widespread capital controls and international financial market regulations. Since 1973, the financial system has grown progressively more fragile with recurrent and increasingly stressful international debt and currency liquidity crises threatening the stability of the global economy.

Why the Change Since 1973?

Keynes's incompatibility thesis can be directly derived from his book *The General Theory of Employment Interest and Money* – an analysis of a money-using, market-oriented, entrepreneurial economy, where liquidity played an essential role in determining real spending decisions. Unfortunately, despite the adoption of many Keynesian policies in the years after the war, Keynes's analytical system was never incorporated into orthodox economic theory. Accordingly, by the 1960s, mainstream classical economists were developing closed and open economy models based on three classical axioms that Keynes had suggested were too restrictive for a general theory of employment.[1] By invoking these restrictive classical axioms, a special case model was resurrected whose 'characteristics happen not to be the economic society in which we live with the result that its teaching is misleading and disastrous if we attempt to apply it to the facts of experience' (Keynes, 1936, p. 3). This *special case* classical (supply-side) model demonstrated that Keynes's incompatibility thesis was wrong because markets are efficient.

Optimum global economic growth, therefore, requires a *laissez-faire* approach to market activities with flexible exchange rates, free trade and free international capital mobility. This special case claims that any regulation to limit financial flows (whether of cross-border capital flows or within a nation) imposes huge costs on society. Free the banking system and all financial markets from onerous government oversight and regulation and, policy-makers were assured, a world of heavenly economic bliss would envelop the planet.[2]

Neoclassical Synthesis (or Old) Keynesians had already adopted micro-foundations developed by Samuelson (1947) that invoked the three classical axioms rejected by Keynes (Davidson, 1984). Joan Robinson dubbed the progeny of this unfortunate marriage of classical axioms with Keynesian macroeconomic jargon and policy 'Bastard Keynesianism'. The logical inconsistency between their micro-foundations and their macroeconomics made these Bastard Keynesians easy prey for the classical counter-revolution. Nevertheless, this successful academic resurrection of the classical system would not have been sufficient to alter the policy mix if it were not for events of the 1970s.

The 1973 oil price shock created huge international payments imbalances and unleashed inflationary forces in oil-consuming nations. The resulting economic dislocation placed policy-makers in a difficult position. Without having to admit that they did not know what to do, policy-makers threw away the institutions that had accommodated Keynes's incompatibility thesis and used the 1960s classical model to rationalize their behaviour. Then if anything went wrong, policy-makers could suggest that they could not be blamed because, after all, the efficient marketplace 'knows' best, as Nobel prize winners Friedman,[3] Lucas, Merton and Scholes continually assured us.

The exchange rate itself became an object of speculation. Since the mid-1970s, international financial transactions have grown substantially faster than the growth in international trade (Felix, 1997–8). International financial flows dominate trade payments. Currently banks transact over US$1.5 trillion daily in foreign exchange markets, almost 70 times the volume of daily international trade in goods and services. Exchange rate movements reflect changes in speculative positions rather than changes in trade patterns.

Since the 1970s, Tobin (1974) has been almost the only voice with significant visibility in the economics profession warning that free international financial markets with flexible exchange rates can be extremely volatile and can therefore have a 'devastating impact on specific industries and whole economies' (Eichengreen, Tobin and Wyplosz, 1995). Exchange rate movements affect the international competitive position of domestic *vis-à-vis* foreign industries and therefore tend to depress the inducement to invest in large projects with irreversible sunk costs. Volatile exchange rates undermine entrepreneurs' confidence in their ability to appraise the potential profitability of any large investment project. Every exchange rate increase not only threatens domestic industries with significant loss of export-market share but also home-market share loss, as imports become less expensive. Managers realize that any upward blip in the exchange rate during the lifetime of any contemplated investment project can saddle their enterprises with irreversible costly idle capacity. Downward blips can reduce expected real profits. Consequently the marginal efficiency of investment is reduced (Pindyck, 1991, p. 1139). The greater the uncertainty regarding future exchange rates, the less investment globally – just as Keynes's (1936, Chapter 17) analysis of liquidity preference and investment predicted.

Since 1973, trade and real investment spending in open economies have become the tail wagged by the international speculative exchange rate dog. Consequently, the annual growth rate in investment in plant and equipment in OECD nations fell from 6 per cent (before 1973) to less than 3 per cent (since 1973). Less investment growth means a slower economic growth rate in OECD nations (from 5.9 to 2.8 per cent) while labour productivity growth declined even more dramatically (from 4.6 to 1.6 per cent).

Alternative Theories of Financial Markets

Are capital and exchange rate markets *inherently* destabilizing and fragile or is today's financial today's financial fragility the result of market 'liberalization' policy decisions taken since 1973? In these days of Asian contagion, Russian bears, and reeling Brazilian reals, we are being haunted by Minsky's frightening financial fragility question 'Can it happen again?'.

Peter L. Bernstein is the author of the best-selling book *Against The Gods* (1996), a treatise on risk management, probability theory and financial markets. Bernstein noted that since World War II 'the number of stock markets around the world has grown from 50 to just over 125 – even the Chinese, nominally still socialists have seen fit to establish stock markets on their territory'. Accordingly, we might first ask, if financial markets are, as Minsky suggests, so fragile and destabilizing, why are so many emerging economies using them?

How we respond to these queries depends on the underlying economic theory that is explicitly, or implicitly, used to explain the role of financial markets in an entrepreneurial economy. There are two major alternative – and incompatible – theories of financial markets: (i) the classical efficient market theory (EMT) and (ii) Keynes's liquidity preference theory (LPT). Proponents of EMT urge liberalization of financial markets, while those favouring LPT suggest the need for vigilant regulation with institutions and rules constraining and affecting the behaviour of market participants.

EMT is the backbone of conventional economic wisdom whose mantra is that 'the market knows best' how to optimally allocate scarce capital resources and promote maximum economic growth. This EMT view is succinctly epitomized in US Treasury Secretary Summer's statement: 'the ultimate social functions [of financial markets are] spreading risks, guiding the investment of scarce capital, and processing and disseminating the information possessed by diverse traders . . . prices will always reflect fundamental values . . . The logic of efficient markets is compelling'[4] (Summers and Summers, 1989, p. 166).

In contrast, the logic of Keynes's LPT is that the primary function of financial markets is to provide liquidity for asset holders. Because a liquid market must be an *orderly* one, rules and institutions must be developed to guarantee orderliness. If Keynes's LPT of orderly financial markets is relevant, then financial markets can never deliver, in either the short or long run, the efficiency promises of EMT. *In the real world, efficient markets are not liquid and liquid markets are not efficient.*

Bernstein argues that EMT is *not* the relevant theory for the world in which we live. Bernstein states 'The fatal flaw in the efficient market hypothesis *is that there is no such thing as an [efficient] equilibrium price . . . [and] a market can never be efficient unless equilibrium prices exist and are known'* (1998a, p. 8, emphasis in original; also Bernstein, 1998b). Bernstein (1998a, p. 7) endorses Keynes's LPT as the relevant explanation for the global growth of financial markets when he argues 'a stock market without liquidity ceases to be a market'.

Claims of Efficient Market Advocates and the Post-War Facts

Since the 1970s, EMT has provided the rationalization for dismantling the ubiquitous post-war regulations of financial markets. Liberalization, it is claimed, produces lower real costs of capital and higher output and productivity growth rates compared to growth rates experienced between the end of the Second World War and 1973, when international capital flow controls were practised by most countries of the world, including the USA.[5] Do the facts support this EMT argument for financial liberalization?

Comparing the historical record since 1700, Adelman (1991) has characterized the post-war pre-1973 period as a 'Golden Age of Economic Development . . . an era of unprecedented sustained economic growth in both developed and developing countries'. Adelman (1991, p. 15) found that the *average* annual growth rate of OECD real GDP per capita from 1950 to 1973 was 'almost precisely double the previous *peak* growth rate of the industrial revolution period. Productivity growth in OECD countries was more than triple (3.75 times) that of the industrial revolution era'. The resulting prosperity of the industrialized world was transmitted to the less developed nations (LDCs) through world trade, aid and direct foreign investment. From 1950 to 1973, *average* growth in per capita GDP for *all* LDCs was 3.3 per cent, almost triple the *average* growth rate experienced by the industrializing nations during the industrial revolution. Aggregate GDP of the LDCs increased at almost the same rate as that of the developed nations, i.e. 5.5 and 5.9 per cent respectively.

Since 1973 the world's growth in real GDP per capita has been less than 1.5 per cent, while, as already noted, OECD real GDP per capita growth, investment in plant and equipment, and labour productivity growth rates declined by more than half of the rates experienced before liberalization. Clearly financial liberalization since 1973 has not produced the achievements its advocates claimed. Global financial market performance has been fragile. The global economy has stumbled from one economic liquidity crisis to another, e.g. the 1970s stagflation, the 1980s Latin American and African debt-liquidity problems, and the 1990s international currency crises, i.e. the 1992 EMS currency crisis, the 1994–95 Mexican pesos crisis, the 1997 Asian crisis, the 1998 Russian debacle, and the 1998–99 Brazilian crisis. Despite liberalization, for most nations, economics has once more become the dismal science.

A Lesson from the Gold Standard Era

From 1880 to 1914, the gold standard provided the world with a fixed and credible exchange rate system. During this period there were many banking crises 'but they rarely turned into currency crises, except at the Latin American periphery . . . despite very large international capital flows' (Skidelsky, 1999, p. 3). Even though defaults occurred, global investment continued as London, acting as the clearing-house for international trade, made 'sterling the main vehicle currency in both international payments and investments. *It was the absence of alternative currencies to hold that reduced the speculative element in short-term money flows'* (Skidelsky, 1999, p. 5, emphasis added).

In this period, bouts of inflation, unstable political conditions and revolution, or a collapse of export (commodity) prices led to recurrent currency crises in the Latin America periphery. But 'debt collectors moved in, with rescheduling and fresh loans . . . as soon as service on the bonds was resumed, the investors came back . . . The crucial point in all this was that the gold standard was stable at the centre, unstable at its Latin American periphery . . . As a rule, currency crisis hit second class countries, not first class ones' (Skidelsky, 1999, pp. 8–9).[6]

This changed in the inter-war period when international capital flow crises struck the core countries as well as the periphery. In the 1920s, even as core countries attempted to return to the gold standard, the resulting exchange rate peg was not credible. Competition between financial centres in London, Paris and New York made multilateral clearing cumbersome and difficult, especially when there were persistent imbalances in international payments. Only the continual recycling of US current account surplus by American banks prevented the collapse of the world economy. Meanwhile the USA adopted tariffs that made it very difficult for Europeans to run a balanced trade position or to earn dollars to repay post-war dollar loans.

In 1928, when US funds were diverted from international loans to Wall Street speculation, the international payments system started to crumble. Money began flowing from deficit to surplus countries as reserves were liquidated to service debts to the USA. When commodity prices collapsed, the periphery defaulted on these loans, but this time 'the contagion spread to Europe' as Germany tried to balance its international payments by severely depressing its economy. As unemployment rose drastically, a German default occurred in 1931. 'A deflationary hurricane swept over the world, as investors scrambled for liquidity' (Skidelsky, 1999, p. 13). Huge speculative waves attacked the core currencies. Interbank credits could not stem these assaults. The result was to end private foreign investment flows for decades. Can this happen again as the euro and the yen compete with the US dollar as an international reserve currency, especially if the world's largest debtor slips into recession in the near future and the world relies on liberalized financial markets to finance payments imbalances?

Proposed Solutions and the 'Third Way'

Minsky (1975, 1982) argues that financial markets are inherently fragile and destabilizing. Old and New Classical economists, on the other hand, believe in the absolute robust efficiency of free financial markets where speculation is inherently stabilizing. Mainstream Keynesians appear to be trying to keep one foot in the Minsky camp and the other in the classical camp. They argue that information about the future is difficult and costly to obtain and therefore, at least in the short run, a flexible exchange rate system can be destabilizing.

Consequently there is a search for a 'third way', occupying the middle ground between the Minsky view – that markets are inherently fragile – and the classical view – that financial markets are always efficient and speculation is stabilizing. This 'third way' approach has become the conventional wisdom of America's 'New Democrats', Britain's 'New Labour' and Germany's 'New Social Democrats' political leaders and their economic advisors. The third way admits that in the long run free markets are efficient and stable (i.e. revert to the mean) but, in the short run, twentieth-century free-market capitalism has not quite yet attained the state of perfection claimed by New Classical theorists. Accordingly, there is a role for a small army of skilled technicians (recruited from the graduate students of third way economics professors) who, by making information readily and inexpensively available, will keep the efficient free market machine from being pushed off its tracks by scoundrels, wastrels, shirkers, cronies and fools.

The financial instability of the Asian tigers and other peripheral nations is attributed to the lack of transparency, i.e. the difficulty of obtaining full information regarding the foolish actions of bankers, capitalist cronies, dishonest and/or incompetent government employees, etc., who flourish in a world of asymmetric information. For example, at a 1998 conference at the Jerome Levy Institute on the 'fragility of the international financial system', the then Federal Reserve Vice-Chair Alice Rivlin recommended a policy involving 'two key prescriptions, one relating to transparency' and the other 'increased supervision and monitoring of emerging financial markets'.

Rivlin's two keys imply that sufficient transparency and Central Bank auditing procedures (similar to what exists in the US banking system) is the policy fix for the financial fragility of emerging markets. The Federal Reserve (but apparently not the Bank of Japan), we are led to believe, has the fragility problem well in hand. In Euroland, the Bundesbank also had the situation well in hand, but there are doubts about the new European Central Bank.

No one can be against more information and uniform public auditing procedures to prevent criminal fraudulent practices. Financial fragility, however, would not disappear in a world of uncertainty if only we have more transparency. After the Mexican crisis of 1994–95, the World Bank and the IMF, as well as the US Treasury and the Federal Reserve, had professional technicians continually monitoring financial activities occurring in Southeast Asia, Russia and Brazil. Despite the scrutiny of all these professionals, no warning flag was apparently raised within their respective agencies until after each crisis developed. Nor did the transparency, banking regulations, auditing controls and uniform bankruptcy laws of the USA prevent (i) the 1982 oil patch crisis from threatening major US banks such as Continental Illinois, (ii) the mid-1980s Savings and Loan Bank crisis, and (iii) the 1998 Long Term Capital Management hedge-fund crisis. In all these cases, only after the crisis had developed did US authorities take action, e.g. the 'too big to fail' doctrine in the first case, the Resolution Trust Company in the second, and brokering of an equity take-over of Long Term Capital Management by a syndicate of its banker-creditors.

This evidence suggests that transparency, oversight and market discipline alone do not solve financial market instability problems. To be for transparency and discipline is the moral equivalent of being for motherhood and peace. No self-righteous person can be against motherhood, and by implication neither can one be against the provision of more information, i.e. transparency.[7] Transparency *per se*, however, is not the solution, for as *The Economist* (13 March 1999, p. 90) notes, the term 'transparency' is merely jargon an economist invokes to 'regain the initiative' whenever 'an economist is falling behind in an argument'.

Despite their willingness to accept the 'compelling logic' of EMT, the common sense of Old Keynesian Tobin and some of his New Keynesian followers such as Summers and Summers (1989) and Stiglitz (1989) regarding real-world financial markets cannot help but break into their logical models – with injury to their logical consistency. To solve today's international monetary problems, these Keynesians, at least in their academic writings, have advocated a 'Tobin tax' where governments limit market volatility by increasing the transactions costs on all international payments via a small *ad valorem* tax (Tobin, 1974). Unfortunately, although Tobin's assessment of the problem is correct, the empirical evidence is that any increase in the financial transactions costs significantly increases rather than decreases measured market volatility (Davidson, 1998). Moreover, a Tobin tax does not create a greater disincentive for short-term speculators than for long-term traders as some have claimed (Davidson, 1997). Hence, the 'Tobin tax' solution is the wrong tool to solve the growing international financial market volatility problem.

Since the Mexican peso crisis of 1994, pragmatic policy-makers have advocated a lender-of-last-resort (LOLR) as *crisis manager* to stop international financial market liquidity haemorrhaging and to 'bail out' the international investors, despite the moral hazard problem these bail-outs are supposed to cause. In 1994, US Treasury Secretary Rubin encouraged President Clinton to play this LOLR role. With Clinton's liquidity facilities exhausted, the IMF stepped into this lender role when the Asian crisis of 1997 and the Russian default occurred in 1998. When the IMF appeared to be near the end of its liquidity rope after the Asian, Russian and Brazilian crises, IMF Director Stanley Fischer (1999) suggested that the G-7 nations provide financing for an international lender-of-last-resort (LOLR). Fischer's cry for a G-7 LOLR collaboration is equivalent to recruiting a volunteer fire department to douse the flames after someone has cried fire in a crowded theatre. Even if the fire is ultimately extinguished there will be many innocent casualties. Moreover, every new currency fire requires the LOLR to pour more liquidity into the market to put out the flames. The goal should be to produce a permanent fire prevention system, not to rely on organizing larger and larger volunteer fire-fighting companies with each new currency crisis. In other words, crisis prevention rather than crisis management should be the policy goal.

Economists Rudi Dornbusch and Steven Hanke have recommended a currency board solution for Latin American and Asian nations. A currency board fixes the exchange rate so that the domestic money supply does not exceed the amount of foreign reserves a nation possesses.[8] Thus, if and when investors panic and rush to exit from a nation, the currency board maintains the exchange rate by selling foreign reserves and reducing the domestic money supply by an equivalent sum. A currency board solution, therefore, is equivalent to the bloodletting prescribed by seventeenth-century doctors to cure a fever. Enough blood loss can, of course, always reduce the fever but often at a terrible cost to the body of the patient. Similarly, a currency board may douse the flames of a currency crisis but the result will be a moribund economy. Jeffrey Sachs and others have suggested a return to completely flexible exchange rates. Unfortunately whenever there is a persistent international payments imbalance, free market exchange rate flexibility can make the situation worse. For example, if a nation is suffering from a tendency towards international current account deficits due to imports exceeding exports, then free market advocates argue that a decline in the market price will end the trade deficit. If, however, the Marshall–Lerner condition does not apply, then a declining market exchange rate worsens the situation by increasing the magnitude of the payments deficit.[9]

If the payments imbalance is due to capital flows, there is a similar perverse effect. If, for example, country A is attracting a rapid net inflow of capital because investors in the rest of the world think the profit rate is higher in A, then the exchange rate will rise. This rising exchange rate creates the expectations of even higher profits for foreign investors and contrarily will encourage others to rush in with additional capital flows, pushing the exchange rate even higher. If suddenly there is a change in sentiment (often provoked by some ephemeral event), then a fast exit bandwagon will ensue, pushing the exchange rate perversely down.

Liquidity, Uncertainty and the Stability of Markets

By providing liquidity in a world where the future cannot be reliably predicted, financial markets can encourage savers to provide funding for durable investment projects that they would not furnish if their investment was illiquid. A liquid market permits investors to have a *fast exit* strategy where they believe that they can close out their position at little cost the moment they are dissatisfied with the way in which matters are developing. A liquid market means that the asset holder has the 'ability to reverse [immediately] a decision at the lowest possible transactions cost' (Bernstein, 1998b, p. 16).

Financial assets typically represent liquid claims on expected future income streams generated by illiquid real investment projects. If today's market price is to reflect 'fundamentals', then the market must use existing data to make a statistically reliable forecast of the entire future stream of quasi-rents associated with the underlying illiquid investment project. Strictly speaking, to make such a prediction requires us to draw samples from the future and calculate the statistical moments around the mean. Because this is impossible, efficient market theorists invoke (usually implicitly) the ergodic axiom.[10] This ergodic presumption is that statistical averages calculated from existing historical cross-sectional *or* time series data provide reliable estimates of the same statistics that can be calculated from samples drawn in the future. Consequently, by invoking the ergodic axiom, EMT proponents are claiming that the future is merely the statistical shadow of the past.

Keynes took a dim view of the ability of people to reliably forecast the future in an uncertain world. Instead, market prices of liquid assets are dominated by a convention. 'The essence of this convention – though it does not, of course, work out quite so simply – lies in assuming that the existing state of affairs will continue indefinitely, except if we have specific reasons to expect a change' (Keynes, 1936, p. 152).

In normal times, the conventional wisdom is that financial markets are stable, or at least have a high degree of built-in inertia. This simple-minded Keynesian convention has been translated by a highly sophisticated econometric technology into a search for unit roots and a random walk down Wall Street. Of course, if most market participants presume that the existing state of affairs will continue indefinitely (in the absence of evidence of a change in what people call market fundamentals), then most of the time financial market activity should be neither fragile nor destabilizing. But if the future is uncertain in the sense that it cannot be reliably predicted, doesn't this imply inherent fragility and instability?

In a letter, Keynes (1973, p. 137) admonished Joan Robinson, saying 'You must not confuse instability with uncertainty. It is true that the future . . . [is] uncertain but this does not mean that the present . . . is in a technical sense unstable'. Market conditions will be stable in normal times as long as market participants expect no 'surprises' in the near future.

Abnormal times of instability can readily occur, however, when the market's

> conventional valuation . . . is established as the outcome of the mass psychology of a large number of ignorant individuals, [then it] is liable to change violently as the result of a sudden fluctuation of opinion due to factors which do not really make much difference to the prospective yield . . . In abnormal times in particular, when the hypothesis of an indefinite continuance of the existing state of

affairs is less plausible . . . the market will be subject to waves of optimistic and pessimistic sentiment which are unreasoning and yet in a sense legitimate where no solid basis exists for reasonable calculation.

(Keynes, 1936, p. 154)

Liquidity and Orderly Markets

Financial markets furnish liquidity by providing an orderly environment where assets can be readily resold for cash. (The underlying real reproducible assets, however, do not possess the 'essential [elasticity] properties' that Keynes associated with the attribute of liquidity.[11]) Market orderliness requires a private or a public institution, a 'market maker', that regulates the net flows into and out of the market. Orderly liquid financial markets, however, encourage each investor to believe they can always make a fast exit (or entrance).

Orderliness, therefore, promotes the separation of ownership and control-management (Keynes, 1973, pp. 150–1; Davidson, 1972; Bernstein, 1998b). With a liquid capital market, owners have no legal or moral commitment to stick around long enough to make sure their capital is used efficiently. If capital markets were completely illiquid then there would be no separation of ownership and control. Once capital is committed, the owners have an incentive to use the existing facilities in the best possible way, no matter what unforeseen circumstances might arise. Perhaps then capital markets might behave more like the efficient markets of mainstream theory.[12] Bernstein's (1998b, p. 23) homily that 'An efficient market is a market without liquidity' is a lesson that policy-makers must be taught. Judicious use of capital controls can promote efficient use of capital resources by constraining any sudden change in the demand for liquidity that can adversely affect the real economy.

Because financial markets are primarily organized to provide liquidity, then when bullish sentiment about the uncertain future dominates financial markets, rising market prices encourage savers to readily provide the funding that induces entrepreneurial investors to spend sums on new investment projects that (i) far exceeds their current incomes and (ii) induce exuberant expectations of future returns. The result is an investment boom. If some time in the future, doubts suddenly arise concerning the reliability of these euphoric expectations, then bearish sentiment will come to the fore and the investment boom will turn into a bust.

When the bearish view of the future becomes overriding, an excessive demand for liquidity can develop that will impede the production of new investment capital even when real resources are idle and therefore readily available to produce new real capital goods. The basic message of Keynes's *General Theory* is that too great a demand for liquidity can prevent 'saved' (i.e. unutilized) real resources from being employed in the production of investment goods. These resources will be involuntarily unemployed.

Unlike Old and New Keynesians, Keynes explicitly recognized that the introduction of sand in the wheels of liquidity-providing financial markets via a transactions tax is a double-edged sword. Keynes (1936, p. 160) noted that a financial transactions tax 'brings us up against a dilemma, and shows us how the liquidity of investment markets often facilitates, though it sometimes impedes, the course of new investment'.

What are the market conditions that in normal times create stable financial market prices? 'It is interesting that the stability of the [financial] system and its sensitiveness . . . should be so dependent on the existence of a variety of opinion about what is uncertain. Best of all that we should know the future. But if not, then, if we are to control the activity of the economic system . . . it is important that opinions differ' (Keynes, 1936, p. 172). In other words, an ergodic system would provide the 'best of all' possible worlds for financial market stability. Then the future can be reduced to actuarial certainty, i.e. 'we should know the future'. Market efficiency would be assured as long as agents operated in their actuarially known self-interest. There would be no need for a fast exit strategy.

If the system is non-ergodic, however, then actuarial certainty and the possibility of rational probabilistic risk spreading which, according to New Classical and New Keynesian economists is an essential function of efficient markets, is impossible. Nevertheless, market stability is possible if substantial numbers of market participants either (i) hold continuously differing expectations about the future or (ii) believe the current price is the correct price and that there is a *credible* institution that will take whatever steps are necessary to assure non-volatile changes in the (correct) current price. Under these conditions, any small upward change in the market price brings about a significant bear reaction, while any slight downturn induces a bullish reaction. The result is to maintain spot financial market (resale) price orderliness over time and therefore a high degree of liquidity.[13]

Irrational Exuberance and Bandwagon Behaviour

If at any time increased volume in financial markets is associated with the 'irrational exuberance' behaviour that central banker Alan Greenspan once spoke of, then many similar thinking 'irrational' participants suddenly will have dominated the market. If there is a sudden market swing to a bandwagon consensus, then there is an abrupt lack of market participants with differing expectations about the future. Liquidity can dry up until there is a sufficiently large movement in the market price to break down the bandwagon consensus mentality and create a diversity of bull-bear views.

Whenever there is a sudden shift in the private sector's bull-bear disposition, what I call a bandwagon effect,[14] then price stability requires capital regulations to prevent the bears from liquidating their position too quickly (or the bulls from rushing in) and overcoming any single agent (private or public) who has taken on the responsible task of market maker to promote 'orderliness'. Capital controls serve the same function as laws that make it a crime to yell fire in a crowded theatre. In the absence of such social constraints on free speech, the resulting rush to the exit may inflict more damage than any potential fire. In the absence of laws permitting governments to invoke capital controls to prevent a crush due to fast exit (or entry), unruly financial market behaviour can inflict severe damage on innocent bystanders.

In the absence of a credible market maker with sufficient liquid resources and/or regulatory controls to stem a bandwagon, enterprise becomes the bubble on the whirlpool of speculation (Keynes, 1936, p. 159). Disruptive speculation involves sharp and profound changes in the *ex post* moving average secular trend.[15]

Bandwagons are induced often by some 'surprising' event that encourages portfolio holders to expect that others will now expect a change in the exchange rate. If an institution can be developed that assures portfolio managers that exchange rates will be stable over time no matter what unforeseen events occur, then this will do more to inhibit speculative short-term round tripping than any small Tobin tax.

Conventional wisdom is that if the psychology of the market is not changing there will be an inertia in market valuations.[16] Accordingly, a policy designed to reduce, if not eliminate, disruptive speculation must involve building institutions that assure market participants that the 'correct' market psychology is a belief in a persistent, stable (moving average) trend in market prices over time.[17] For example, if market participants believe that a market maker exists who can guarantee an unchanging spot market price (or changing only within very small boundaries) over time under preannounced and readily understood rules of the game, then the existence of this credible market maker provides an anchor for 'market psychology'. For participants to believe in the market maker's ability to maintain the target market price trend, however, the market maker must have a sufficient inventory of money and the asset that is being sold in the market. In a foreign exchange market for example, this implies that the domestic monetary authority has credibility (and a sufficient inventory of foreign reserves or easy access to additional reserves) and has announced that it will use its reserves to maintain an orderly market at the 'proper' exchange rate. That is the explanation of why currency boards with reserves equal to the domestic money supply can fix the exchange rate and, in normal times, can maintain the exchange rate.

To prevent disruptive speculation requires a buffer stock policy practised by a market maker and the power to institute financial flow regulations. The majority of market participants must believe in the institution's ability to enforce civilized behaviour similar to the prohibition of not yelling fire in a theatre. Then any speculation that occurs will be small 'bubbles on a steady stream of enterprise' (Keynes, 1936, p. 159).

Such considerations led Keynes to suggest an outright prohibition of all 'hot money' international portfolio flows through the creation of a supranational central bank and his bancor plan. At this stage of economic development and global economic integration, a supranational central bank is not politically feasible. Accordingly what should be aimed for is a more modest goal of obtaining an international agreement among the major trading nations that insures orderly international monetary markets. To be economically effective and politically feasible, this agreement, while incorporating the economic principles that Keynes laid down in his bancor plan, should not require any nation to surrender control of local banking systems or its domestic fiscal policies.

Policy Recommendations

The function of capital controls is to prevent sharp changes in the bull-bear sentiment from overwhelming a market maker and inducing rapid changes in price trends, for such volatility, especially in foreign exchange markets, can have devastating real consequences.

There is a spectrum of different capital controls available. At one end of the spectrum are controls that primarily impose administrative constraints either on a case-by-case basis or expenditure category basis. These controls include administrative oversight and control of individual transactions for payments to foreign residents (or banks) often via oversight of international transactions by banks or their customers.[18]

Other capital controls include (a) policies that make foreign exchange available but at different exchange rates for different types of transactions, and (b) the imposition of significant taxes (or other opportunity costs) on specific international financial payments, e.g. Chilean speed bumps or the 1960s US Interest Equalization Tax which discriminated against foreign securities being sold in domestic markets. Finally there can be many forms of monetary policy decisions undertaken to affect international payment flows, such as raising the interest rate to slow capital outflows, raising bank reserve ratios, limiting the ability of banks to finance purchases of foreign securities, and regulating interbank activity.

The experience of the IMF, as lender-of-last-resort imposing the same conditions on all the Asian contagion nations requiring international liquidity loans, should have taught us that in discussing policy prescriptions one size does *not* fit all. Accordingly, the type of capital regulations a nation should choose from the spectrum of tools available will differ depending on the specific circumstances involved. In this brief chapter it would be presumptuous of me to catalogue what capital regulations should be imposed for any nation under any given circumstances. Nevertheless, it should be stressed that regulating capital movements is a necessary, *but not sufficient*, condition for promoting global prosperity.

Elsewhere (Davidson, 1992, 1994, 1997) I have developed in detail a proposal for reforming the entire international payments system via an international clearing union that provides for capital controls and other necessary and sufficient conditions to permit the establishment of a Golden Age in the twenty-first century. The main provisos of my proposal are:

1. The unit of account and ultimate reserve asset for international liquidity is the International Money Clearing Unit (IMCU). All IMCUs are held *only* by central banks, not by the public.
2. Each nation's central bank is committed to guaranteeing one-way convertibility from IMCU deposits at the clearing union to its domestic money. Each central bank will set its own rules regarding

making foreign monies available (through IMCU clearing transactions) to its own bankers and private sector residents.[19]
Ultimately, all major private international transactions clear
between central banks' accounts in the books of the international
clearing institution.

3. The exchange rate between the domestic currency and the IMCU is
   set *initially* by each nation – just as it would be if one instituted an
   international gold standard.
4. Contracts between private individuals will continue to be denominated into whatever domestic currency is permitted by local laws
   and is agreed upon by the contracting parties.
5. An overdraft system to make available short-term unused creditor
   balances at the Clearing House to finance the productive international transactions of others who need short-term credit. The terms
   will be determined by the *pro buono* clearing managers.
6. A trigger mechanism to encourage a creditor nation to spend what
   is deemed (in advance) by agreement of the international community to be *'excessive' credit balances accumulated by running current
   account surpluses*. These excessive credits can be spent in three ways:
   (i) on the products of any other member of the clearing union, (ii)
   on new direct foreign investment projects, and/or (iii) to provide
   unilateral transfers (foreign aid) to deficit members.
7. A system to stabilize the long-term purchasing power of the IMCU
   (in terms of each member nation's domestically produced market
   basket of goods) can be developed. This requires a system of fixed
   exchange rates between the local currency and the IMCU that
   changes only to reflect permanent increases in efficiency wages.[20]
   This assures each central bank that its holdings of IMCUs as the
   nation's foreign reserves will never lose purchasing power in terms
   of foreign produced goods, even if a foreign government permits
   wage-price inflation to occur within its borders.
8. If a country is at *full employment* and still has a tendency towards
   persistent international deficits on its current account, then this is
   prima facie evidence that it does not possess the productive capacity to
   maintain its current standard of living. If the deficit nation is a poor
   one, then surely there is a case for the richer nations who are in
   surplus to transfer some of their excess credit balances to support the
   poor nation.[21] If it is a relatively rich country, then the deficit nation
   must alter its standard of living by reducing the relative terms of trade
   with major trading partners. If the payment deficit persists despite a
   continuous positive balance of trade in goods and services, then there

is evidence that the deficit nation might be carrying too heavy an international debt service obligation. The *pro buono* officials of the clearing union should bring the debtor and creditors into negotiations to reduce annual debt service payments by [i] lengthening the payments period, [ii] reducing the interest charges, and/or [iii] debt forgiveness.[22]

Proviso #2 permits capital controls. Proviso #6 embodies Keynes's innovative idea that whenever there is a persistent (and/or large) imbalance in current account flows – whether due to capital flight or a persistent trade imbalance – there must be a built-in mechanism that induces the surplus nation(s) to bear a major responsibility for eliminating the imbalance. The surplus nation must accept this burden for it has the wherewithal to resolve the problem.

In the absence of #6, under any conventional system, whether it has fixed or flexible exchange rates and/or capital controls, there will ultimately be an international liquidity crisis (as any persistent current account deficit can deplete a nation's foreign reserves) that unleashes global depressionary forces. Thus, proviso #6 is necessary to ensure that the international payments system will not have a built-in depressionary bias. Ultimately then it is in the self-interest of the surplus nation to accept this responsibility, for its actions will create conditions for global economic expansion, some of which must redound to its own residents. Failure to act, on the other hand, will promote global depressionary forces that will have some negative impact on its own residents.

Some think that my specific clearing union plan, like Keynes's bancor plan, a half-century earlier, is Utopian. But if we start with the defeatist attitude that it is too difficult to change the awkward system in which we are trapped, then no progress will be made. Global depression does not have to happen again if our policy-makers have sufficient vision to develop this post-Keynesian approach. The health of the world's economic system will simply not permit us to muddle through.

Conclusion

Liquid markets cannot be expected to be efficient. In an uncertain world, it is not surprising therefore that liberalized international financial markets have undergone so many currency (liquidity) crises in recent years.

Conventional mainstream wisdom, if and when it recognizes the possibility of currency crises in an efficient market model, usually rationalizes the appearance of such international liquidity crises as a necessary *disciplinary device*. For example, DeAngelis (1999–2000) argues that in 'the context of a global economy geared towards production for profit, liquidity crunches have a systemic function in that they help ensure the standards of competitiveness or movements towards further global integration are *enforced*'.

In other words, as classical economists have always claimed, recessions and depressions are a good laxative for the economic system as they cleanse the economic body of the inefficiencies that have built up in an era of prosperity. A classic example of this classical prescription is revealed in the memoirs of Herbert Hoover. Treasury Secretary, Andrew Mellon, always offered the same advice to President Hoover: 'Mr. Mellon had only one formula. Liquidate labor, liquidate stocks, liquidate the farmer, liquidate real estate. It will purge the rottenness out of the system . . . People will work harder, lead a more moral life' (Hoover, 1952, p. 30). Today's conventional wisdom espoused by the IMF and many other mainstream economists still affirms Mellon's puritanical cathartic view of the value of a liquidity crisis.

On the other hand, Keynes believed that a liquidity crunch was not a necessary purgative for restoring economic health. Rather liquidation processes and the resulting unemployment involved a 'public scandal of wasted resources' (Keynes, 1936, p. 381). Keynes believed that the two major faults of the entrepreneurial system in which we live are 'its failure to provide for full employment and its arbitrary and inequitable distribution of income and wealth'. He claimed that his 'general theory' had an important 'bearing' on ameliorating both these 'outstanding faults' (Keynes, 1936, p. 372).

In the closed economic system of his *General Theory*, Keynes (1936, p. 379) insisted that his analysis 'is moderately conservative in its implications. For whilst it indicates the vital importance of establishing central controls [over the level of effective demand] . . . there are wide fields of activity which are unaffected'. Our argument has extended Keynes's principle of effective demand to an open economy setting. In an open system, changes in the exchange rate affect the level of aggregate demand for domestically produced goods through its impact on exports and imports, the interest rate and the rate of domestic investment. Accordingly, Keynes's principle of effective demand indicates (i) the need for central controls over the exchange rates and (ii) international agreements that place the major responsibility for resolving international payments imbalances on the creditor nation(s). Only then will Keynes's 'moderately conservative' analysis point the way to a golden age for the global economic system of the twenty-first century.

Notes

1. These classical axioms are the neutrality of money axiom, the gross substitution axiom, and the ergodic axiom (Davidson, 1982–3).
2. Only the supply side limitations of available resources and the level of technical progress would prevent the immediate achievement of a Garden of Eden on Earth.
3. In a recent article in the *Wall Street Journal*, Friedman (1998) argues that with market-determined exchange rates, exchange rate pressures will always be dissipated, despite the long-known argument that in the absence of the Marshall–Lerner condition, market forces would exacerbate exchange rate problems. For a further discussion see page 21.
4. In an EMT world, economic fundamentals such as price/earnings ratios determine stock market prices.
5. In July 1963, the USA introduced the Interest Equalization Tax (IET) on purchases by residents of foreign (other than Canadian) fixed-rate securities. The tax rate varied from zero to 150 basis depending on maturity. In August 1971 dollar convertibility was suspended and in 1973 Nixon closed the gold window. In 1974 the IET was formally abolished.
6. Does not this experience appear to have some similarities to events in the post-1973 era when the world was on a dollar standard?
7. The sound bite word 'transparency' however, is a canonization of the misleading and potentially devastating New Keynesian economic position that markets would be efficient in the short run except for the fact that reliable full information about the future is not free. In other words, asymmetric information-driven behaviour is a prime cause of the current financial market crises that have devastating real impacts. In my recent invited lecture to a plenary session of the Royal Economic Society (Davidson, 1998) I developed why I believe this asymmetric information scenario is logically inconsistent as well as inapplicable to the world in which we live.
8. A currency board is the modern equivalent of the gold standard where US dollars are the 'gold'. The gold standard worked only when there were no bandwagon effects. It always failed when there was a bandwagon effect for a fast exit.
9. The Marshall–Lerner condition requires that the sum of the price elasticities for exports and imports exceed unity for a depreciating exchange rate to reduce the payments deficit. The textbook J-curve for a depreciating exchange rate recognizes that in the short run the payments deficit worsens (the downward part of the J-curve). The J-curve ultimately turns upward because it is *assumed* that in the long run, price elasticities are approximately infinite.
10. For an explicit statement of the need for the ergodic axiom see Samuelson (1969) and Lucas and Sargent (1981).

11. Keynes (1936, p. 241n) argues that the 'attribute of liquidity' of an asset is by no means independent of the presence of two essential properties, namely that the asset is not reproducible via the employment of labour and cannot be substituted for the producible output of industry.

12. In the absence of a liquid financial market '[t]here is no object in frequently attempting to revalue an investment to which we are committed' (Keynes, 1936, p. 151) for there can be no fast exit strategy.

13. Only in the non-ergodic world that is our entrepreneurial economic system is it sensible to organize complex and lengthy production and exchange processes via the use of nominal contracts (Davidson, 1994) in order to give entrepreneurs some control of cash flows over an otherwise uncertain future. In such a world, the primary function of organized financial markets is to provide liquidity by permitting the resale of assets in an orderly market. Only secondarily do modern super-efficient financial markets affect the allocation of new capital amongst industries and to the extent it apportions capital, this distribution is not predetermined by some long-run immutable real economic fundamentals.

14. Some speak of a 'herd' effect. However, except for moments of stampede, herds are usually docile and tend to move slowly from one grazing place to another.

15. The dictionary defines secular as 'lasting from century to century'.

16. *Ex post* we can always calculate a moving average for any time series of market prices and, if we accept what Samuelson has called the ergodic hypothesis, the resulting market valuation over time can be attributed to being determined by some underlying 'fundamental'.

17. In fact, all markets in liquid assets require the institution of one or more credible 'market makers' who follow some preannounced rules of the game to ensure orderliness in the market. The more orderly the market maker keeps the market, the less the moment-to-moment volatility. It is only when market makers fail in their responsibility to maintain orderly markets that volatility becomes disorderly and speculation can have real disruptive effects.

18. Mayer (1998, pp. 29–30) has argued that the Asian problem was due to the international interbank market that created the whirlpool of speculation and that what is needed is a 'system for identifying . . . and policing interbank lending' *and* banks' contingent liabilities resulting from dealing in derivatives. Echoing our non-ergodic theme, Mayer (1998, p. 31) declares 'The mathematical models of price movements and covariance underlying the construction of these [contingent] liabilities simply collapsed as actual prices departed so far from "normal" probabilities'.

19. Correspondent banking will have to operate through the International Clearing Agency, with each central bank regulating the international relations and operations of its domestic banking firms. Small-scale smuggling of currency across borders, etc., can never be completely eliminated. But such movements are merely a flea on a dog's back – a minor, but not debilitating, irritation. If, however, most of the residents of a nation hold and use (in violation of legal tender laws) a foreign currency for domestic transactions and as a store of value (e.g. it is estimated that Argentineans hold more than US $5 billion), this is evidence of a lack of confidence in the

government and its monetary authority. Unless confidence is restored, all attempts to restore economic prosperity will fail.

20. The efficiency wage is related to the money wage divided by the average product of labour, i.e. it is the unit labour cost modified by the profit mark-up in domestic money terms of domestically produced GNP. At this preliminary stage of this proposal, it would serve no useful purpose to decide whether the domestic market basket should include both tradable and non-tradable goods and services. (With the growth of tourism more and more non-tradable goods become potentially tradable.) I personally prefer the wider concept of the domestic market basket, but it is not obvious that any essential principle is lost if a tradable-only concept is used, or if some nations use the wider concept while others the narrower one.

21. This is equivalent to a negative income tax for poor fully employed families within a nation.

22. The actual programme adopted for debt service reduction will depend on many parameters including: the relative income and wealth of the debtor *vis-à-vis* the creditor, the ability of the debtor to increase its per capita real income, etc.

References

Adelman, I. (1991) *Long Term Economic Development*, Working Paper No. 589, Berkeley, CA, California Agricultural Experiment Station.

Bernstein, P. L. (1996) *Against the Gods*, New York, John Wiley & Sons.

Bernstein, P. L. (1998) 'Why the Efficient Market Offers Hope For Active Management', Keynote address to the European Federation of Financial Analysts Society, September.

Bernstein, P. L. (1998a) 'Stock Market Risk in a Post Keynesian World', *Journal of Post Keynesian Economics*, 21(1):15–24.

Davidson, P. (1972) *Money and the Real World*, London, Macmillan.

Davidson, P. (1982–3) 'Rational Expectations: A Fallacious Foundation for Studying Crucial Decision-Making Processes', *Journal of Post Keynesian Economics*, 5:182–95.

Davidson, P. (1984) 'Reviving Keynes's Revolution', *Journal of Post Keynesian Economics*, 6:561–75.

Davidson, P. (1992–3) 'Reforming the World's Money', *Journal of Post Keynesian Economics*, 15:1–25.

Davidson, P. (1994) *Post Keynesian Macroeconomic Theory*, Cheltenham, Elgar.

Davidson, P. (1997) 'Are Grains of Sand in the Wheels of International Finance Sufficient To Do the Job When Boulders are Often Required?', *Economic Journal*, 107:671–782.

Davidson, P. (1998) 'Volatile Financial Markets and the Speculator', *Economic Issues*, 3: 1–18.

DeAngelis, M. (1999–2000) 'Capital Movements, Tobin Tax and Permanent Fire Prevention', *Journal of Post Keynesian Economics*, 22:345–65.

Eichengreen, B., Tobin, J. and Wyplosz, C. (1995) 'Two Cases for Sand in the Wheels of International Finance', *Economic Journal*, 105(428):162–172.

Felix, D. (1997–8) 'On Drawing Policy Lessons', *Journal of Post Keynesian Economics*, 20:220–35.

Fischer, S. (1999) 'On The Need For An International Lender of Last Resort', paper delivered to Allied Social Science Association Convention, January, San Francisco California.

Friedman, M. (1998) 'Markets to the Rescue', *Wall Street Journal*, 13 October 1998.

Hoover, H. (1952) *The Memoirs of Herbert Hoover; The Great Depression 1929–1941*, New York, Macmillan.

Keynes, J. M. (1936) *The General Theory of Employment Interest and Money*, London, Macmillan.

Keynes, J. M. (1973) *The Collected Writings of John Maynard Keynes*, Vol. 14 (edited by D. Moggridge), London, Macmillan.

Lucas, R. E. and Sargent, T. J. (1981) *Rational Expectations and Econometric Practices*, Minneapolis, University of Minnesota Press.

Mayer, M. (1998) 'The Asian Disease: Plausible Diagnoses, Possible Remedies', *Levy Institute Policy Brief*, No. 44, pp. 10–15.

Minsky, H. P. (1975) *John Maynard Keynes*, New York, Columbia University Press.

Minsky, H. P. (1982) *Can it Happen Again?* Armonk, NY, M. E. Sharpe, Inc.

Pindyck, R. S. (1991) 'Irreversibility, Uncertainty and Investment', *Journal of Economic Literature*, 29:1110–48.

Samuelson, P. A. (1947) *Foundations of Economic Analysis*, Cambridge, Harvard University Press.

Skidelsky, R. (ed.) (1999) 'Historical reflections on capital movements' in *Capital Regulation: For and Against*, London, The Social Market Foundation.

Stiglitz, J. G. (1989) 'Using Tax Policy to Curb Speculative Short Term Trading?' *Journal of Financial Services*, 3:101–13.

Summers, L. H. and Summers, V. P. (1989) 'When Financial Markets Work Too Well: A Cautious Case For A Securities Transactions Tax', *Journal of Financial Services*, 3:163–88.

Tobin, J. (1974) 'The New Economics One Decade Older', *The Janeway Lectures on Historical Economics*, Princeton, Princeton University Press.

3
Reforming the International Financial Architecture: An Asian Perspective

M. G. Quibria and Joy Quitazol

> In the aftermath of every crisis, whether war or currency collapses, there is a soul-searching effort to build a better world. Just such an effort, short lived and without leaving a trace, got underway after the Mexican debacle. Another one is being conducted just now. Asia's collapse and Japan's implosion are the obvious triggers. This is a great occasion for bad ideas, or just impractical ones, to draw attention and gain respectability.
>
> (Dornbusch, 1998)

Introduction

In the wake of the Mexican financial crisis in 1994–95, policy-makers began to realize that global financial institutions and rules have not kept pace with the speed of integration in international capital markets. Although it had evolved over the years, the existing Bretton Woods architecture had originally been designed for a world where capital mobility was limited. Since the Halifax Summit of the G7 leaders in 1995, but especially after the Asian financial crisis, official discussions on an international financial architecture have proliferated and an increasing number of organizations have become involved. In addition, a number of individual academics and other commentators have put forward their own reform proposals. The result is a plethora of ideas.

Some of these ideas envisage a radical reform of the existing architecture, while others call for marginal changes. The British Prime Minister Tony Blair has appealed for a new Bretton Woods for the next millennium: a world financial authority that merges the International Monetary Fund (IMF), the World Bank, and the Bank for International

Settlements. The hedge fund guru and philanthropist George Soros (1998) has proposed establishing an international debt insurance corporation. The Wall Street insider Henry Kaufman (1998) recommended the setting up of an international credit rating agency. Jeffrey Garten (1998) has proposed the creation of an international central bank. Jeffrey Sachs (1995, 1998), a fervent critic of the IMF, has suggested abolishing the IMF and establishing an international bankruptcy court. On the other hand, deputy managing director of the IMF, Stanley Fischer (1999), has pointed to the need to create a lender-of-last-resort and, of course, would like to see the IMF play that role. Other suggestions that do not embody such grandiose plans are those that would place restrictions on the free movement of capital – either on capital outflows or inflows. Paul Krugman (1998) has emphasized the controls on outflows and Barry Eichengreen (1999a) on inflows.

The next section of this chapter describes the fundamental dilemma in devising an international financial architecture. The following section critically analyzes the various proposals that have been advanced to reform the existing international financial architecture. In conclusion, we offer a consolidated set of suggestions to improve the existing architecture.

The Trilemma of International Financial Architecture

The financial architecture has to reconcile a number of desirable, but not necessarily mutually congruent, goals of greater economic integration. Lawrence Summers (1999) recently referred to them as the 'integration trilemma'. He noted that in the years ahead the central task of international political economy will be to reconcile satisfactorily three desiderata: greater integration, proper public management and national sovereignty. In effect, policy-makers would like the international financial system to foster greater capital market integration, devise efficient supervision and regulation of international financial markets just as national markets are regulated and supervised, and maintain national sovereignty. Unfortunately, these three goals are incompatible: maintaining national sovereignty in a world of free capital means forfeiting market regulation and support. Conversely, to create regulations and a lender-of-last-resort at the international level implies overriding national sovereignty. The only way that a country can regulate and support its financial markets while maintaining national sovereignty is by controlling capital flows.

This trilemma is particularly striking in the area of exchange rate management. Policy-makers want the benefit of financial market integration; they want exchange rate stability; and they want monetary independence.[1] Unfortunately, they cannot have them all simultaneously.[2]

To illustrate, suppose a country wants a stable exchange rate as well as financial integration (i.e. free access to international capital). To achieve these goals, it must either establish a currency board or join a monetary union. In either case, it means giving up the monetary policy independence associated with a flexible exchange rate. Suppose the country wants to maintain monetary sovereignty as well as derive the benefit of integration. It has to give up exchange rate stability. In a world of freely mobile capital, fixed (but adjustable) exchange rate pegs are unsustainable, because they would immediately be tested by currency speculators. Finally, suppose the country wants to maintain sovereignty in pursuing monetary policy and maintain currency stability. The only way a country can do so is by restricting capital flows, i.e. by sacrificing the benefits of integration. This was the combination – macroeconomic policy sovereignty and currency stability – chosen by policy-makers under the original Bretton Woods regime. For the first 25 years after the Bretton Woods agreement, the global financial architecture was based on a system of fixed exchange rates and strict capital controls.

During the 1960s, however, private investors gradually began to evade these capital controls, and international capital movements increased. As capital mobility increased, countries were forced to choose between the ability to maintain macroeconomic policy independence and exchange rate stability. The breakdown of the Bretton Woods system of fixed exchange rates in the early 1970s shows that industrial countries chose to maintain independence by forfeiting fixed exchange rates. Since then, the world's major currencies – the US dollar, the yen and the European currencies – have all floated.

In developing countries, capital flows remained tightly controlled for much longer. However, in the 1980s, and particularly in the 1990s, the trend toward greater capital mobility has spread worldwide. Thus ever more countries face the choice between exchange rate stability and policy independence. Most have moved toward exchange rate flexibility. In 1976, for instance, almost 90 per cent of developing countries pegged their currency to a single currency (such as the US dollar or the French franc) or to a basket of currencies. Twenty years later the percentage of developing countries that still have pegged exchange rates has fallen to less than 50. The Asian financial crisis, as well as the recent crises in Brazil, Mexico and Russia, hit economies with pegged exchange rates and large inflows of foreign capital. They illustrated in a stark, cruel way the interplay of the integration trilemma. Thus at the heart of the debate on improving the international financial architecture is the thorny question of which of the three goals is to be sacrificed.

Proposals for Strengthening the Architecture

Proposals for strengthening the international financial architecture differ significantly in their nature and scope. Some proposals are radical and demand a total overhaul of the existing structure; some are conservative and relatively easy to implement within the existing structure; some rely on more forceful responses from the international community; while others would like to see greater involvement of the market for crisis resolution. The following section reviews a set of salient proposals.

Controlling Capital Flows

A set of financial reform proposals hopes to solve the open economy trilemma by controlling capital mobility. Some economists, such as Jagdish Bhagwati (1998) and Dani Rodrik (1998), argue that benefits from free mobility of capital are not the same as the benefits from free trade. They do not see the necessity of free movement of capital to enhance economic efficiency or economic growth as free trade alone would suffice to achieve these objectives. They put forward two arguments to support this view. First, countries can reap the benefits of free trade in goods and services without simultaneously opening up their financial markets to foreign competition. Second, the theoretical benefits of free capital flows, such as increased investment and more efficient use of funds, do not occur in reality, because the efficiency gains that a country reaps from opening up to foreign capital are more than offset by increasing uncertainty and greater risk of financial crises. As financial markets are plagued by imperfect information and a tendency to overshoot, international financial integration often brings developing countries more risks – in the form of creditors' panic and financial crisis – than rewards. These economists claim that there is no solid empirical evidence in support of the view that countries perform better with capital mobility than without. In particular, Rodrik (1998) finds that for a cross-section of developing countries, there is no correlation between capital account liberalization and economic growth. These arguments have been countered on both a priori theoretical and empirical grounds. First, countries that try to pursue free trade while maintaining capital controls suffer a number of problems as people try to evade the capital controls. Importers, for instance, often over-invoice their shipments to smuggle capital out of the country. As economies develop and become more open, capital controls not only foster corruption, but they also restrict the growth of trade.

Second, increasing global financial integration increases uncertainty. However, this also occurs as trade is liberalized. Terms of trade shocks – the sudden rise or fall in a key export or import price – are potentially as unsettling as the contagious spread of financial crises. Similarly, the claim that there is no empirical evidence of any measurable impact of capital account liberalization on a country's welfare is overstated. Indeed, the empirical evidence in this area is ambiguous. For example, Rossi (1999) finds that capital controls are associated with significantly slower growth.

Third, market integration is essentially a multilateral process. While analyzing the costs and benefits for a single economy is possible, the ultimate benefits of integration will depend on policies followed by all countries and their evolution over time. While one country might not suffer excessively by slowing or reversing its capital mobility, the negative impact of many countries doing this could be much greater. For all these reasons, reforms of the financial architecture that are predicated on greater restrictions on capital mobility make little sense.

However, this does not imply that all capital account liberalization is good. The record of financial crises, especially in Asia, shows that ill-planned liberalization of capital flows – without the appropriate market reforms – can result in financial instability and imply large economic costs. The Asian crisis showed that when countries open their capital accounts without effective supervision and regulation of financial intermediaries, they become more vulnerable to crisis, because the access to foreign capital magnifies the weaknesses and distortions of the domestic financial system.

This suggests that financial liberalization must be carefully sequenced. A number of architectural reform proposals are designed to assist that process. Some concentrate on improving market regulation, bank supervision, and transparency standards. Others concentrate on minimizing the risks associated with capital flows, focusing on measures to discourage short-term borrowing in foreign currency, which is widely regarded as the most dangerous form of foreign capital.

The goal is not to proscribe international financial transactions, but simply to increase their relative cost – or, in the famous words of James Tobin (1978), 'to put some sand in the wheels' of international capital markets. This can be done in a number of ways.[3] The most widely supported is to tax foreign borrowing. Chile is the most well-known example of this approach. From May 1992 until May 1998, any company that borrowed abroad had to place 30 per cent of the proceeds at the central bank for one year. This unremunerated reserve requirement was the equivalent of a hefty tax on short-term borrowing. Over a longer-term horizon it became much less punitive. In addition, only Chilean companies with a credit rating equivalent to that of the sovereign government could borrow abroad. Alternative ways to discourage short-term borrowing include placing limits on open foreign currency positions by domestic banks and instituting high-risk weights in the capital requirements for foreign currency loans to domestic firms.

These proposals raise a number of questions. First, should the rules apply only to banks or also to the broad corporate sector? Banks are clearly the most vulnerable institutions, but a regulation narrowly focused on banks might simply shift the foreign borrowing to firms. Second, how can such rules be effective in a financial system that lacks adequate supervision and regulation? Third, how can such prudential regulations be implemented without jeopardizing a country's broad commitment to liberalization? Finally, and most importantly, do they work? Evidence from Chile suggests that the main effect of the controls was not on the level of incoming flows, but on their distribution across assets of different maturities. In other words, as observed by Valdes-Prieto and Soto (1997), while overall capital inflows were not affected, short-term inflows were effectively discouraged.[4]

While prudential controls on capital inflows may help prevent a crisis, they are not much use once a crisis occurs. However, some commentators, such as Paul Krugman (1998), suggest that a different type of capital control – on outflows – may be an important component of crisis resolution. In the face of a crisis, the country that attempts to safeguard the currency through sharp increases in the interest rates risks damaging the banking system and the economy. Similarly, a country that allows a sharp depreciation of the currency jeopardizes the health of the domestic banking and corporate sectors. Imposing controls on capital outflows allows policy-makers to sever the links between domestic interest rates and exchange rates. Thus they can lower interest rates and stimulate the domestic economy without incurring the cost of currency devaluation. While capital controls themselves do not solve the fundamental economic problems underlying a currency crisis, their proponents argue that they can give policymakers time to address the relevant reform issues.

Such a strategy carries considerable risks. First, there is the risk of a strongly negative market reaction. Once a country resorts to controls on capital outflows, investors will worry that politicians could introduce them again. They will therefore demand higher returns to invest in that country again. Worse, the introduction of capital outflow controls could unsettle markets more broadly and have negative consequences for the market access of other developing countries.

Second, capital outflow controls create the incentives for corruption – the trapped-in investor with a large sum of money will be inclined to bribe the local officials for his exit – and reduce the pressure for politicians to introduce politically unpopular structural reforms. If 'temporary' controls on capital outflows remain in place for long, they generate many adverse economic consequences. For all these reasons, proposals to sanction the liberal use of capital outflow controls are unlikely to find broad support among international financial architects. However, the use of capital controls as a last-resort measure now seems to have gained wider acceptance, including by the IMF. Indeed, the apparent success of Malaysia with capital controls attests to the fact that capital controls are more workable than is commonly presumed.

Improving Regulatory Standards

One of the main causes of the Asian financial crisis was poor regulation and supervision of financial institutions. Hence it is not surprising that much of the effort to improve the international financial architecture has concentrated on finding ways to improve international standards of financial regulation and supervision.

Two of the G22 working group reports were concerned with these issues: one concentrated on transparency and accountability (G22, 1998a), the other on strengthening financial systems (G22, 1998b). The report on transparency contained a variety of suggestions ranging from the uncontroversial (for instance, that private firms should adhere to national accounting standards) to the ambitious (that wide-ranging data on the international exposure of financial institutions and firms should be compiled and published). While increased transparency can help promote efficient global markets, it cannot prevent financial collapse in the presence of weak fundamentals. As long as the financial system has maturity and currency mismatches, it will be vulnerable to runs (Cole and Kehoe, 1998). Indeed, Morris and Shin (1998) show that excessive transparency can sometimes intensify, rather than ease, the problem of financial instability.

The report on strengthening financial systems enumerated major weaknesses in many domestic financial sectors, such as inadequate risk management, faulty deposit insurance schemes, and mismatched assets and liabilities. It found that international consensus existed in many areas of banking supervision and securities regulation, but that in some areas best practices and standards needed to be defined. The report also noted that standards should be defined in a collaborative manner so that both industrial and developing countries have a voice.

The Basle capital accords are widely regarded as a model for international supervisory standards. Although originally agreed on by the G10, the Basle standards for minimum capital adequacy for banks are now widely accepted. To ensure that banks are adequately capitalized, the Basle standards are measured against banks' risk-adjusted assets rather than their total assets. The Basle capital accords provide a framework for classifying assets according to their risk categories, specifying different risk weights for different risk categories, and calculating risk-adjusted assets. Since 1997 they have been supplemented by a broader set of core principles of banking supervision.

One way to encourage countries to adopt such standards is through IMF surveillance. The G22 working committees, for instance, recommended that the IMF issue a transparency report along with its regular Article IV economic assessment of member countries. Another approach is to improve coordination between regulatory bodies, or even to introduce a system of peer review, whereby national regulators could supervise each other. Improved regional surveillance would be another option. Recently, the Asian Development Bank has established a Regional Economic Monitoring Unit to support the surveillance activities of the ASEAN.

Another set of reform proposals focuses on improving existing regulatory standards. Some suggestions concentrate on tightening the rules on foreign borrowing in developing countries. Others focus on changing the incentives lending banks face, in particular by updating the Basle capital adequacy accords. Regulating lending banks has two positive effects. The first is realism: regulators of borrowing banks (in developing countries) are generally less sophisticated than those of lending banks (in industrial countries). The second effect is that better regulation might improve the incentives facing lending banks. The existing Basle capital standards contain several perverse incentives. For instance, risk weightings for short-term loans are considerably lower than for long-term loans, which gives lending banks a clear incentive to supply short-term rather than long-term loans to emerging markets. The ongoing revision of the Basle capital standards may well contain changes to these risk weightings.[5] The Basle supervisors are also considering the issue of banks' internal risk assessment for regulatory purposes. As the banks themselves should have the strongest incentive to act with prudence, some economists and policy-makers have argued that the greater use of banks' own methods of risk assessment (value-at-risk models) can be extremely useful for this purpose. Also under discussion in this regard is the need for regulatory purposes of increased reliance on market discipline through the mandatory issuance of subordinated debt, that is, debt that has a 'junior' claim on a firm's assets in the event of bankruptcy.

Compared with banking regulation, the problem of regulatory standards becomes much more severe when it comes to auditing and accounting, insolvency codes, and corporate governance. In these areas, a number of private sector bodies are active. The International Accounting Standards Committee, a committee with members from more than 100 countries, formulates international accounting standards. The International Federation of Accounts and the International Organization of Supreme Audit Institutions formulate auditing standards and issue auditing guidelines. Committee J of the International Bar Association has been concerned with bankruptcy laws and insolvency guides. The International Corporate Governance Network deals with issues of corporate governance. While all these organizations have done a considerable amount of work, much still remains to be done in improving standards in these areas.

To improve regulatory standards in the financial and corporate sectors internationally, some have suggested that the international financial organizations should work in harmony with these private sector entities. The international financial organizations should recognize these standards, urge adoption by their memberships, and monitor compliance. This decentralized approach to regulatory reform has much to warrant its recommendation.

Among the more radical regulatory reform ideas is the creation of global regulatory institutions. Proposals include a world financial authority that would be the equivalent of the World Trade

Organization for financial institutions (United Nations, 1998) and a board of overseers of international financial markets (Kaufman, 1998).[6] In each case, given that the goal is to create a global supervisor and regulator consistent with global capital markets, countries would have to surrender substantial amounts of national sovereignty, a requirement that renders these ideas unrealistic. On the other hand, if enforcement is left largely to national authorities, it is likely to be lax and defeat the very purpose of creating the organization.

Finally, in this regard, a recent institutional innovation of the G7 has been the creation of the Financial Stability Forum. This forum, which will bring together central bankers, finance ministers, financial regulators, and representatives of multilateral organizations, has an ambitious mission – to assess the issues and vulnerabilities affecting the global financial system and to identify and oversee the actions needed to address them. It is too early to say what role the forum will play in the evolving international financial architecture. However, if it can create a mechanism for improving information sharing, surveillance of and agreements on standards, codes of conduct, and transparency requirements, then it would significantly increase the efficiency of global financial markets and reduce systemic risks.[7] To achieve this objective successfully, the forum will need to expand its membership to emerging economies. The latest meeting of the Forum invited four new members – Australia, Hong Kong, the Netherlands and Singapore. Its progress so far has been rather slow.

Rethinking Exchange Rate Regimes

The Asian crisis has shown that pegged, but adjustable, exchange rates are difficult to sustain in a world of increasing capital mobility. Sooner or later they are likely to be tested by a speculative attack, forcing – at the very least – high interest rates and budget cuts. The Asian crisis has also reinforced another traditional argument against fixed, but adjustable, exchange rates: by creating an illusion of permanent currency stability, they reinforce the incentive for financial institutions and firms to borrow from abroad without hedging.

Given these problems, the emerging consensus now among economists is that only the extremes of exchange rate management are likely to succeed.[8] Today's conventional wisdom suggests that countries must either rigidly and irrevocably tie their currency to another by adopting a currency board or entering into a currency union, or they must allow their currency to float.

Three related arguments support flexible exchange rate regimes. First, countries with floating currencies are less likely to suffer sudden crises of investor confidence. By definition, they will not waste precious reserves defending an exchange rate peg. Empirical studies confirm that serious currency crises are generally associated with the collapse of a fixed exchange rate regime. On average, countries that see a sudden depreciation of a floating currency suffer less macroeconomic distress.

Second, a flexible exchange rate regime allows the government more room to act as a lender-of-last-resort to the financial sector. Countries committed to defending a currency peg cannot provide domestic liquidity freely without risking a loss of reserves. Countries with a flexible rate need not worry about losing reserves, because the exchange rate will simply depreciate as more domestic liquidity is created. This flexibility does not mean that countries with a flexible exchange rate can prevent financial crises generated, for instance, by large capital outflows. In fact, if the burden of external debt is high, the scope for increasing liquidity domestically may be limited.

Third, a flexible exchange rate allows a country more autonomy with regard to its macroeconomic policy. This is the classic argument in favour of floating rates (see the earlier discussion of the integration trilemma). However, exaggerating this benefit, especially for developing countries, is easy. A developing country with significant policy autonomy may have trouble gaining credibility in international financial markets. Too often in the past governments have used their discretion to pursue imprudent, inflationary policies. Countries with floating exchange rates often have to keep interest rates high to maintain investors' confidence. Mexico's experience in mid-1998 demonstrates this point. The peso fell by 20 per cent in response to turmoil in Asia and Russia, yet Mexican interest rates were considerably higher than those in Argentina, a country with an extremely tough currency board.

The choice of currency regime will depend on a country's size, history and geographical location. In Europe, for instance, it is likely that more countries will ultimately adopt the euro. In Latin America, Argentine policy-makers are seriously considering the adoption of the dollar as the national currency (dollarization). In Asia, driven by the bitter experience of the recent crisis, more and more countries are embracing a more flexible exchange rate regime, while Hong Kong continues to uphold the currency-board system. India and China, the two goliath economies of the region, still maintain an intermediate regime, which is only flexible with respect to current account transactions. There have been talks of a possible currency union in Asia. However, the future remains uncertain as the political and practical hurdles to any regional currency union remain high.

A number of observers (Cooper, 1984; Garten, 1998) have advocated the creation of a global currency union and a global central bank to oversee the global currency. There is no doubt that a single currency would do away with the problem of instability of currency values and will facilitate trade and cross-border investment. However, given that such an innovation requires a much greater degree of political integration than exists today, the idea cannot be implemented in the near future. Even if such an idea were politically feasible, it is not clear whether the entire world is really an 'optimal currency area'[9] and represents a better arrangement than a world with multiple currencies. Indeed, more than one currency may be desirable to promote competition among currencies and to hold inflation in check. In addition, different regions may need to follow different monetary policy stances as different countries are subject to 'asymmetric shocks', and therefore, the nature of macroeconomic problems and policies may differ significantly across the regions.

Creating an International Lender-of-Last-Resort

A number of reform proposals focus on preventing contagion in international financial markets by creating an international lender-of-last-resort (for example, Mishkin, 1994; Meltzer, 1998; Garten, 1998; Calomiris, 1998a; Giannini, 1999; Fischer, 1999). The argument in favour of an international lender-of-last-resort is based on an analogy with the role central banks play in national economies. When a banking panic hits a domestic financial system, the central bank can limit contagion by providing liquidity to the system. In a world of integrated capital markets, many argue that a similar institution is needed at the international level. By providing limited liquidity in return for policy conditionality, the IMF already plays a similar, if highly circumscribed, role. Most advocates of an international lender-of-last-resort suggest that the IMF should play this role.

However, the proposal to create an international lender-of-last-resort is plagued with numerous conceptual and practical difficulties. Conceptually, scholars do not agree on exactly what a lender-of-last-resort does. The classic definition stems from Bagehot (1873), which states that the lender-of-last-resort should lend freely, at a penalty rate, on good collateral in a time of financial panic. Thus the lender-of-last-resort must be able to distinguish between healthy and insolvent institutions, intervening only to stop unwarranted panics and leaving normally insolvent institutions to fail.

Extending these conditions from banks to countries and from national authorities to international institutions is a rather strenuous process. The first problem is that of distinguishing between illiquidity and insolvency. An international lender-of-last-resort should provide limitless liquidity in the case of the former, and demand restructuring and adjustment in the case of the latter; but as the Asian crisis highlighted, distinguishing between the two is extremely difficult.

The second problem is that of moral hazard. National central banks put in place prudential regulations on domestic financial institutions to limit reckless behaviour. They also retain the power to close or merge insolvent or weak financial institutions. Neither capacity exists at the international level. As yet, no binding global rules of financial behaviour exist, and the IMF certainly cannot close down a recalcitrant country.

The final issue relates to resources. If necessary, a domestic central bank can provide limitless liquidity simply by printing money (unless it is constrained by a fixed exchange rate regime). The IMF has no capacity to issue fiat money. Its resources are limited, and despite the recent capital increase and introduction of the New Arrangements to Borrow (an emergency credit line from donor countries to the IMF), they are insufficient to make it a credible lender-of-last-resort. To fulfil this role the IMF would need a substantial increase in its resources. Indeed, the real resources at the command of the IMF (as a percentage of world GNP) have declined over the years since its creation at the end of the Second World War.[10] In addition, it seems unlikely that the world community is prepared to make available to the IMF the kind of resources that will be required to make it an effective international lender-of-last-resort.

Some observers suggest that only countries which meet a stringent set of requirements, especially with respect to their banking systems, should have access to IMF funds (Calomiris, 1998b). To those countries that fulfil the requirements, the IMF should lend without policy conditionality, but should demand collateral in the form of government bonds. Dornbusch (1998) suggests that only countries which have complied with an agreed risk control strategy should qualify for IMF funds. These suggestions suffer from the problem that few countries would fulfil the requirements. Given the contagious nature of financial crises, it is unlikely that large countries would be left unaided even if they failed to meet the criteria. Moreover, by announcing that a country no longer fulfilled the criteria for assistance, the IMF might actually precipitate a crisis. However, charging countries with lower financial standards higher interest rates for assistance can reduce this risk (Fischer, 1999).

A proposal put forward by the USA in September 1998, and subsequently endorsed by the G7 and finally approved by the IMF's Executive Board in April 1999, moves the IMF cautiously in the direction of being a lender-of-last-resort. The goal is to set up a contingency credit facility, called Contingency Credit Line (CCL), where countries in good economic health, i.e. meeting certain macroeconomic and regulatory standards, can set up a precautionary credit line with the IMF to reduce the chances of being hit by financial contagion. This credit line, which will be more expeditiously processed than other IMF loans, will be front loaded and disbursed in large amounts. Repayment maturities will be short and the interests will be high to discourage misuse of this facility. The problem with this facility is that it is difficult to implement in practice, because the distinction between unwarranted panic and fundamental economic problems are often very arbitrary. Depending on how the access conditions are enforced, the facility may become irrelevant or harmful. If the facility is too easily accessible, then it could become a fruitful source of moral hazard; if it is too strictly enforced, it can never become activated and would therefore be rendered irrelevant. Finally, rather than being viewed as a sign of strength, it is widely believed that accessing the CCL by a country can trigger speculative attacks on its currency and unleash new waves of macroeconomic stability. For these reasons, despite the IMF pressure on several countries to make use of this facility, no country has so far availed itself of the CCL.

Finally, George Soros (1998) has proposed the establishment of a new international authority to insure the international investors against debt default.[11] When floating loans, borrowing countries would buy an insurance against such defaults. Such an international authority would set limits on how much each country would be allowed to borrow, and any amount in excess of this limit would be uninsured and would not qualify for bail-outs, should a default occur. However, such an idea has some shortcomings. It is not clear how the global authority would determine the limits on how much should be loaned and how much is the appropriate insurance fee would be. Second, it is difficult to bestow any real power on the international regulatory authority without compromising national sovereignty. Finally, the threat that there will not be any bailing out for the default of the uninsured amount is not credible because the proposal does not change the basic incentives that drag debtor countries into the crisis.

Establishing the Regional Monetary Funds

Whether there should be a 'deep pocket' lender-of-last-resort is a subject of considerable controversy on account of both feasibility and desirability. However, there is very little controversy over whether there should be some crisis manager(s) to contain and manage the sudden eruption of a financial crisis. What is however controversial is whether the role should be vested on a single entity or a plurality of entities. In other words, whether crisis should be managed by a single global entity like the IMF or a set of regional entities complementing the role of the IMF.

Japan has recently proposed the creation of 'regional currency support mechanisms' – the regional monetary funds – to complement the role and function of the IMF (Miyazawa, 1998). The 'mechanisms' are institutions that would provide liquidity in times of financial crisis. These mechanisms, which can be established in Asia, the Western hemisphere and Eastern Europe, could be regionally funded by countries that are economically interlinked by trade, investment, etc., and are engaged in policy dialogue with each other. Non-regional countries with political and economic interests in the region could also participate. A number of economic arguments have been advanced in favour of the regional Fund[12] (Ito, Ogawa and Sasaki, 1999; Quibria, 1999). First, currency and financial crisis have strong cross-border spillover effects: macroeconomic and financial instability can fairly easily spread to neighbouring economies even if economic fundamentals are sound. While the recent Asian crisis may have something to do with economic fundamentals, it has a lot to do with investor panic. The disproportionate regional nature of cross-border repercussion justifies supplementary regional response. Second, given its vantage position of an insider organization, a regional institution is likely to have a comparative advantage in its diagnosis of the problem, devising appropriate solutions, monitoring and surveillance of possible financial difficulty and bringing peer pressure for corrective action. Third, a regional institution would be geared to quick action, as it is likely to be more receptive to regional needs than a large global organization like the IMF with more than 180 members. As local organizations are more receptive to local problems than the remote central organization, a regional fund will be more receptive to local needs than the global IMF. Fourth, a global institution with limited reserves is ill-equipped to meet the challenges of today's complex financial crises. During the Asian crisis, the IMF had to rely on additional resources from other international and bilateral donors. Therefore, the availability of a larger pool of funds in the form of a regional IMF could be useful in extinguishing such a crisis.[13] Finally, a regional institution would create a kind of competitive pluralism in the market-place for ideas, to which the affected countries could turn in times of need and could benefit from. The idea of a regional fund, which is based on a number of strong economic arguments, enjoys wide support among Asian leaders.

'Bailing in' the Private Sector

Another popular goal among the architects of international financial reform is that of 'bailing in' the private sector, i.e. forcing the creditors to share the burden of a financial crisis. The idea is to minimize moral hazard and spread the burden of financial crisis by ensuring that private investors and banks bear some of the cost.

One approach that Argentina has successfully pioneered is to set up private sector credit lines before a crisis. Argentina has negotiated US $6.7 billion worth of repurchase arrangements with 13 inter-national banks. Against the collateral of an equivalent amount of domestic bonds, these arrangements give Argentina access to capital in the event of a financial crisis. Mexico and Indonesia have negotiated similar facilities with international banks (although in both cases, these facilities are pure credit lines). They are, in effect, a limited form of private lender-of-last resort. Such arrangements have considerable potential, particularly if multilateral development banks guarantee some portion of the risk involved, and thereby encourage more private banks to participate in such schemes. However, this type of facility is likely to be available to countries with relatively weak policies, and the amount may often be less than sufficient.

More controversial are proposals to forcibly 'bail in' private investors once a crisis has struck. One proposal, advocated by the G22, is to encourage 'lending into arrears' by the IMF. Since the 1980s the IMF has been able, in certain circumstances, to lend to a country that was in arrears on its commercial bank debt. Now this idea has been extended to countries that are in default to other private creditors, including bond-holders. Provided that the country is willing to under-take strong policy adjustment and is making good-faith efforts to work with creditors to solve its financial problems, the IMF can lend to the country. This effectively sanctions default. The goal behind this approach is to encourage recalcitrant creditors to negotiate, and thereby to promote orderly and responsible debt restructuring rather than chaotic default. The G22 working group also recommended that bond contracts be modified to facilitate restructuring. By including so-called collective action clauses, such as the collective representation of creditors, designating a trustee to speak for creditors, binding majority decisions, and formulas for sharing the costs of workouts in all sovereign bond offerings, involving the private sector in the resolution of financial crises would be easier. While an orderly workout is clearly superior to a disorderly one, the risk involved in changing bond contracts is that the market for such bonds will shrink and the cost of funds will rise.

More radical proposals along similar lines include imposing 'haircuts' (mandatory losses) on investors if they withdraw during a financial crisis. One proposal by Williem Buiter and Anna Siebert (1998) suggests a mandatory debt rollover option with a penalty on all foreign currency lending. This option would entitle the borrower to extend or roll over the debt at maturity for a specified period, say three or six months, at a penalty rate. The penalty would have to be big enough to ensure that the borrower would not want to exercise the rollover option under orderly market conditions. If crisis conditions still prevailed when the rollover period expired, the option could be exercised again at an even higher penalty. This proposal would only be useful when otherwise solvent borrowers are unable to roll over their foreign currency debt because of a liquidity crisis or credit crunch. It only helps when a country is solvent, willing to pay, but prevented from doing so because international financial and credit markets are temporarily closed to it. Given the difficulty of distinguishing between insolvency and illiquidity, it is not clear that a market for such options would emerge. This proposal, too, might simply raise the cost of capital for borrowing countries. Finally, it has been suggested that the power to activate the mandatory rollover option should lie with a third party like the IMF. The IMF will activate only in the case of a pure liquidity crisis rather than a crisis rooted in fundamentals. However, even then it is less clear whether the IMF is in a better position than market participants to distinguish between illiquidity and solvency crises. In addition, should the IMF be lending to the country, it may not fairly qualify as the disinterested party to make that decision.

The most radical ideas for 'bailing in' the private sector focus on creating an international bankruptcy court. Just as domestic bankruptcy courts can prevent creditor grab-races, decide on a hierarchy of claimants, and allow an insolvent but viable firm access to new financing, so some commentators such as Jeffrey Sachs (1995) suggest there should be an international bankruptcy court to restructure countries' debts. This idea stands little chance of being implemented. First, it would demand a huge surrender of national sovereignty. A domestic court can seize a company's physical assets and fire its board of directors. The country equivalence of these acts would entail seizing sovereign assets and firing sovereign governments! Second, national bankruptcy codes differ enormously, and reaching international agreement on a single code is highly unlikely.

Conclusions

The Asian financial crisis has prompted scores of proposals for a new international financial architecture. Many of these ideas are interesting, yet impractical. Many are innovative, but often inconsistent with each other. The reason is that different reformers choose different combinations of national sovereignty, financial market regulation and support, and capital mobility. Given these incompatible goals, international policy-makers are unlikely to agree on radical changes to today's financial architecture.

The idea of large global institutions regulating financial markets and institutions is interesting. However, it collides head on with the notion of national sovereignty and signifies a move toward creating a centralized architecture, founded on mega-bureaucracies. Nevertheless, there is no denying the need for appropriate institution(s) for global crisis management. What is, however, contentious is whether the institutional framework for crisis management should be a centralized or a decentralized one. That is, whether a single global body, like the IMF, or a host of regional institutions should manage crisis is an open question. This chapter argues that there is a strong case for such decentralization,[14] and advocates the creation of regional funds that will be more sensitive to local needs, provide a number of solutions and bring to bear peer pressures to address local problems.

In addition to decentralization of the global financial architecture, a number of other important reforms appear to be warranted. First, minimum international standards of financial practice need to be negotiated. Despite considerable progress at creating international norms, auditing and accounting practices still vary considerably across countries.

This makes it difficult for lenders to gauge the financial conditions of borrower banks and corporations. Differences in corporate governance practices, investor protection laws, and laws relating to insider trading in securities markets also make international capital markets less transparent and more dangerous than they need be. While individual countries should implement reforms in these areas as they deem appropriate, minimum international standards would help prevent national problems spilling over to the international level.

Second, prudent regulation of capital accounts should be introduced. While developing countries should aim for integration into the international financial system, this should not imply a reckless rush to capital account convertibility. The gradual and cautious removal of capital controls may be appropriate for countries whose domestic capital markets are underdeveloped and whose capacity to regulate excessive risk-taking by domestic institutions is limited. For many developing countries, Chilean-style taxes on capital flows may be helpful.

Third, exchange rate regimes have to be reformed. The options for emerging economies seem to have narrowed significantly to the extremes, i.e. a fully flexible exchange rate regime and the currency board. A sudden collapse in the exchange rate peg and large unexpected swings in the currency value can bring serious financial distress to domestic banks and corporations with unhedged debt exposure. This problem can to a large extent be circumvented in two ways. First, a floating exchange rate will induce banks and corporations to hedge their foreign currency debt. Second, a currency board or currency union will permanently eliminate unexpected currency fluctuations. International financial institutions can push the agenda of an appropriate exchange rate regime without any fundamental institutional change.

Fourth, there is a need to create the framework for an orderly restructuring of problem debts. Debt restructuring today is a difficult, protracted process. Modest changes, including clauses for majority voting and the provision of a trustee to represent and coordinate creditors, could easily be introduced. If industrial countries included such provisions in their bond contracts, they could become standard practice, then developing countries would not incur a price penalty when they introduced them.

Fifth, private sector credit lines should be encouraged. Given the IMF's limited resources and the conceptual difficulties surrounding the notion of an official international lender-of-last-resort, limited credit lines with the private sector appear promising. Argentina's contingency finance arrangements with private banks seem to have served it well. With multilateral guarantees this approach might prove useful for more countries. The reform proposals suggested in this chapter do not envisage the creation of a centralized architecture through the establishment of global regulators nor do they call for the New Bretton Woods for the new millennium. Rather, this chapter proposes an opposite approach, which emphasizes the decentralization of the existing international financial structure, along with a number of relatively simple innovations. The innovations suggested here are by no means new. What is perhaps new about this chapter is that it pieces together a coherent body of proposals. The suggested proposals, if implemented, would ensure not only a more efficient allocation of capital worldwide but also a relatively stable global financial environment, from which all countries would benefit.

Acknowledgements

The authors would like to express their gratitude to Koichi Hamada, John McCombie, Soonam Oh and Purnima Rajpakse for helpful comments, suggestions and encouragement. However, none of the above is responsible for any errors, omissions and deficiencies in this chapter. The chapter draws on the Asian Development Outlook 1999, of which Quibria was the lead author. The opinions expressed herein are of the authors and not of the Bank.

Notes

1. The idea indeed goes back to the earlier work of Nobel Laureate Robert Mundell (1968), who introduced the concept of 'impossible trinity'. This implies that a country cannot simultaneously achieve free movement of capital, a fixed exchange rate and an effective monetary policy; it has to pick two of the three goals.
2. See Asian Development Bank (1999) for further discussion.
3. See Eichengreen (1999a) for a discussion of the different policy guidelines for capital account liberalization.
4. However, Edwards (1998) argues that the success of Chile in avoiding speculative pressures and discouraging short-term volatile flows has little to do with Chile's system of capital controls. It is largely due to a constellation of favourable conditions, including the presence of a well-developed system of prudential banking regulation in the country.
5. The Basle Committee on Banking Supervision has drafted a new set of proposals for capital adequacy requirements that are stricter than before. The most controversial requirement is that the lending agencies must use credit ratings from the international credit agencies, such as Moody's and

Standard and Poor's. In countries such as Germany and Japan, domestic corporations are not normally rated by external agencies. This would reduce the lending by Japanese and German banks *vis-à-vis* US banks (Business Week article by Fairlamb, 4 October 1999).

6. As recommended by the United Nations Committee for Development Planning, the World Financial Organization would oversee international capital flows and negotiate debt repayments in crises (World Bank, 1999). In contrast, Kaufman's proposed world financial regulator would be run by investment experts from the private sector who would specifically oversee both banks and non-bank financial intermediaries.

7. The Forum has put together a compendium of standards and best practices, which are now available on its web site.

8. This has now come to be known as the 'hypothesis of the vanishing intermediate regime', which is in effect a corollary of the 'impossible trinity'. However, there are a few dissenting voices, such as Jeffrey Frankel (1999) and John Williamson (1998), who contend that the hypothesis is not yet proven and the consensus is far from forged. Frankel points out that a majority of the countries under IMF membership still follow an intermediate exchange rate regime.

9. The seminal work on the optimal currency area was done by Robert Mundell (1968).

10. To date, the IMF only has approximately US$200 billion in loanable resources which, if taken as a percentage of world GNP, would amount to less than one-fifth the figure the IMF had at its inception. In view of the resource constraint, an independent task force, sponsored by the Council on Foreign Relations, recommended that the IMF should abandon large financial rescue packages. The Fund should lend less and concentrate on crisis prevention, restricting itself to a leaner agenda of monetary, fiscal and exchange rate policies and foreign sector reform (a press release by the Council on Foreign Relations, 17 September 1999).

11. The Soros proposal of creating a sort of an international Federal Deposit Insurance Corporation (FDIC) for country debt highlights in some sense an important economic principle – of taxing risky activities that generate negative externalities.

12. The theoretical work on the incentive mechanism of international financial organizations has only recently begun (see for example, Bagwell and Staiger, 1997; Dixit, 1996; Hamada, 1999). They pose the problem of the incentive issue facing an international financial institution from the common agency perspective. There are many countries that are members of the institution. The countries are the principals who monitor the common agent, the institution. Within this framework, Hamada shows that under fairly non-restrictive conditions, the existence of more than one institution would improve the welfare of the members, if they offer goods that have more of the characteristics of private goods, such as rescuing the crisis countries. However, if the good that is being served is predominantly public good, then the existence of a single entity may be more helpful. If the goods offered by the institutions are more private in nature, then the existence of more than one institution will be welfare-enhancing. According to Hamada, 'a kind of Tiebout equilibrium by voting with feet'

will take place (p. 9). In this connection he went on to argue, 'if the major role of the IMF and the Asian Monetary Fund is . . . to rescue crisis countries, and accordingly has more private good characteristics, then the coexistence of two institutions may be beneficial to the world. If Japan cannot represent its wishes in proportion to its financial contributions . . . and the United States does not fully cooperate with the IMF with respect to payment of subscription, Japan's intention to establish another fund can be substantiated' (p. 10). In sum, the message that seems to emerge from the theory is that if the good that is being offered is a pure public good, then a single global institution is optimal. If the good being offered has more private good property, then there is a case for plurality of suppliers and decentralized production.

13. The IMF can be in charge of providing goods, which are more in the nature of public goods such as global standards, issues in exchange management and orderly capital account convertibility, etc.

14. The basic rationale for regional development banks is based on such notions of advantages of regional proximity and decentralization. The World Bank, which seems to have recognized the advantages of such decentralization, is in the midst of efforts to decentralize its operations regionally, including the budget.

References

Asian Development Bank (1999) *Asian Development Outlook 1999*, Hong Kong, Oxford University Press for the Asian Development Bank.

Bagehot, W. (1873) *Lombard Street: A Description of the Money Market*, London, William Clowes and Sons.

Bagwell, K. and Staiger, R. W. (1997) 'Multilateral Tariff Cooperation during the Formation of Free Trade Areas', *International Economic Review*, 38(2):291–319.

Bhagwati, J. (1998) 'The Capital Myth: The Difference between Trade in Widgets and Dollars', *Foreign Affairs*, 77 (May/June):7–12.

Buiter, W. and Siebert, A. (1998) 'UNDROP or You Drop: A Small Contribution to the New International Financial Architecture', unpublished manuscript, Department of Economics, Yale University, New Haven, CT.

Calomiris, C. (1998a) 'The IMF's Imprudent Role as Lender of Last Resort', *Cato Journal*, 17(3):275–95.

Calomiris, C. (1998b) 'Blueprints for a New Global Financial Structure', unpublished manuscript, Columbia University, New York.

Cole, H. and Kehoe, T. (1998) 'A Self-Fulfilling Debt Crisis', *Staff Report*, 211 (July). Federal Reserve of Minneapolis.

Cooper, R. (1984) 'A Monetary System for the Future', *Foreign Affairs*, 63:166–184.

Council on Foreign Relations (1999) 'International Financial Architecture', a press release (17 September). [Online]. Available from: http://www.foreignrelations.org/public/pubs/IFAPressRelease.html/

Dixit, A. (1996) *The Making of Economic Policy: A Transaction-Cost Politics Perspective*, Cambridge, Massachusetts Institute of Technology.

Dornbusch, R. (1998) 'After Asia: New Directions for the International Financial System', unpublished manuscript, Massachusetts Institute of Technology, Boston.

Edwards, S. (1998) 'Capital Flows, Real Exchange Rates and Capital Controls: Some Latin American Experiences', Working Paper No. 6800 (November), National Bureau of Economic Research, Cambridge, MA.

Eichengreen, B. (1999a) *Toward a New International Financial Architecture: A Practical Post-Asia Agenda*, Washington, The Institute for International Economics.

Eichengreen, B. (1999b) 'Taming Capital Flows', a paper prepared for a special issue of *World Development* edited by Irma Adelman (August).

Fairlamb, D. (1999) 'International–Special Report: A Big Brouhaha in the Banking World', *Business Week* (4 October). [Online]. Available from: http://www.businessweek.com/1999/99_40/b3649036.htm/

Fischer, S. (1999) 'On the Need for an International Lender of Last Resort', paper presented at the annual meetings of the American Economic Association and the American Finance Association, 3 January, New York.

Frankel, J. A. (1999) 'No Single Currency Regime is Right for All Countries or at All Times', Working Paper no. 7338 (September). National Bureau of Economic Research, Cambridge, Massachusetts. [Online]. Available from: http://www.nber.org/papers/w7338/

G22 (Group of 22) (1998a) 'Report of the Working Group on Transparency and Accountability', International Monetary Fund, Washington, D.C.

G22 (Group of 22) (1998b) 'Report of the Working Group on Strengthening Financial Systems', International Monetary Fund, Washington, D.C.

Garten, J. (1998) 'In This Economic Chaos, A Global Central Bank Can Help', *International Herald Tribune* 8 (25 September).

Giannini, C. (1999) 'Enemy of None but Friend of All? An International Perspective on the Lender of Last Resort Function', Working Paper WP/99/10, Washington, DC, International Monetary Fund.

Hamada, K. (1999) 'Incentive Mechanisms Surrounding International Financial Institutions', *Asian Development Review*, 16(1):

Ito, T., Ogawa, E. and Sasaki, Y. N. (1999) 'Establishment of the East Asian Fund', in The Institute for International Monetary Affairs (ed.) *Stabilization of Currency and Financial Systems in East Asia and International Financial Coordination*, Tokyo, Institute for International Monetary Affairs, Chapter 3.

Kaufman, H. (1998) 'Preventing the Next Global Financial Crisis', *Washington Post* A17 (28 January).

Krugman, P. (1998) 'Saving Asia: It's Time to Get Radical', *Fortune* (7 September): 74–80.

Meltzer, A. (1998) 'Asian Problems and the IMF', Testimony prepared for the Joint Economic Committee, US Congress, 24 February.

Mishkin, F. (1994) 'Preventing Financial Crises: An International Perspective', Working Paper no. 4636 (February), Cambridge, MA, National Bureau of Economic Research.

Miyazawa, K. (1998) 'Towards a New International Financial Architecture', a speech delivered at the Foreign Correspondents Club of Japan, 15 December.

Morris, S. and Shin, H. Y. (1998) 'Unique Equilibrium in a Model of Self-Fulfilling Currency Attacks', *American Economic Review*, 88 (June):587–97.

Mundell, R. A. (1968) *International Economics*, New York, Macmillan.

Quibria, M. G. (1999) 'The Case for Asian Fund', *Asia Week* (25 June):56.

Rodrik, D. (1998) 'Who needs capital account liberalization?', in P. B. Kenen (ed.) *Should the IMF Pursue Capital Account Convertibility?* Essays in International Finance No. 207. Princeton, NJ, Princeton University, Department of Economics, International Finance Section.

Rossi, M. (1999) 'Financial Fragility and Economic Performance in Developing Economies: Do Capital Controls, Prudential Regulations and Supervision Matter?', Working Paper WP/99/66, Washington, DC, International Monetary Fund.

Sachs, J. (1995) 'Do We Need an International Lender of Last Resort?', paper prepared for the Frank Graham Memorial Lecture, Princeton University.

Sachs, J. (1998) 'Fixing the IMF Remedy', *The Banker*, 148 (February):16–18.

Soros, G. (1998) *The Crisis of Global Capitalism*, New York, Public Affairs Press.

Summers, L. (1999) 'Reflections on Managing Global Integration', Lecture delivered at the Annual Meeting of the Association of Government Economists, New York, 4 January.

Tobin, J. (1978) 'A Proposal for International Monetary Reform', *Eastern Economic Journal*, 4:153–9.

United Nations (1998) 'Bretton Woods and UN Move Closer', *Development Update*, 25 (September–October).

Valdes-Prieto, S., and Soto, M. (1997) 'The Effectiveness of Capital Controls: Theory and Evidence from Chile', unpublished manuscript, Universidad Catholica de Chile, Santiago.

Williamson, J. (1998) 'Crawling Bands or Monitoring Bands: How to Manage Exchange Rates in a World of Capital Mobility', *International Finance* 1 (October):59–80. Washington, The Institute for International Economics. [Online]. Available from: http://www.iie.com/TESTMONY/ifwills2.htm/

World Bank (1999) 'UN Calls for Body to Monitor Quicksilver Capital', *Development News* (9 April). [Online]. Available from: http://wblnoo18.worldbank.org/news/devnews.nsf/

4
An Agenda for a New Bretton Woods*

John Grieve Smith

Introduction

The 1944 Bretton Woods Agreement established the International Monetary Fund and the World Bank, and laid down for the first time an agreed framework of rules for international finance. The aim was to avoid a recurrence of the devastating economic crises and mass unemployment of the inter-war years. Over the years, however, the accelerating growth of financial markets and the abandonment of fixed exchange rates has led to major changes in the international financial scene. Short-term capital movements and fluctuating exchange rates have become a major source of instability, making it increasingly difficult for companies involved in international trade and investment to plan ahead, as national currencies alternate between being over-valued or under-valued – as British industry has found to its cost. More recently, with growing financial liberalization of capital markets, developing and transition economies have been hit by a series of crises, first in Asia, then in Russia and Brazil, which have culminated in financial failure and massive rises in unemployment, with millions of people in countries such as Indonesia slipping back into dire poverty.

The time has come for a fundamental review of international arrangements to tackle these problems. Globalization means that it is more important than ever for governments to work together to establish the international machinery needed to guarantee financial stability and ensure that the new forces of globalization become a force for

---

* This chapter is a condensed version of the *Report On An Agenda For A New Bretton Woods* by a Robinson College Working Group, convened by the author.

progress, not a threat of disaster. This chapter discusses the broad principles that should underlie such a new regime and possible ways of implementing them.

Unstable Capital Flows

The 1997 East Asian crisis affected what appeared to be some of the best performing economies in the world. The onset of the crisis was almost totally unexpected, as were its severity and the speed and extent of the subsequent contagion (Singh, 1999; Grabel, 1999). The economic and social effects on the worst affected countries have been extremely serious. The World Bank estimates that Indonesia's GDP fell by 15 per cent in 1998, Korea's by 7 per cent and Malaysia's by 5 per cent, leading to sharp falls in employment and real incomes. Unemployment in Indonesia, Korea and Thailand combined is estimated to have risen to about 18 million at the end of 1998, compared to 5 million at the end of 1996. As a consequence, 17 million more people in Indonesia alone are expected to fall below a poverty line of US$1 a day (World Bank, 1998/9). The poorer and more vulnerable groups in those countries will be the worst affected, even though they did not contribute to the problem.

Causes of the Crisis

Why were these economies suddenly shaken by such major currency and financial crises? Clearly there were important weaknesses in their domestic financial systems, particularly in their banking systems, which were not appropriately regulated. There had been poor monitoring and regulation of short-term private debt, incurred both by banks and by corporate borrowers. The form in which the capital accounts were liberalized also encouraged short-term flows. Furthermore, several had pegged their currencies to the US dollar, which made them less competitive when the US dollar appreciated sharply *vis-à-vis* the Japanese yen. Because Japan is such an important trading and investment partner for the East Asian countries, this was particularly damaging.

The damage that can be done by sharp changes in capital flows is is greater if a high proportion of the inflows are short-term and easily reversible. In the case of the East Asian crisis, the reversal of private capital flows was quite dramatic. According to figures from the Institute of International Finance (IIF), the five East Asian countries hardest hit by the crisis (South Korea, Indonesia, Malaysia, Thailand

and the Philippines) experienced in a single year a turnaround of US$105 billion, a shift from an inflow of US$93 billion in 1996 to an estimated outflow of US$12 billion in 1997, an outflow that continued in 1998. Most of this swing occurred in commercial bank lending, followed by short-term portfolio flows, whilst foreign direct investment remained constant. The turnaround of US$105 billion in the five Asian economies represented more than 10 per cent of their combined GDP (higher than the 8 per cent shift that occurred in Latin America in the early 1980s).

A major factor in all such crises is the tendency for investors to 'follow the herd' and fall in with whatever is the currently fashionable trend. Individual short-term investors, lenders or fund managers try to choose the investments or loans that are most likely to be chosen by other investors or lenders. This leads to self-fulfilling attacks, i.e. crises arising without obvious current policy inconsistencies. In such cases, the attitude of speculators and investors is crucial to whether an attack occurs. Good macroeconomic fundamentals are not a sufficient condition for avoiding such crises.

Stabilizing Capital Flows to Developing Countries

The instability of capital movements lies at the heart of recent financial troubles. It has been widely argued that free capital flows benefit all countries – especially the developing countries where there is a capital shortage. But in practice flows of productive investment have been swamped by speculative movements in short-term capital and portfolio investment; and even productive capital does not necessarily flow into the developing countries that most need it, nor in the most appropriate form. Indeed, the reduction of official flows during the last decade or so, in the belief that the development of international capital markets reduces the need for such flows, has only aggravated this problem: a cruel reminder of this is the absence of capital inflows into Africa, despite all the liberalization and opening-up measures that the continent has taken during the last decade or so.

Despite the potentially important roles of FDI and portfolio investments in providing private long-term capital in developing countries, they tend to be geographically concentrated in the middle-income countries, with a considerably higher degree of concentration in the case of portfolio investment. Middle-income developing countries received an average share of 58 per cent of FDI and 87 per cent of portfolio investments in developing countries in the period 1991 to 1996 (World Bank, 1998).

Even in countries where there is an inflow, there is no guarantee that foreign capital will go into the sectors most important for long-term economic development, without some regulation by the national governments. In Latin America, additional capital inflows typically did little more than finance a huge consumer boom feeding on imported goods. In the crisis-stricken Asian countries, governments that had previously imposed some controls on real estate investments or investment in industries where there was a danger of excess capacity, abandoned such practice under IMF pressure in the 1990s, consequently creating asset bubbles and/or excess capacity.

This problem must be tackled on a number of fronts. The first is to re-examine the principles and rules affecting developing countries' ability to control the flow of capital into and out of their countries. The second is to consider what international action can and should be taken to encourage and stabilize the flow of capital to developing countries, particularly those in most need. Care must be taken, however, that the measures adopted contribute to broadening access by all developing countries to capital flows, particularly long-term ones. In this context, foreign direct investment is potentially beneficial, as it is not only a source of capital, but can also contribute technological and managerial know-how, as well as better access to markets.

Capital Controls

In tackling the question of controlling capital flows, it is important to distinguish between short-run and long-run movements. Short-run capital flows, by their very nature, are more volatile. Long-run capital flows in the form of foreign direct investment are much less likely to be reversed. A variety of short-run controls have been tried to regulate the capital inflow or at least to make it costly to move capital in and out a country quickly. 'Evaluation of these controls suggests that in most cases they were effective to varying degrees: inflows significantly declined as a percentage of GDP after their imposition except in Brazil and Columbia, with short-term inflows actually becoming negative for a time in Chile and Malaysia: and in Chile and Columbia there was shift away from short-term in the composition of inflows' (UNCTAD, 1988).

A fundamental review is required of the possible scope for capital controls in an international regime where they are no longer ruled out. The optimal degree of financial openness and the appropriate capital controls differ between countries, depending on such factors as their size, stage of development, the sophistication of their existing financial sector, and the competence of their administrators. No single recipe or model will fit them all, but there needs to be an agreed set of principles and rules governing the use of such controls, to avoid accusations of favouritism or discrimination between lenders or borrowers.

Development Capital

The two basic objectives of any reforms must be to provide an adequate flow of development capital to those countries that need it and ensure that the benefits of such capital flows are not destroyed by speculative capital inflows and outflows. To achieve the first objective the current role of the World Bank needs to be reconsidered. Its original remit (set out in Article 1 of the Bretton Woods Agreement) was 'To promote private foreign investment by means of guarantees or participation in loans and other investments made by private investors; and when private capital is not available on reasonable terms, to supplement private investment by providing, on suitable conditions, finance for productive purposes out of its own capital, funds raised by it and other resources'.

Portfolio investment in developing countries, in the form of debt and equity, was increasing sharply before the crisis. Bond issues, certificates of deposits and commercial paper, equities and commercial bank loan syndications increased from 18 per cent of total net long-term resource flows to developing countries in 1990 and 1991 to more than 39 per cent in the period 1992 to 1997.

The growth of portfolio investment reflects the increased depth and sophistication of the participation of developing countries in international capital markets, as well as the participation of foreign companies in the emergent equity and bond markets in some developing countries. The sources of capital, however, are expected to decline in the short to medium term, owing to the collapse of domestic capital markets and the restricted access of developing countries to international capital markets. But in the longer term, it is likely to recover in importance. The speed and extent of the recovery will depend, however, on the restoration of confidence in the crisis-hit countries, including the reform and strengthening of the financial systems. The problem is the ease with which such inflows can be reversed.

Foreign direct investment in developing countries has also grown rapidly in significance in both absolute and relative terms during the 1990s, particularly since 1993 when it surpassed official development finance in value and became the single largest component of net long-term resource flows in these countries. It now forms a substantial component of private long-term flows, with an average share of 52 per cent in the period 1990 to 1997.

Foreign direct investment is not only the least unstable source of capital, it can also be a major source of technology transfer and skill diffusion to the host countries. The success of foreign direct investment, however, depends heavily on the ability of the host country to absorb and effectively utilize the imported know-how and technology, which calls for an educated workforce and good infrastructure – both of which require public expenditure. Without a healthy economic climate, foreign direct investment can inhibit the growth of domestic industry. Moreover, under adverse circumstances, there is the danger that foreign companies' 'branch factories' may be the first to close. Nevertheless direct investment does not carry the risks of drastic outflows that are associated with portfolio investment.

Official development finance supports the growth of long-term private capital flows in developing countries, indirectly through grants and loans for the accumulation of basic social capital such as public utilities which are a prerequisite for private productive investment, as well as directly through the provision of guarantees and investment insurance for productive capital investment. Since the mid-1980s the flow of official development finance to developing countries, in the form of loans and grants, has declined dramatically, from an average share of two-thirds of total net resource flows in the period 1986 to 1990 to over one-quarter in the period 1990 to 1997 – with grants remaining more important than loans. With the decline in private investment following the Asian crises, official development finance assumes increasing importance and new ways need to be found to fund it.

The Tobin Tax

One measure which could both significantly reduce the volume of speculative foreign exchange transactions, and raise money for international purposes, would be a 'Tobin tax', i.e. a tax levied on all foreign exchange dealings (for a detailed examination of the Tobin Tax see ul Haq, Kaul and Grunberg, 1996; Arestis and Sawyer, 1997; Grieve Smith, 1997). A tax of the order of 0.1 per cent would yield significant sums of money, which could be used to provide additional development funds, particularly for low-income developing countries that do not at present attract much in the way of foreign capital.

Such a tax would reduce the attraction of very short-term movements in and out of currencies, which account for a high proportion of transactions. A tax of 0.1 per cent would mean that a movement in and out of currency for less than 7 days would not be worthwhile if there was an interest rate differential of less than 10 per cent. In addition, a reduction in the volume of transactions would mean that the reserves of Central Banks would be greater relative to the volume of transactions and hence may make Central Bank intervention in foreign exchange markets somewhat more effective. Such a tax would not, however, deter speculation against major changes in exchange rates.

There is little doubt that the Tobin tax would have considerable tax-raising powers. Revenue of the order of over US$200 billion a year could be generated through a modest transactions tax (Arestis and Sawyer, 1997). It is clear, however, that the collection of a Tobin tax on a purely national basis would generate (on the present pattern of exchange transactions) large disparities in revenue raised by different countries, with the UK and the USA collecting nearly half of the total revenue. It is essentially an international tax, of which only part should be kept by collecting countries and the remainder used to support international activities (or be subject to some redistribution mechanism whereby the revenue collected in those countries was redistributed to other countries).

There is widespread agreement that the tax would have to be implemented on a coordinated (and virtually universal) international basis. This may well be the most important practical obstacle to its implementation. It would clearly require the cooperation of all countries with significant foreign exchange dealings within their borders (and those with the potential to develop foreign exchange dealing centres), and agreement on a common rate of tax. Levying the tax on the basis of the location of the transaction would, however, give every country with a foreign exchange market an incentive to levy the tax.

The workings of the tax could be reinforced by making the administration of a tax on currency transactions a condition of membership of the IMF and the BIS; although this in itself might not be sufficient to prevent the growth of offshore dealing because a small country might feel it had little to gain from membership of the IMF. It might therefore be necessary to have a punitive tax on dealings with offshore markets.

The appropriate definition of the transaction would be any transaction that involved the exchange of a financial asset denominated in one currency for a financial asset denominated in another currency, which is in line with Tobin's initial suggestion. Any other less inclusive definition would create readily exploitable loopholes and provide ways of financial transactions being disguised as trade. The introduction of the tax may be complex, but it is doubtful whether it would be any more complex than existing taxes on income and expenditure. It would be relatively easy to collect because the number of financial institutions involved is limited and the necessary calculations would be built into their computer systems. It could well be the first of an eventual series of international taxes on financial transactions to damp down speculation and raise money for international purposes, such as development, humanitarian aid, and even peace-keeping.

Reforming the Exchange Rate System

Although developing countries have become particularly vulnerable to speculative capital movements, the problem of instability is by no means confined to them. Reforming the global financial system so as to achieve greater exchange rate stability and make capital markets less volatile would be of benefit to both industrialized and developing countries. The two objectives – more stable exchange rates and less speculative activity – are mutually reinforcing, as exchange rate movements are a major factor in market activity.

In searching for a solution to the problem of exchange rate instability, the objective must be to devise a system that facilitates adjustments in rates in response to fundamental factors such as changes in relative costs or shifts in a country's desirable payments surplus or deficit, but to prevent fluctuations in rates due to variations in short-term capital movements and currency speculation. This points inevitably to some form of managed, as opposed to floating, rates. But managing rates successfully depends on solving two basic problems: securing agreement between the countries concerned on changes in rates; and preventing currencies being driven off their agreed parities or bands by speculative forces.

The problem of agreeing changes in parities in any form of managed system stems from the conflict of interest which arises because such changes will affect countries' relative competitive position and hence their trade. This is most acute when large changes are made that substantially alter existing relativities. The problems of securing mutual agreement and minimizing speculation both suggest that small and relatively frequent changes in parities should be easier to manage than large and infrequent ones. This view is reinforced by considering the practicalities of changing parities in a target zone system with agreed bands of ± *x* per cent around parities, as in the ERM (i.e. a system in which a change in parity involves a corresonding movement in the band). If changes in parity are sufficiently small to allow the new parity to lie within the old band, the spot rate will not necessarily go down (or up) the morning after the change. For example, with a band of ± 2.5 per cent and a 1 per cent reduction in parity, the new parity would be well within the old band (and even a rate 1 per cent below the new parity would still be within the old band). If rates were reviewed monthly, and changes limited to, say, 1 per cent, there would still be enough scope to adjust rates to allow for differing inflation rates etc. in all but exceptional circumstances. Such an approach to changing rates would be similar to that now adopted by many central banks in changing key interest rates, i.e. monthly meetings and small changes.

The main reason for changing rates in the short term would be differing rates of inflation between countries. The basic aim would be to maintain stable exchange rates in real terms, which is what is important for industry and trade. The fact that some countries' exchange rates would be depreciating and others appreciating would be consistent with similar differences in their interest rates, i.e. countries would have comparable real rates of interest. Such stability would not, however, be compatible with the active manipulation of interest rates to counteract business cycles, if the cycles were out of phase in different countries. An example of this is the recent use of high interest rates to combat inflation in the UK, when continental Europe had lower interest rates and relatively depressed demand, the net result of which was a damaging strengthening of the pound. Managed exchange rate systems, like currency unions, imply that demand management to cope with differing cyclical conditions in different countries must be a task for primarily fiscal, rather than monetary, policy. This means a reversal of the present fashion of eschewing active fiscal policies. But such a change may well be on the way, as it becomes apparent that lower interest rates on their own will not be enough to stave off recession – as we already see in Japan.

Automatic Stabilization

For such a system of managed rates to be successful, there must be effective means of keeping rates within their specified bands. This depends on some system of *automatic* (rather than discretionary) intervention. In principle this could be achieved by an obligation on the key central banks to intervene as required. But in practice it is difficult to make central bank intervention automatic, when any concrete action requires a number of banks to discuss and agree what should be done. Certainly if there is no automatic obligation to intervene, as in the ERM, everything depends on the willingness of the key central bank to do so – in the ERM case the Bundesbank. When that support was not forthcoming, devaluation was inevitable. Moreover central bank resources nowadays are limited in relation to turnover in currency markets: official foreign exchange reserves and gold holdings are now equal to approximately one day's global turnover. There is therefore a strong case in any managed rate system for establishing a special stabilization fund with power to borrow from central banks in order to intervene as required. The mere existence of such a fund should in practice obviate the need for it to take action, and the existence of an organization with this obligation might facilitate agreement on realistic rates – it should certainly reduce the prevailing bias towards maintaining excessively high rates. For if the central institution, such as the IMF, has the obligation to intervene when rates are threatened, they will have a clear incentive to use their influence to see that rates remain realistic.

A Two-Tier System

A purely global approach, as at Bretton Woods, seems impractical for a flexibly managed, rather than fixed rate system. There are just too many currencies involved. There needs to be a two-tier approach with both regional and global arrangements. Indeed there are already blocs based on the dollar and the euro, and the question of managing the rate between them, and their relation with the yen, cannot be evaded indefinitely.

The question is then: how far would the proposed formula be appropriate for arrangements (a) *within* regional groups such as the EU or NAFTA, and (b) *between* regional groups, based on say the euro, the dollar and the yen? A relatively close-knit regional group such as the EU would seem perfectly capable of setting up and operating a formal system of this nature. It has been suggested that such a system should be introduced to manage the link between the euro and the pound, together with the currencies of other EU countries that are not members of the EMU.

Arrangements within regional groups might differ from case to case. Where there is a leading currency such as the dollar or yen, and a potentially dominant partner, such as the USA or Japan, the other currencies would tend to be linked to that currency, but should be linked flexibly, rather than pegged. The regional arrangements would then be concerned with provisions for changing rates *vis-à-vis* the leading currency. This flexibility is important to ensure that changes in rates, between the yen and dollar for instance, do not result in an inappropriate rate for, say, the Korean won. Automatic intervention within the dollar or yen zones would in practice be largely the responsibility of the USA or Japan. In other cases the arrangements might be more genuinely multi-lateral. Regional stability funds might be developed in parallel with regional development banks.

It would also seem feasible for a limited number of major currencies, such as the dollar, yen and euro (cum sterling), or regional groupings based on these currencies, to start up a major currency stabilization club. Indeed, stabilizing rates within regions would be much easier if rates between regions were also being kept stable. For example, there would be fewer problems in stabilizing the pound against the euro, if the euro were stable against the dollar. To manage rates between three or more regional groups, there would have to be either an anchor currency in each group, or a numeraire in the form of a basket of currencies in the region (such as the former ECU), and an appropriate body responsible for securing agreement on the rates between them. There would also need to be a global (or tripartite) intervention fund. This would eventually require amendments to the IMF constitution. Regional differences and the difficulties of making such a system universal from the start (e.g. including Africa) would suggest, however, that any new constitution for the IMF should provide for the formation of regional groupings over a period of years and thus a gradual increase in the number of such groups participating in a new global management system. The width of bands, the limits on parity changes and the frequency of meetings of the managing board would all need to be capable of change and not carved in stone in any new international agreement. A two-tier managed rate along these lines might initially be constituted on an informal basis, but eventually a new Bretton Woods agreement would be desirable, provided it was elastic enough to allow for the evolution of varying arrangements in different regions, albeit with certain common guiding principles.

Payments Strategy

Any system of managed exchange rates is only sustainable if it is based on a measure of agreement about the desired pattern of payments between the countries involved, i.e. their current surpluses or deficits together with long-term capital movements. The most obvious omission today is the lack of any coherent view of the desirable resolution of the problems of the Japanese and US balance of payments, and hence whether the yen should be stronger relative to the dollar or *vice versa* – or even in some quarters recognition that such a problem exists. For the USA to continue indefinitely running deficits of the magnitude in recent years seems unsustainable. There is always a danger that a major loss of foreign confidence in US securities or the dollar could lead to a potentially disastrous outflow of funds from New York and the present system could collapse virtually overnight. The creation of the euro will provide an alternative safe haven and far from helping to stabilize the world economy a strong euro could destabilize the dollar. But apart from the financial dangers, it does not make sense for a major industrial power like the USA to be absorbing resources in exchange for financial claims on its assets, rather than running a balance of payments surplus combined with a substantial flow of aid and productive investment to the rest of the world, particularly developing countries. It would, however, be disastrous at the present time for the USA to try to remove its balance of payments deficit by deflationary measures which reduced demand and activity in the US economy. On the contrary the immediate need is for the prosperous industrial countries to be prepared to run deficits to keep up demand in the Asian economies and help them restore their exchange reserves. In the longer term, any reduction in the US balance of payments deficit needs to be aimed at reducing corresponding surpluses elsewhere, not driving countries already in deficit further into the red. This means that such a reduction must for the most part be matched by a reduction in the Japanese surplus.

Mutually consistent objectives are needed for both the US and Japanese balance of payments to provide a rational basis for any agreement on the desired relativity between the dollar and the yen. These objectives need in turn to be part of a world payments strategy setting out a consistent and desirable pattern of trade, aid and productive investment between key areas, which would in turn provide a rationale for a pattern of agreed target zones. This is not, of course, to imply either that there is one ideal world payments scenario, or that anyone can calculate precisely what set of exchange rates would achieve it. Rather that, without a broad concept of the direction in which we are aiming to go, there is little rational basis for any agreement on exchange rates. In practical terms any such exercise would, initially at any rate, concentrate particularly on the interplay between the three major players: the USA, EU and Japan or the corresponding regional groupings.

Guiding Principles

To sum up, the guiding principles for both global and regional arrangements for managing exchange rates should be as follows:

1. Exchange rate management should be compatible with economic stability and the maintenance of full employment and low inflation.
2. Exchange rates should be as stable as possible in real terms, subject to adjustment to meet changes in relative costs or other factors affecting the desired flow of foreign trade and productive investment.
3. The pattern of rates should be based on an agreed strategy for the broad magnitude of trade surpluses or deficits and the flow of long-term capital between or within regions.
4. Changes in rates should be small, and if necessary, relatively frequent, rather than large and infrequent.
5. To achieve this, the general pattern of management would be to establish target zones of suitable widths and change parities in steps of less than half the width of the zone, so that the new parity would be in the old zone.
6. Automatic stabilization arrangements should be established to ensure that currencies, or groups of currencies, remain within their agreed zones.
7. While design of automatic stabilization arrangements may differ globally and regionally, the objective should be to establish an international fund or funds rather than rely on agreements between central banks.

Any new arrangements must be based on recognition of the need for a fundamental change in attitude towards exchange rate management. In formulating what were to become the Bretton Woods proposals, Keynes tried unsuccessfully to establish the principle that surplus as well as deficit countries had a responsibility for achieving equilibrium. But in practice the onus has always remained on those with a deficit because they are the ones in difficulty. A similar asymmetry exists in the case of exchange rates. At present a country's exchange rate is regarded solely as its own responsibility, with some help from international sources if it runs into difficulties. This is increasingly unrealistic. Exchange rates reflect the terms on which two countries, or a group of countries, conduct their mutual trade and affect all those concerned. The achievement of exchange rate stability must be regarded as a matter of continuing mutual concern and international cooperation rather than unilateral action.

Regulation and Crisis Management

In the field of prudential regulation (which is now receiving widespread attention) there is a need for closer scrutiny of borrowing and lending institutions, both nationally and internationally. The first requirement is greater transparency, and the collation of the facts about risk exposure in individual institutions at an international level to make them fully aware of the total exposure to particular countries, banks and companies. This should be backed up by the requirement that banks and other financial institutions should face higher capital or cash backing when dealing with counter-parties who fail to reveal their own exposures fully.

The key instrument of the regulators is their ability to lay down capital backing requirements for particular types of loans. Both the general level of these safety requirements, and the pattern of percentage backing for different types of loan, need to be reviewed. Consideration also needs to be given to the feasibility of giving international regulators the power to vary backing requirements in the light of knowledge about exposure to particular countries or institutions.

There should be a bias towards *raising* such requirements, as a general cautionary measure and as a means of reducing the leverage in the financial system. One of the fundamental factors behind the asset price bubbles, which pose such a danger today, is the extent of the leverage available for speculation either in the form of the availability of credit or the use of derivatives.

Basle Committee Proposals

Some broadly similar ideas have been put forward in a consultative paper issued by the Basle Committee on Banking Supervision (BCBS) in June 1999. The paper suggests that risk weights on banks claims might be set in a more graduated fashion according to a relatively objective assessment of creditworthiness, instead of the present blunt and arbitrary distinction between OECD and non-OECD countries. The weights attaching to sovereign credits and claims on banks would be set in five bands (0, 20, 50, 100 and 150 per cent) by reference to a government's (or bank's) credit rating as established by a recognized external credit rating agency or by G10 export credit insurance bodies. Because such credit ratings may be altered in the light of circumstances, the risk weights themselves would be, in principle, variable over time. The BCBS also propose that, for claims to qualify for risk weights below 100 per cent, the borrowers would have to meet the relevant international disclosure standards.

Another welcome feature of the BCBS paper is the proposal that the preferential risk weights attaching to short-term claims on non-OECD banks (or bank-guaranteed credits) should be similarly graduated, ranging from the present 20 per cent up to 100 per cent, and that short term might be redefined as 'up to six months' rather than 'up to one year'. This proposal, taken together with the BCBS's proposed five bands for risk weights on normal claims, would result in a differential in favour of short-term claims, expressed in terms of the capital backing required, ranging from zero (for low-risk countries) to 4 per cent (for high-risk countries), compared with the present standard differential of 6.4 per cent. While this reduction in regulatory bias towards short-term lending is to be welcomed, it would however still leave a significant incentive for lending to higher-risk countries to be short term, because that would attract only half the capital backing required for longer-term claims.

Any new agreement should redefine responsibilities for international regulation, and the relationship between international and national institutions. There is a case for developing the new G7 Forum for Financial Stability into an international body coordinating all financial regulatory activity; but here, as elsewhere, it is important to build on existing strengths, in particular the experience of the BIS.

Crisis Management

Whatever improvements may be made in prudential regulation and other fields, financial crises may still arise from time to time and contingency plans are needed to deal with them. A distinction must be made between three inter-related aspects of such crises:

1. The danger of insolvency of banks or companies and the need for measures, particularly the provision of liquidity, to avert bankruptcies. This is in the first instance a responsibility of national central banks and governments, but in the case of large institutions operating on a global scale, there may be a need for international action.

2. The danger of a crisis incurring sovereign debt default by national governments, which is likely to require debt restructuring and may also require immediate support from the IMF.
3. Foreign exchange crises, which nowadays are more likely to originate from an outflow of capital, rather than (as in the past) a current balance of payments deficit. Such foreign exchange crises face countries both with a shortage of reserves, and devaluation or a falling exchange rate.

These three elements need to be considered separately, although they will often occur together. Dealing with the threat of insolvency of private institutions might well be primarily a function of the regulators, who should be in the best position to know the facts. Dealing with sovereign debt crises could be a formal responsibility of the IMF or its successor, as well as the provision of foreign exchange reserves in times of threatened or actual crisis. But as proposed above in our consideration of exchange rate management, there is also a need to recognize the responsibility for exchange rate *stabilization* as a new international function in its own right requiring active market intervention – a function that is distinct from the traditional IMF function of providing foreign exchange to national central banks in difficulties.

A New Bretton Woods

The institutional consequences of the various proposals discussed in this report need careful consideration. The key operating bodies involved are clearly the IMF, the World Bank, the BIS and other regulatory authorities. But there is a multiplicity of other international organizations both under the UN umbrella and outside, in particular the OECD, which have little or no operational responsibilities, but which absorb considerable professional and other resources. At some point there is a strong case for streamlining these bodies and integrating them into the machinery of the UN. This would, amongst other things, raise the influence of the developing countries whose relative voting power within the Bretton Woods institutions has diminished over the years. There are, however, considerable political and human problems in achieving such institutional reforms and this would be an appropriate topic for a high-powered international commission to review.

The more urgent task is to change the principles and policies on which these organizations work. One such change should be recognition of the need for diversity under a global system. The neo-liberal 'Washington Consensus', and the IMF's standard formulae for borrowing countries assume that all countries, whatever their economic situation, social structure or national tradition should follow a single pattern. With the recent crisis in Asia, this pressure has taken on a new dimension. The IMF programmes previously focused on macro-economic targets, but this time the problems have been diagnosed as 'structural' and 'institutional', and explicit attempts have been made to reform the Asian institutions and economies in the Western image. These programmes, especially that for Korea, have included demands for institutional reforms in areas that have been hitherto regarded as beyond international pressures, such as employment practices and corporate takeover rules. Privatization has been another key feature of recent IMF prescriptions. This enforced uniformity is not only undemocratic but economically inappropriate.

Any new agreement must restate the original Bretton Woods objective that the international finance regime and the economic policies of individual countries should help to promote and maintain 'high levels of employment and real income' and 'the development of the productive resources of all members'. To this end the system must encourage a stable flow of resources from the richer to poorer countries.

The new Bretton Woods must be based on the belief that international financial activity should not be regarded as an end in itself, but as a means of facilitating world trade and productive and social investment. It must tackle the inherent instability of financial markets by more effective prudential regulation and other measures to damp down speculative activity. Greater exchange rate stability must be a central objective.

Exchange rates are the most fundamental price-mechanism in the international economy. They should provide a stable and rational basis for comparing the costs of goods and services when making decisions on trade and investment. The development of a system of managed exchange rates on a regional and global basis should lie at the heart of the new regime.

Globalization can and should be a positive factor in the development of the world economy and the abolition of poverty and hunger. But it will only be so if governments cooperate more vigorously to make international institutions effective in the pursuit of these aims.

Summary and Conclusions

The recent financial crises in Asia and elsewhere, and the changes in the world financial system over the last 50 years, call for a fundamental review of the 1944 Bretton Woods Agreement. Such a review needs to go wider than measures to improve the prudential regulation of financial institutions, which have so far been the principle focus of attention in G7 and elsewhere. The inherent instability of global financial markets poses a continuing threat to us all.

Premature liberalization of capital flows into developing countries was a major contribution to the recent crises and there is a need to reconsider the means by which such countries can control the inflows (and hence outflows) of short-term capital. There is a corresponding need to take measures to increase and stabilize the flow of long-term finance for development, particularly to low-income countries.

The volatility of capital movements and exchange rates are closely inter-related. A prime objective of any new system should be to establish greater exchange rate stability, without a return to fixed or 'pegged' rates that can only be adjusted in crisis conditions. This calls for a system of managed, but flexible, rates, with small adjustments at relatively frequent intervals in order to cut down the scope for speculative gains. Such a system should be based on mutually agreed target zones with automatic stabilization arrangements for intervention to keep rates within their stated zones.

The introduction of a managed rate regime would require a two-tier approach with both regional and global arrangements; starting with regional arrangements based on the dollar, yen and euro (cum sterling) and global arrangements to manage the rates between these three major currencies.

The prudential regulation of financial institutions requires radical rethinking in the light of the high correlation of lending risks to different institutions and countries evidenced by the recent crises. This calls both for improving information and tighter backing requirements. The fundamental need is to reduce the leverage available to financial institutions and other investors in order to reduce the volatility and risks in currency and asset markets. The creation of the Financial Stability Forum is a welcome step down this road.

No improvements in the system can rule out crises altogether and better arrangements are needed for crisis management, with provision for speedy action to supply liquidity and stabilize markets. Fundamental changes are needed in the policies of the IMF to avoid the prescription of unwarranted deflationary action as a condition for supporting countries in difficulty or political interference in their economic structure.

International financial activity should not be regarded as an end in itself, but as a means of facilitating world trade and productive and social investment. This can only be achieved if governments cooperate more effectively to strengthen international economic institutions.

References

Arentis, P. and Sawyer, M. (1997) 'How Many Cheers for the Tobin Tax?' *Cambridge Journal of Economics*, November.

Grabel, I. (1999) 'Rejecting exceptionalism: Reinterpreting the Asian financial crises' in J. Michie and J. Grieve Smith (eds) *Global Instability*, London, Routledge, pp. 37–67.

Grieve Smith, J. (1997) 'Exchange Rate Instability and the Tobin Tax' *Cambridge Journal of Economics*, November

Singh, A. (1999) 'Asian capitalism and the financial crises' in J. Michie and J. Grieve Smith (eds) *Global Instability*, London, Routledge, pp. 9–36.

ul Haq, M., Kaul, I. and Grunberg, I. (eds) (1996) *The Tobin Tax: Coping with Financial Volatility*, Oxford, Clarendon.

UNCTAD (1988) *Trade and Development Report*.

World Bank (1998) 'Middle income developing countries' in which 1996 GNP per capital was between $786 and $9,635, *Global Development Finance*.

World Bank (1998/9) *Global Economic Prospects and the Developing Countries*.

5
Will the Euro Bring Economic Crisis to Europe?

Philip Arestis and Malcolm Sawyer

Introduction

The initial introduction of the euro has, against many expectations, been accompanied by a decline in its value (notably *vis-à-vis* the dollar and sterling). It has also been introduced at a time of high levels of unemployment within most of the European Union (EU). This chapter explores how the economies of the EU may suffer from the introduction of the euro, specifically from the policy and institutional arrangements within which the euro is embedded.

It is the argument of this chapter that the eurozone will face considerable economic difficulties. These difficulties will take a number of forms, but we focus on two rather different aspects that could qualify for the term crisis. First, the euro has been launched at a time of high levels of unemployment (of the order of 10 per cent of the workforce) and with particularly severe disparities in unemployment experience and in standards of living. At the end of 1998, the rate of unemployment was over 20 per cent in Spain, and in double figures in Finland, France, Germany, Ireland and Italy. It is argued here that these high levels of unemployment are likely to continue in the foreseeable future, and that the policy arrangements that surround the operation of the euro, notably the objectives of the European Central Bank (ECB) and the workings of the *Stability and Growth Pact*, will have a deflationary bias. These levels of and disparities in unemployment could be termed a crisis. Second, the introduction of the euro and the associated institutional setting could well serve to exacerbate tendencies towards financial crisis including the volatility and subsequent collapse of asset prices and runs on the banking system. There may be some additional forces of instability arising from the relationship between the dollar and the euro as two major global currencies and the current trade imbalances. Further, the operating arrangements of the European System of Central Banks (ESCB) can be seen as inadequate to cope with such financial crises.

The Institutional Policy Framework

The institutional policy framework within which the euro has been introduced and will operate has four key elements. First, the ECB is the only effective federal economic institution. The ECB has the one policy instrument of interest ('repo') rate to pursue the main objective of low inflation.[1] The Governing Council of the ECB[2] agreed on the main features of their stability-oriented policy strategy (ECB, 1998). The single monetary policy will have a euro area-wide perspective. The president of the ECB, at a press conference on 13 October 1998, clearly stated that monetary policy 'will not react to specific regional or national developments'. A quantitative definition of price stability was adopted: the annual increase in the Harmonized Index of Consumer Prices (HICP) for the euro area should be less than 2 per cent. This is to be achieved through the policy weapon of the rate of interest, and by announced quantitative reference values for the growth of the broad M3 monetary aggregate set at 4.5 per cent. Being a reference level, there is no mechanistic commitment to correct deviations in the short term, although it is stated that deviations from the reference value would, under normal circumstances, 'signal risks to price stability'. It has also been agreed that a broadly-based assessment of future price developments will be undertaken, but not publicly announced.

Second, the ECB and the national central banks are linked into the ESCB with a division of responsibility between them. The ECB has the responsibility for setting interest rates in pursuit of the inflation objective and the national central banks responsibility for regulatory matters. In order to achieve its objectives, the ECB will conduct open market operations, it will offer standing facilities (overnight lending against eligible assets and deposit facilities to the institutions subject to minimum reserves with national central banks), and it will impose minimum reserve requirements. The latter will be interest-rate bearing (at the repo rate) on institutions holding accounts with it. The reserve ratio will be 2 per cent of eligible liabilities,[3] and the reserves will be lodged with national central banks.

One notable feature of the operation of the ESCB is the apparent absence of the lender-of-last-resort facility. The Protocols under which the ECB is established enables, but does not require, the ECB to act as a lender-of-last-resort. The relevant article of the Protocol suggests that 'In order to achieve the objectives of the ESCB and to carry out its tasks, the ECB and the national central banks may: operate in the financial markets by buying and selling outright (spot and forward) or under repurchase agreement and by lending or borrowing claims and marketable instruments, whether in Community or in non-Community currencies, as well as precious metals; conduct credit operations with credit institutions and other market participants with lending being based on adequate collateral. The ECB shall establish general principles for open market and credit operations carried out by itself or the national central banks, including for the announcement of conditions under which they stand ready to enter into such transactions' (from Protocol, No. 3, on the *Stature of the European System of Central Banks and of the European Central Bank*).

A lender-of-last-resort function requires that base money is essentially provided on request to the banking system by the Central Bank, and in particular would be supplied if reserves were low following an expansion of broader money. More generally, the lender-of-last-resort function recognizes the role of a central bank in securing a stable financial system, but that specific objective of the stability of the financial system is not included in the remit of the ECB. It is clear that on occasions, the lender-of-last-resort function may require base money to be supplied when pursuit of a price stability target would point in the opposite direction.

Third, the ECB is intended to be independent of the EU Council and Parliament and of its member governments. Thus there is a complete separation between the monetary authorities, in the form of the ESCB, and the fiscal authorities, in the shape of the national governments comprising the EMU. National governments are given the objective of keeping any budget deficit below 3 per cent according to the *Stability and Growth Pact* (see below for more details). It follows that there can be little coordination of monetary and fiscal policy. Apart from the separation of the monetary and fiscal authorities, there is also the requirement cited below that national governments (and hence the fiscal authorities) should not exert any influence on the ECB (and hence the monetary authorities). Any strict interpretation of that edict would rule out any attempt at coordination of monetary and fiscal policies.

Fourth, a key relationship between the EU and national governments relates to the restrictions placed on national economic autonomy in that interest rates are set at the EU level and fiscal policy is constrained by the 3 per cent of GDP upper limit on fiscal deficits. This is the *Stability and Growth Pact*, which details 'escape' clauses that allow a member state that has an excessive deficit to avoid sanction. If there is an economic downturn and output has fallen by more than 2 per cent, then the member state will escape sanction automatically but the deficit should be corrected once the recession has finished. If output falls between 0.75 and 2 per cent then the Council can use discretion when making a decision on an excessive deficit, other factors will be taken into account such as the abruptness of the downturn, the accumulated loss of output relative to past trends and whether the government deficit exceeds government investment expenditure. The notion that 'excessive' deficit is one which is more than 3 per cent of GDP will mean that a government seeking to ensure that its budget deficit does not go above 3 per cent of GDP during recession will have to aim for an average deficit that is much lower.

In light of the swings of budget deficit over the course of a business cycle, we would reckon that the average level of the budget deficit would have to be of the order of 0 to 1 per cent of GDP, given the swings in the size of the deficit over the business cycle. It would also mean that for many countries the primary budget position (that is excluding interest payments) would be one of a surplus. The ability of national governments to run deficits will be circumscribed by that Pact. A country which fails to keep its budget deficit within the 3 per cent limit will have to pay in the first instance a penalty equivalent to the payment of a non-interest-bearing deposit. If the situation persists the penalty becomes a fine equivalent to between 0.2 and 0.5 per cent of GDP, depending on the size of the 'excess' deficit. The penalty clause would add to the deficit it is meant to cure, and as such it could generate national opposition. This constraint on the budget deficit effectively precludes the use of national fiscal policy for demand management purposes. The budget position can clearly fluctuate over the business cycle in a stabilising manner, but there would be difficulties in dealing with severe recessions, noting that, for example, the deficit in the UK rose to near 8 per cent of GDP in the early 1990s.[4]

The budget of the EU itself is relatively small. It represents around 1.5 per cent of EU GDP, and there is a requirement that it is in balance, with revenue from member governments determined so as to cover planned expenditure. The EU is thus constrained to run a balanced budget on an annual basis. Articles 199 and 201 of the amended Treaty of Rome (EU, 1998) require that 'the revenue and expenditure shown in the [Community] budget shall be in balance' and that 'the budget shall be financed wholly from own resources'. It follows that in no sense can the EU be seen to constitute 'big government' and act to stabilize the level of economic activity. Consequently, the scale and balanced budget nature of EU expenditure clearly means that there is no role for fiscal policy at the EU level (even of a passive form whereby budget deficits vary with the business cycle).

In order to meet the upper limit of 3 per cent of GDP on national budget deficits during a recession, it is likely that member governments would need to run significant surpluses during economic upswings, and over the course of the business cycle the average budget deficit will be small or perhaps zero. The 3 per cent of GDP rule for budget deficits may well mean that over the business cycle the budget position is balanced or in surplus. This means that 'National governments will need to aim at a balanced budget or surplus, or the deficit limit of 3 per cent could well prevent the proper working of fiscal stabilisers over the economic cycle'. It also means that 'governments could be required to raise taxes, or cut government spending, as the economy moves into recession, thereby exacerbating the downturn' (Currie, 1997, p. 13). In the past decade, the budget position in the UK has swung from a surplus of 1 per cent of GDP to a deficit of nearly 8 per cent. If a comparable swing in the budget position occurred in the future, with the largest deficit constrained to 3 per cent, then the surplus would be 6 per cent, with an overall surplus averaging around 1 per cent of GDP. A more cautious government, aiming for, say, a maximum deficit of 2 per cent to provide a margin of error, would clearly run a somewhat larger surplus.

A government budget deficit can be financed by borrowing or by issuing base money (M0), and the expansion of the economy involves some expansion of the stock of money. Credit has to be available to permit the expansion of expenditure to be financed, and an expansion of national income will usually generate a greater transactions demand for money. The expansion of the form of money (say M1) which is largely used to finance transactions is of particular significance. It is necessary for government to run a budget deficit which was partially monetized in order that base money (M0) increased. A growing economy required an expansion of the stock of money (say M1), and such an expansion requires the underpinning of a growth in M0 to prevent a continuous decline in the reserve ratio (between M0 and M1 in this instance). In the context of EMU, there is a complete separation between the fiscal authorities and the monetary authorities, and moreover the appropriate fiscal authorities are barred from running any deficit.

As the EU budget must be balanced each year, there can be no (base) money creation from that direction. It may well be that over the cycle there would be no net budget deficit (for the reasons indicated above). But in any case deficits run by member states must be covered by borrowing as they cannot be monetized because that would require credit to be granted to the national government by the ECB. This is clearly prohibited: 'Overdraft facilities or any other type of credit facility with the ECB or with the central banks of the Member States (hereinafter referred to as 'national central banks') in favour of Community institutions or bodies, central governments, regional, local or other public authorities, other bodies governed by public law, or public undertakings of Member States shall be prohibited, as shall the purchase directly from them by the ECB or national central banks of debt instruments' (Article 104 of the Treaty of Rome).

There would seem to be three possible responses by the ECB to this apparent inability of the ECB to create high-powered euros. The first is that in effect the ECB does actually monetize national government debt through open market operations. The quote from Article 104 of the Treaty of Rome given above rules out the direct monetization of national government deficits (the prohibition of 'purchase directly') but leaves open the possibility of indirect purchases, that is through open market operations. Bonds would be sold by national governments, and then at some later stage sold on to the ECB (or to one of the national central banks). The ECB could justify this on the grounds that their stated objective is price stability, which is compatible with growth of the stock of money in line with the growth of national income.[5] Under this scenario, the ECB would gradually accumulate the bonds of national governments: the interest on the bonds being paid by the national governments to the ECB, which then makes a profit, which is paid to its 'shareholders', the national governments (see also Article 32 of the Protocol).

The second is that the ECB permits the ratios of broader money (e.g. M1, M3) to base money (M0) to grow over time. This would mean that the ECB foregoes the imposition of any reserve ratio requirement which would run counter to their announced reserve ratio for M3. The growth of these broader measures of money would be driven by the demand for those moneys, and in particular the growth of M1 would be driven by transaction requirements. This could only continue if the banks were willing to collectively become less liquid over time in the sense that the ultimate source of liquidity is base money, and the ratio of base money to broader measures of money would decline.

The third is that the ECB imposes reserve ratio requirements on banking and other financial institutions as it is permitted to do under Article 19 of the Protocol, which prevents the reserve ratios from falling. The ECB has announced a reserve ratio on M3 of 2 per cent. The clear consequence of this would be that the necessary monetary expansion to underpin economic growth could not occur (unless M1 grew even though the broader notion of M3 did not). Even if real growth did occur, it would have to be accompanied by price deflation. This is not to accept any simple quantity theory formulation, but rather to accept that expansion of the economy requires credit creation. Further, the ability of the European financial system to grant credit to finance investment and expansion would be severely limited. A post-Keynesian approach would stress the role of credit creation in investment, and without the credit creation investment would be blocked off, and thereby any hope of economic growth.

Chick and Dow (1995) indicated that there are large differences in the ratio of reserves to deposits between banks in different countries. Within the EU countries, Greece appears as an outlier with a reserve ratio of over 40 per cent, but other countries have reserve ratios ranging from less than 1 per cent (UK), and Italy and France at less than 2 per cent, to over 7 per cent (Portugal and Denmark).[6] The current reserve ratios would not generally be constrained by the requirements of national central banks, but rather reflect the commercial banks' calculations on risk and attitudes to liquidity. However, it is likely that the reserve ratios will fall in many countries because the holding of reserves imposes costs on the banks. The pressure of competition of banks from other countries could well put downward pressure on the reserve ratios. It can be readily calculated that relative small movements in the reserve ratio would have substantial impacts on the money stock (for given reserves): for example, a move from 30 per cent reserve ratio to 20 per cent involves a 50 per cent increase. This would suggest the potential for rapid increases in the stock of money, but any increase in the stock of money requires a demand for loans to provide a mechanism by which the money stock expands and an increased demand for money.

The conclusion we can draw from this quick sketch of the policy framework of the euro is that there are likely to be significant deflationary pressures. These arise from the constraints on national fiscal policy, the absence of any significant EU fiscal policy and the tendency of the ECB towards deflation. However, there may be some tendency for commercial banks to expand loans and the stock of money (as reserve ratios fall) but there appears to be an absence of any mechanism by which base money can expand. The liquidity position of banks can then be expected to deteriorate.

The Problematic Nature of the Institutional Policy Framework

Asymmetric Shocks

An important problematic aspect of the policy framework is the symmetry or otherwise of shocks. Given the one-instrument-only nature of monetary policy within the eurozone, the extent of asymmetrical shocks becomes paramount. If shocks are indeed asymmetrical the one-policy framework cannot tackle effectively even the one-target objective of price stability. From the perspective of the business cycle, it could be argued that Ireland with output above trend to the extent of over 3 per cent of GDP and Italy with output below trend to the extent of nearly 4 per cent of GDP, require quite different macroeconomic policies.[7]

The optimists tend to believe that the introduction of the euro and the continuing effects of the single market will lead to further integration between the national economies. This integration could then be reflected in some convergence between national business cycles and to a reduction in the extent of asymmetric shocks (that is shocks which impact on some economies but not on others). If there was full integration between the national economies then a unified economic policy would be appropriate, although we would argue that a single policy instrument such as interest rates is not sufficient to achieve multiple objectives. It is too soon to be able to assess whether the single market has indeed generated more integration in the sense in which we have indicated. One simple measure is the variation between countries in terms of the business cycle, and for this we can look at, for example, the standard deviation of the output gap across countries. On OECD figures, this was 1.69 per cent in 1998 as against an average of 1.77 per cent over the period 1982 to 1998.[8] This does not suggest (albeit on a very simple measure) much convergence of the business cycles across the EU countries.

The results generated by Fatas (1998), which relate to the period 1960 to 1996, suggest that there are significant asymmetric shocks which have lasting effects on GDP of individual countries relative to the EU average. The results imply that relative GDP is far from being a stationary variable, and fluctuations in GDP growth are lasting, with permanent shocks being large and frequent.

Funke, Hall and Ruhwedel (1999) report a decline in the importance of country-specific shocks over the past 20 years, although they were only looking at manufacturing industries. However, they conclude that 'not all countries are equally far along this path [of convergence] and so the implication is that, if European governments are prepared to trade the costs of surrendering the exchange rate as a policy instrument for the benefits of a common currency, monetary union should only include a small core group of countries that have reached the symmetric league (Germany and the Netherlands and possibly France and Austria; certainly not Greece or Portugal, and the UK is probably not fully ready yet)' (pp. 63–4).

The degree to which countries (and regions) suffer from asymmetric shocks and are at different points of the economic cycle raises significant questions for economic policy. The present arrangements are deficient in at least two respects. First, as already suggested, the single policy instrument of interest rate cannot be set in a manner appropriate for different regions suffering from different shocks and/or at different points of the economic cycle. A particular concern here would be that the interest rate may be set more with regard to those regions that are viewed as 'overheating' rather than to those regions that are 'freezing'. Second, the constraints on national and EU level fiscal policy, outlined above, clearly operate against the active use of fiscal policy and even place constraints on passive fiscal policy (which would involve allowing budget deficits to vary counter-cyclically).

An important piece of evidence relating to asymmetric shocks is provided by Arrowsmith, Barrell and Taylor (1999). This study concentrates on the volatility of the euro and its possible asymmetric effects. The sole objective of price stability suggests that monetary policy will have serious implications for the euro exchange rate stability. The non-availability of national exchange-rate adjustment for shocks that have differential effects on the eurozone economies will have serious implications. The euro interest rate will have to cope with these shocks, implying uncomfortable consequences for the exchange rate. This exchange rate volatility will have uneven impacts on the eurozone economies. The study by Arrowsmith *et al.* (1999) simulates the impact of exogenous exchange rate disturbances on individual economies under the assumption of the ECB pursuing the single objective of price stability. Their results confirm these propositions unambiguously.[9]

Channels of Monetary Policy

Monetary policy is often discussed in essential monetarist terms, namely that the stock of money can be changed (or targeted) by the Central Bank, and the growth of the stock of money determines the rate of inflation, leaving output and employment determined on the supply-side of the economy (invoking the classical dichotomy between the real and monetary sides of the economy). But whatever is the rhetoric, the reality is that the relevant stock(s) of money are bank deposits (whether narrowly defined as demand deposits or broadly defined to include time deposits) which are created by banks but remain in existence only when there is a demand to hold them. Further, and of particular significance here, is that monetary policy operates through interest rates. A change in the 'repo' rate works through the effect on the spectrum of interest rates and thereby on demand and supply of loans and the willingness of the public to hold money. From these rather obvious observations, three considerations arise.

First, the basis of the classical dichotomy is undermined. In particular, it would be anticipated that variations in the rate of interest would have an impact on the level of investment (and thereby future productive capacity) and the exchange rate. Monetary policy in the form of interest rates is viewed as operating through the effect of the level of economic activity and thereby on the rate of inflation. In so far as interest rate changes are effective in influencing the pace of economic activity, they can be seen to do so through exchange rates (and thereby on demand for import and exports) and through investment.

Second, there is a range of reasons for thinking that monetary policy will have a differential impact across regions and countries. As the Monetary Policy Committee (1999) recognizes, monetary policy 'sets one interest rate for the economy as a whole and can only take account of the impact of official rate changes on the aggregate of individuals in the economy' (p. 7). Monetary policy is undifferentiated in that a single official rate will apply. But there are differences in financial structures between countries in the eurozone, and in particular differences in the extent of variable rate and fixed rate borrowing and in the effect of interest rate changes on economic activity. The effects of interest rate changes will be far from uniform across eurozone countries. An interest rate rise may succeed in slowing down economic activity in some countries but not in others; it may have little effect on inflation in some but act to speed it up in others.

Third, there is the question of how effective the interest rate is as an (or the) instrument of demand management policy. To begin with, the ECB will have no choice but to raise interest rates when the prospect is of inflation rising. The ECB may operate on evidence of prices rising faster or any evidence such as unemployment falling below the estimated non-accelerating inflation rate of unemployment (the NAIRU) or some combination of factors. Interest rates are likely to be a rather blunt instrument for this purpose. There are questions over how much impact a rise in interest rates will have on the rate of change of the money supply, and further whether changes in the money supply have a causal effect on changes in prices. It is also the case that increases in interest rates raise prices, whether directly through impact on mortgage payments (particularly significant in the UK) or indirectly through impact on firms' costs. Furthermore, whether interest rates have the direct effect postulated depends on the way in which the consumer price index is constructed. But it is also of relevance how people regard interest rate rises. If they are perceived as having caused prices to rise, whether or not recorded in the official statistics, there may be some impact on other prices and on wages.

A number of problems are expected to surface in view of the architecture of the EU banking systems and financial markets. The banking systems are at different stages of development with different characteristics where the capacity of banks to create credit depends on their stage of evolution (Chick and Dow, 1995). Banking systems in the peripheral countries (Greece, Portugal, Spain, Ireland) differ substantially from the ones in the core countries in this respect. There are also important differences within the core countries, which are particularly pertinent. For example, the distinction between bank-based (for example Germany) and capital-market-based (UK is a good example) financial systems is pertinent in this context. These institutional and behavioural characteristics across EMU countries, along with differences in the timing and amplitude of cycles, are expected to have serious implications for the transmission mechanism and thus channels of monetary policy, throughout the EMU area. They are significantly different across the member states. The ECB monetary policy is thus expected to have asymmetric effects across the Union. So that 'differences in the responsiveness of other financial markets to changes in money market interest rates and differences in the net financial positions and interest sensitivities of personal, corporate or financial sectors will mean that the burden of adjustment will not be evenly distributed' (Arrowsmith, 1995, p. 84).

The available empirical evidence on the transmission mechanism is on balance supportive of the view that monetary policy will have different effects across the EMU countries. Empirical studies which are based on large multi-equation econometric models suggest significant differences, while studies based on small VAR-type models suggest insignificant differences. Table 5.1 provides a summary of the findings of an empirical assessment of the impact of monetary policy on output in various eurozone countries (including the UK for comparative purposes). They clearly support the suggestion just alluded to. Dornbusch, Favero and Giavazzi (1998) when reviewing the evidence conclude that in view of the usual difficulties associated with the interpretation and origins of reduced-form relationships, the evidence adduced from large-scale models is more reliable. Further support of the argument of asymmetric effects of monetary policy, is the possibility that consumers display different responses to interest rate changes across the EU. For example, consumers in the UK may be more sensitive to interest rate changes than in some other countries in the EU, due in part to the system of mortgage finance. Additional institutional differences, such as the system of equity markets, may also account for differences in behaviour. Evidence based on simulations with macroeconomic models run by national central banks, confirm the differential impact of interest rate changes across the EU. The following example is an interesting and relevant result that makes the point about the differential impact of interest rate changes on economic activity. It suggests that 'for the UK, the impact of an interest rate change on domestic demand after two years is four times the EU average', so that 'the impact of any change in European monetary policy would be disproportionately channelled through the UK' (CEPR, 1997, p. 17).

The channels of monetary policy are likely to change. Especially so in view of the pressures the financial sector is likely to come under, crucially in terms of credit allocation. Table 5.2 makes the point vividly. Private sector balance sheets in five euro-area countries show that whilst the net assets of both households and enterprises as a percentage of GDP are fairly similar across countries, the composition of gross assets and liabilities varies significantly. In addition, the response of lending rates to changes in policy interest rates also varies. Increasing competition amongst financial institutions will thus give a significantly wider choice of financial instruments. Financial institutions themselves will inevitably react to these developments. As a result, more emphasis is likely to be on interest rates and less on credit availability (OECD, 1998, p. 143).

Table 5.1: Empirical assessments of the impact of monetary policy on output in various European countries (impact on real GDP, percentage deviation from baseline in second year after shock)

Study	Type of shock	Germany	France	Italy	United Kingdom	Spain	Netherlands
Single-country Macro Models[a]							
National Central Bank models (BIS, 1995)	1	-0.4	-0.4	-0.4	-0.9	0.0[a]	-0.2
Multi-country Macro Models[b]							
Fed MCM model (BIS, 1995)	1	-0.7	-0.7	-0.3	-1.2	–	–
IMF Multimod standard multiplier	2	-0.5	–	–	-0.5	–	–
Quest II (Commission Services)	2	-0.4	-0.4	-0.3	-0.4	-0.4	-0.3
Taylor (1995)	2	-0.4	-0.4	-0.4	-0.1	–	–
Small structural models							
Britton and Whitley (1997)[c]	1	-0.5	-0.5	–	-0.3	–	–
Britton and Whitley (1997)[d]	1	-0.4	-0.4	–	-0.4	–	–
Reduced form equation							
Dornbusch, Favero and Giavazzi (1998)[e]	3	-0.5	-0.5	-1.1	-0.5	-0.4	–
Dornbusch, Favero and Giavazzi (1998)[f]	3	-1.4	-1.5	-2.1	-0.9	-1.5	–

Table 5.1: (Continued)

Study	Type of shock	Germany	France	Italy	United Kingdom	Spain	Netherlands
Structural VARs							
Ehrman (1998)	4	-0.6	-0.4	-0.1	-0.2	-0.1	-0.0
Ramaswamy and Sloek (1997)[g]	4	-0.6	-0.4	-0.5	-0.5	-0.3	-0.6
Barran, Coudert and Mojon (1996)[h]	4	-0.6	-0.4	-0.3	-0.4	-0.4	-0.3
Gerlach and Smets (1995)[i]	4	-0.3	-0.2	-0.2	-0.6	–	–
Gerlach and Smets (1995)[j]	1	-1.0	-0.5	-0.5	-0.7	–	–

[a]Fixed ERM rates for Germany, France and Italy; endogenous exchange rate for United Kingdom.
[b]Endogenous exchange rates.
[c]Each country estimated separately.
[d]All countries estimated jointly.
[e]Effect after 8–12 months. Response variable is monthly output data.
[f]Effect after 2 years. Response variable is monthly output data.
[g]Baseline model.
[h]Baseline model (model 1).
[i]1 standard deviation shock.
[j]1 per cent interest rate hike for 2 years.
Types of monetary shock: Type 1: 1 per cent joint rise in short-term interest rates sustained for at least two years; Type 2: 1 per cent permanent decrease in money target; Type 3: 1 per cent simultaneous permanent increase in short-term interest rates; Type 4: 1 standard deviation interest rate shock which in many cases is close to one percentage point.
Source: OECD (1998), where all the relevant references can also be found.

Table 5.2: Financial position of the private sector in selected eurozone countries

| | 1996, as per cent of GDP | | | | |
	Germany[f]	France	Italy	Spain[g]	Belgium
Non-financial enterprises					
Net assets	−35	−73	−67	−43	−81
Gross assets	70	249	39	80	135
of which:					
Short-term[a]	21	24	9	39	26
Long-term[b]	9	4	4	19	38
Equity	23	176	20	16	71
Gross liabilities[c]	105	322	106	123	216
of which:					
Short-term loans	21	16	25	n.a.	21
Long-term loans	45	42	17	n.a.	63
Households					
Net assets	124	138	163	78	217
Gross assets					
of which:					
Short-term[d]	59	21	44	73	75
Long-term[e]	54	41	60	7	79
Equity	17	71	36	40	102
Gross liabilities					
of which:					
Short-term loans	2	8	7	n.a.	4
Long-term loans	8	32	12	n.a.	36

[a] Cash, deposits and short-term loans and securities.
[b] Bonds and long-term loans.
[c] Including own shares.
[d] Including, in some cases, corporate bonds.
[e] Bonds and net equity of life insurance reserves and pension funds.
[f] Figures relate to 1995.
[g] Data for long vs. short loans are not available. It is assumed that half of total loans on the asset side are short and the other half long.
Source: Financial accounts of OECD countries; OECD (1998).

The implementation of monetary policy involves the major difficulty that the interest rate is unlikely to be appropriate for all areas of a monetary union, and this difficulty is exacerbated in the case of the eurozone with the known differences in banking systems and the responsiveness of the economies to interest rate changes. In the context of a relatively closed economy such as the eurozone, interest rates may influence the exchange rate but that change would have relatively little influence on aggregate demand. But interest rates may well operate on investment, and the use of interest rates as a counter-inflation policy may well harm investment and hence future productive capacity.

Income and Interest Rate Elasticity of Demand for Money

A further problematic aspect of the institutional policy framework relates to the possibility of differential income and interest rate elasticities of the eurozone demand for money. Under this possibility, significant differences in income levels and variation of the rate of interest by the ECB will have differential effects throughout the zone. If the income elasticity of demand for money is different, then the national requirements of money stock expansion would be different even if income growth converges. If the interest rate elasticity is different, then monetary policy would not be uniformly effective throughout the eurozone. Under the assumption of exogenous money supply, low interest rate elasticity makes monetary policy very effective; high interest rate elasticity, by contrast, would imply an ineffective monetary policy. In addition, using interest rate changes to target the stock of money would have differential effects. The percentage change in the ECB interest rate would be associated with different percentage changes in euro demand for money. A further implication of possible marked differences in income and interest rate elasticities follows within the traditional theoretical perspective (which appears to be the theoretical framework the ECB has based its policy on). This approach suggests that differences between the rate of growth of the stock of money and of the demand for money would generate inflation. Hence differences in the growth of the demand for money, and a single rate of interest as the monetary policy instrument, would potentially generate differential inflation outcomes.

A number of studies have attempted to estimate the magnitude of interest rate elasticity and Table 5.3 provides a summary of a number of studies which have attempted to estimate it econometrically. We report the results of a number of studies in addition to our own estimates. We have utilised the M3 definition of money stock throughout, since this is the one targeted by the ECB. Four interest rate variables have been employed: short- and long-term, 'own' rate and 'spread' between the own rate and an opportunity cost rate. We have utilized

Table 5.3: Interest and income elasticities for M3 demand for money

Author	Country	Sample period	Method of estimation	Income elasticity	Short-term interest rate elasticity+	Long-term interest rate elasticity	ECM coefficient
This chapter (1999)	AT	1980–98	Johansen, OLS1[One-step OLS estimation]*	1	-0.9+ [10.11]++		-0.15
Hayo (1999)	BE	1965–96	Johansen	1.34			
This chapter (1999)		1980–94	Johansen, OLS1	4.86	-7.6	-0.22	-0.11
Fase and Winder (1993)		1971–89	SECM [Single equation error correction model]	1	0.03	-0.03	
This chapter (1999)	FI	1980–90	Johansen, OLS1*	1			
This chapter (1999)	FR	1979–90	Johansen, OLS1*	1	-2.19	-1.61++	-0.22
Fase and Winder (1993)		1971–89	SECM	1	[4.56]++	-0.01	-0.1
Wesche (1997)		1973–93		4.09		0.09	
Henry and Sicsic (1994)		1971–91	Johansen, OLS1	1	-0.9		
This chapter (1999)	DE	1979–98	Johansen, OLS1*	1	3.92 (spread)		-0.12
Fase and Winder (1993)		1971–89	SECM	1	0.01	-0.04	
Hansen and Kim (1995)		1960–92	SECM	1.26		-0.36	
Hansen and Kim (1995)		1974–89	FMOLS [Fully modified OLS]	1.19	0.09	-0.32	
		1974–89	OLS	1.19	0.10	-0.34	
		1974–89	OLS	1.19	0.11	-0.34	
		1974–92		1.19	0.11	-0.33	
Lutkephol et al. (1996)		1975–94	OLS1	1	[4.1]	-4.1	
Deutsche Bundesbank (1995)		1975–95	OLS2 [Two-step OLS estimation]	1.2		-6	
Biefang-Frisancho et al. (1995)		1975–95	Johansen	1		-3	
		1963–90		1.2		-2.3	
Beyer (1994)		1976–89	OLS1	1	3.7	-6.4	

Table 5.3: (*Continued*)

Author	Country	Sample period	Method of estimation	Income elasticity	Short-term interest rate elasticity+	Long-term interest rate elasticity	ECM coefficient
Todter and Reimers (1994)		1975–92	OLS2	1.6		-1.6	
Kole and Meade (1994)		1970–94	OLS1	1.2		-3.6	
Gerdesmeier (1996)		1975–93	Johansen, OLS1	0.8	0.5	-0.5	
von Hagen (1993)		1965–89	OLS1	1.3		-4.5	
This chapter (1999)	IE	1979–97	Johansen, OLS1	2.95		0.22++ (spread)	-0.14
Fase and Winder (1994)		1971–89	SECM	1	0.01	-0.01	
Hurley and Guiomard (1989)		1979–88 (monthly)	OLS	0.27		-0.01	
This chapter (1999)	IT	1979–98	Johansen, OLS1	1	-2.12		-0.21
Wesche (1997)		1973–93		0.93		0.021	
Fase and Winder (1993)		1971–89	SECM	1		-0.01	
This chapter (1999)	NL	1982–98	Johansen, OLS1	5.5		-1.90	–
Fase and Winder (1993)		1971–89	SECM	1	0.05	-0.06	
Fase and Winder (1993)		1971–89	OLS1	1	2.2	-3.4	
This chapter (1999)	PT	1980–96	Johansen, OLS1	1		-1.46 1.35 (spread)	-0.41
Fase and Winder (1993)		1971–89	SECM	1	0.01	-0.01	
This chapter (1999)	ES	1980–98	Johansen, OLS1*	1	-3.35++	–	
Fase and Winder (1993)		1971–89	SECM	1	0.02	-0.01	

+ Figures in brackets represent estimates of the own rate of interest.
++ Not significant at the 5 per cent significance level.
* In these cases, two cointegrating vectors were found. Consequently, the restrictions that were imposed identified the demand for money and income equations.

the recently developed technique of cointegration with the usual tests of integration – with all the variables utilized being I(1). In Table 5.3, our results appear under the row labelled 'This chapter'. It is clear from this table that there are substantial differences in the estimated elasticities. Furthermore, and as can be ascertained from the last column of Table 5.3, there are also substantial differences in the ECM coefficients from country to country within the eurozone, implying that adjustments when off the steady-state vary significantly. It would be very pertinent under this analysis to ask the question of whether further differences in the elasticities may materialise in view of the changes suggested above. The answer to these questions will have to wait until more data become available. One, however, could speculate on the issue and suggest that in view of the expected changing emphasis on interest rates and the differential mark-up on lending rates across the eurozone countries (as a result of risk differentials etc.), the variation in interest rate elasticity of the demand for money should be expected to increase rather than narrow.

A further potential problem relating to the M3 demand for money, is its instability. Even a cursory look at Table 5.3 clearly indicates how unstable this relationship is within each country where more than one study is reported. A study with a different focus but closely related to what has just been argued, is that of Holmes (1999). It is shown that developments in exchange rate policy and capital controls have been important for those eurozone countries included in the sample of the study (Belgium, France, Germany, Italy, Netherlands, Portugal and Spain).These developments affected relative interest rates and income movements in money velocities. Using monthly data for the period April 1972-December 1979, this study suggests that whilst velocities were integrated during the 1970s and the period 1983–92 (the middle of the ERM period), they were not integrated over the period 1992–97.

It is also important to ask whether the possibility of a eurozone-wide stable demand still exists. We may attempt to derive conclusions from studies which concentrate on estimates of EU demand-for-money functions, and which use constructed aggregates. Arnold (1994) summarises these studies to conclude that 'a stable European money demand function exists. In fact, it appears to be more stable than the money demand functions of individual countries' (p. 249). The same study, though, shows that these estimates from constructed aggregate data are overoptimistic in that 'the use of aggregated data presumes that all noise in national demand functions will be reduced in the process of aggregation and will not be "passed on" the aggregate level' (p. 250). The three sources usually quoted as the causes of money-demand instability are particularly relevant in this context. Institutional changes (for example, new substitutes for money, changes in banking regulation), international developments (for example, abolishing capital controls, changes in the exchange rate regime), and monetary policy (changes in view of the Lucas critique and Goodhart's 'law'), are all possible. We have argued in this chapter that the first two sources are expected to materialise in the eurozone; as for the third, whilst we have not analysed it in this chapter, its potential in causing instabilities to the eurozone demand for money is evident.

There is another problem at present in that we have to invoke exogenous money, in view of the fact that the ECB assume an exogenously driven money stock. We may consider the possibility and implications when the stock of money is viewed as demand driven (Arestis, 1997). The estimates of the demand for money suggest that there are substantial differences between countries in respect of the demand for money. The interest rate will in effect be the same in the sense that there is a common 'repo' rate, though the rates of interest offered and charged by banks may vary across countries depending on market power and liquidity preference. Inflation rates are likely to be similar, but there may be some differences in the growth of income. The likelihood is that the growth of demand for euros will vary across countries, and hence the growth of the stock of euros (bank deposits) in each country will vary. Since loans are the other side of the banks balance sheets (to bank deposits), the availability of loans would vary across countries. This availability, though, may not be what national economies require in view of substantial differences in banking structures across the eurozone. In the absence of any intervention to enable the weaker countries to satisfy their demand for loans, an unsatisfied excess demand for loans would be inevitable. This would depress especially those regions that need funding most.

Financial Capital Mobility

The increase in the degree of financial capital mobility within the EMU reveals additional difficulties. Financial institutions within the eurozone area hold about 90 per cent of their portfolios in domestic assets. With the removal of foreign exchange risks and regulations which inhibit holdings of foreign assets, as well as the elimination of currency conversion costs, financial institutions will increase their holdings of euro assets substantially. The clear implication is that the amount of funds moving within the euro area will make a quantum leap. The regulatory and institutional environment will remain national at least during its initial phase when institutions have not adapted to the new environment. Rates of return will differ across EMU members, but banks will be able to borrow at the same interest rate. Under these circumstances financial disturbances are likely to materialise. A stronger boom in, say, Third Italy than in the rest of the EMU, will be associated with asset inflation there, with the ECB being unable to initiate policies specific to the needs of Third Italy. We can envisage that there will be substantial money flows into areas where asset prices are rising and which offer the prospects of high returns. The inflow will generate further rises in asset prices, generating further asset inflation. The boom cannot continue forever, and at some stage the bubble will burst, with asset prices collapsing causing financial distress in the local banking system. Recent experience in the Far East is probably indicative of what may happen.

There may be difficulties emanating from increased volatility of the euro, especially if it were to become reserve currency challenging the dollar. To begin with, investors and borrowers that were not interested previously in European currencies because of the limited size of the money markets, are expected to increase substantially their demand for euros. At the same time, though, the holdings of different European currencies to diversify their risk, will be reduced thus containing the increased demand for euros just referred to. In fact, there is the potential of 'dollar overhang', the possibility of excess supply of foreign exchange reserves within the ESCB, in view of the replacement of the eurozone countries' reserves by the euro. Estimates range from a large excess supply to a possible excess in demand (see Arrowsmith *et al.*, 1999, for more details). A further potential shift into euro is changes in the currency composition of other countries official reserves and of international investors' portfolios. Arrowsmith *et al.* (1999) estimate that 'If the attraction of the euro as a reserve currency to official holders outside EMU were sufficient to restore its share of world reserves to that taken at present by the currencies of the 11 participating members of EMU, their euro holdings would rise by $66 bn; for the euro, over time, to achieve a share equal to that of the US dollar in non-EU countries' reserves would require (assuming the currencies' shares are unchanged) a switch from the dollar to the euro of $260 bn) (in 1996 terms); and, similarly, equality with the dollar in total world reserves would entail a switch to the euro of $360 bn' (p. 9). As for international investors' portfolios, 'a switch of $250 bn into euro deposits would be required' (Arrowsmith *et al.*, 1999, p. 10) to retain the share of euro in total world foreign currency deposits (at the pre-EMU percentage of non-banks' holdings of the EMU-11 currencies as foreign currency deposits). Furthermore, 'to achieve an equal share with the dollar would entail a switch of $180 bn (to give a 27% share in total foreign currency deposits after EMU)' (Arrowsmith *et al.*, 1999, p. 10). Portfolio shifts should also be expected in the international debt market. Arrowsmith *et al.* (1999) argue that 'a movement of $410 bn would restore the euro's share in the international debt market to that presently held by the EMU-11 currencies, while reaching parity with the dollar would require a shift of $320 bn' (p. 11). Similar arguments could be advanced in the case of international borrowers, thus further adding to the uncertainties just alluded to.

Furthermore, and as agreed at the Madrid summit in December 1995, all new government debt issued after 1 January 1999 by EMU members will be denominated in euros. In addition, all the eurozone countries have committed themselves to renominate existing debt into euros from national currencies. It follows that the re-denomination of government and corporate bonds in euros, and the adoption of a uniform set of conventions in the securities markets, provide further support to the argument that significant changes in the eurozone financial markets will take place. More importantly, these developments will result in a market with euro-denominated securities the size of which is expected to be substantial (OECD, 1998, p. 146). An interesting implication of these developments may very well be that the growth of stronger capital markets would transform bank finance which is the traditional form of company finance, towards market finance (that is bonds and stocks). The value of listed companies in, for example, Germany as a percentage of GDP is currently only 40 per cent, when in the UK and the USA is 150 per cent. Elsewhere in the EMU area the percentage is around Germany's. Consequently, the capitalisation in the EMU stock exchanges could easily double or treble in the near future as existing markets expand and new open. Still a further implication of these developments is that the channels of influence of monetary policy will inevitably change throughout the EMU member countries.

Summary and Conclusions

The broad conclusions which we draw from the above discussion are twofold. First, the euro starts with many of the EU countries and regions experiencing high levels of unemployment. The policy framework which accompanies the introduction of the euro (the Stability and Growth Pact and the ECB) is a generally deflationary one, and does not involve any significant attempts to reduce either the level of or the disparities in unemployment. The prospects for unemployment appear bleak, and in that sense the description of a continuing unemployment crisis could be applied.

Second, capitalist economies suffer from financial fragility and periodic financial crisis. The eurozone may become rather more prone to such crises than has been the case in the constituent countries. The split of responsibilities between the ECB and the national central banks and the weak provisions for the ECB to act as lender of last resort are likely to exacerbate financial fragility. This would be reinforced by the far-reaching changes that are expected to take place in the financial and capital markets which would enhance capital mobility in the eurozone. We also suggest that asymmetric shocks, different channels of influence of monetary policy, and differences in its impact, are forces working towards increasing further financial fragility.

Acknowledgements

The authors are grateful to Kevin McCauley for research assistance, and to Iris Biefang-Frisancho Mariscal for helpful discussions on the econometric aspects of the paper.

Notes

1. The use of monetary policy to target the rate of inflation draws on two broad sets of assumptions. The first is that monetary conditions are the cause and inflation the effect, and that interest rates can affect monetary conditions. In the simple monetarist story, the money supply determines the rate of inflation. But if there is reverse causality, whereby inflation influences monetary conditions, then seeking to set the latter becomes much less attractive. The second broad assumption is the classical dichotomy under which there is a separation between the real and the monetary sides of the economy, and under which the monetary conditions do not influence the real side of the economy, either in the short-run or the long-run. The NAIRU is a reflection of this notion, as it represents a supply-side equilibrium rate of unemployment, at which inflation is constant. In its usual representation, the NAIRU is settled by labour market factors, and not influenced by capacity or by aggregate demand.
2. The Governing Council comprises the Executive Board and the governors of the national central banks. The Executive Board of the ECB consists of the President, Vice President and four other members who 'shall be appointed from among persons of recognised standing and professional expertise in monetary and banking matters' (Article 11 of Protocol on the Statute of the European System of Central Banks and of the European Central Bank). The ESCB 'shall be governed by the decision making bodies of the ESCB' (Article 8). It is clear that financial and banking interests will be well represented but there will be no representation of national or regional governments,

trade unions, industrial and business interests. This heavy reliance on banking and financial interests is likely to generate an emphasis on 'sound' money and the pursuit of overly deflationary policies. Little regard will be paid to issues of unemployment or growth.

3. Eligible liabilities are: overnight deposits; deposits with agreed maturity up to 2 years; deposits redeemable at notice up to 2 years; debt securities issued with agreed maturity up to 2 years; and money market paper.

4. For more details on the *Stability and Growth Pact* see Arestis and Sawyer (1999), and, especially, Arestis, McCauley and Sawyer (2001).

5. This should not be read as supporting a monetarist view on inflation, though the ECB and others appear to adhere to an essentially monetarist view of inflation and hence could use an argument akin to growth of money supply equal to growth of national income (see also Eichengreen and Wyplosz (1998).

6. Figures calculated from *International Financial Statistics*, and generally refer to March 1999 and to the clearing banks, and refer to ratio of broad money to reserves.

7. Figures refer to output gap and are taken from OECD *Economic Outlook*, June 1999.

8. The average figure is much influenced by the experience of Finland in the early 1990s, when the economy slumped under the impact of the collapse of the Soviet Union. The figures excluding Finland are 1.62 per cent in 1998 and an average of 1.60.

9. The simulations reported in Arrowsmith *et al.* (1999) are undertaken on the large multi-country model developed and operated by the National Institute of Economic and Social Research, the so-called NIGEM model (see NIESR, 1998).

References

Arestis, P. (1997) *Money, Pricing, Distribution and Economic Integration*, London, Macmillan.

Arestis, P. and Sawyer, M. C. (1999) 'The Economic and Monetary Union: Current and Future Prospects', *Revista*, 5(December): 33–60.

Arestis, P., McCauley, K. and Sawyer, M. C. (2001) 'An Alternative Stability and Growth Pact for the European Union', *Cambridge Journal of Economics*, 25(1): 113–130.

Arnold, I. J. M. (1994) 'The Myth of a Stable European Money Demand', *Open Economies Review*, 5:249–259.

Arrowsmith, J. (1995) 'Economic and Monetary Union In a Multi-Tier Europe', *National Institute Economic Review*, 152(2):76–96.

Arrowsmith, J., Barrell, R. and Taylor, C. (1999) 'Managing the Euro in a tri-polar World', in M. Artis and E. Hennessy (eds) *The Euro: A Challenge and Opportunity for Financial Markets*, London, Routledge, pp. 1–28.

Beyer, A. (1994) 'Die Geldmenge M3 in Deutschland: Geldnachfrage und Geldmengensteuerung – Eine Okonometrische Studie', Johann Wolfgang Goethe Universitat, Frankfurt/M., *Working Paper*, no. 33, Geld Wahrung Kapitalmarkt.

Biefang-Frisancho Mariscal, I., Trautwein, H. M., Howells, P., Arestis, P. and Hagemann, H. (1995) 'Financial innovation and the long-run demand for money in the United Kingdom and in West Germany', *Weltwirtschaftliches Archiv*, 131(2):302–325.

Centre for Economic Policy (CEPR) (1997) *The Ostrich and the EMU: Policy Choices Facing the UK*, 9 May, London.

Chick, V. and Dow, S. C. (1995) 'Wettewerb und die Zukunft des Europaischen Banken und Finazsystems (Competition and the future of the European banking und financial system)' in C. Thomasbenger (ed.) *Europaische Geldpolitik Swischen Marktzwangen und Neuen Institutionellen Regulengen (New Institutions for European Monetary Integration)*, Marburg, Metropolis-Verlag, pp. 293–321.

Currie, D. (1997) *The Pros and Cons of EMU*, London, HM Treasury.

Deutsche Bundesbank (1995) 'Uberprufung des Geldmengenziels und Neuordnung der Mindestreserve', *Monatsberichte der Deutschen Bundesbank*, July: 19–37.

Dornbusch, R., Favero, C. and Giavazzi, F. (1998) 'Immediate challenges for the European Central Bank', in D. Begg, J. Von Hagen, C. Wyplosz and K. F. Zimmermann (eds) *EMU: Prospects and Challenges for the Euro*, Oxford, Blackwell Publishers, pp. 17–64.

Eichengreen, B. and Wyplosz, C. (1998) 'The stability pact: more than a minor nuisance?' in D. Begg, J. Von Hagen, C. Wyplosz and K. F. Zimmermann (eds) *EMU: Prospects and Challenges for the Euro*, Oxford, Blackwell Publishers, pp. 67–113.

European Union (EU) (1998) *Selected Instruments Taken from Treaties*, Brussels, The European Union.

Fase, M. M. G. and Winder, C. C. A. (1993) 'The demand for money in the Netherlands and other EU countries', *De Economist*, 141(4):471–96.

Fase, M. M. G. and Winder, C. C. A. (1994) 'Money Demand within EMU. An Analysis with the Divisia Measure', *Staff Report*, no. 3, De Nederlandsche Bank.

Fatas, A. (1998) 'Does the EMU need a fiscal federation?' in D. Begg, J. Von Hagen, C. Wyplosz and K. F. Zimmermann (eds) *EMU: Prospects and Challenges for the Euro*, Oxford, Blackwell Publishers, pp. 165–203.

Funke, M., Hall, S. and R. Ruhwedel (1999) 'Shock Hunting: The Relative Importance of Industry-specific, Region-specific and Aggregate Shocks in the OECD Countries', *Manchester School*, 67(Supplement):49–65.

Gerdesmeier, D. (1996) 'The Role of Wealth in Money Demand', *Deutsche Bundesbank*, Discussion Paper no. 96/5.

Hansen, G. and Kim, J. R. (1995) 'The Stability of German Money Demand: Tests of the Cointegrating Relation', *Weltwirtschaftliches Archiv*, 131(2):286–301.

Hayo, B. (1999) 'The Demand for Money in Austria', *Working Paper*, University of Bonn.

Henry, J. and Sicsic, P. (1994) 'Breaking Trends, Financial Innovation and the Velocity of French Money Aggregates', *Occasional Paper*, Banque de France.

Holmes, M. J. (1999) 'The Velocity of Circulation: Some New Evidence on International Integration', *mimeo*, Loughborough University.

Hurley, M. and Guiomard, C. (1989) 'Determinants of Money Demand in Ireland 1970 to 1988: Rounding up the Usual Suspects', *Central Bank of Ireland*, Research and Publications Department.

Kole, L. S. and Meade, E. E. (1994) 'Searching for the Holy Grail: An Examination of German Money Demand after Unification', *Federal Reserve Bank*, USA.

Lutkephol, H., Terasvirta, T. and Wolters, J. (1996) 'Modelling the Demand for M3 in the Unified Germany', *Discussion Paper*, no. 24, Humboldt-Universitat zu Berlin.

Monetary Policy Committee (1999) *The Transmission Mechanism of Monetary Policy*, London, Bank of England.

NIESR (1998) *The National Institute World Model Users Manual*, July.

OECD (1998) *Economic Outlook*, December 1998, Paris: OECD.

Todter, K. H. and Reimers, H. E. (1994) 'P-star as a Link between Money and Prices in Germany', *Weltwirtschaftliches Archiv*, 130(2):273–89.

von Hagen, J. (1993) 'Monetary Union, Money Demand and Money Supply', *European Economic Review*, 37:803–836.

Wesche, K. (1997) 'The Stability of European Money Demand: An Investigation of M3H', *Open Economies Review*, 8(4):371–391.

6
Globalization, the Distribution of Power, and Full Employment

John Cornwall and Wendy Cornwall

Introduction

Power and conflict have virtually no role in mainstream economics, the main reasons being the pervasive influence of the competitive model and the difficulty in incorporating power quantitatively in formal models. However, two important contributions to our understanding of the impact of power on the economy are Kalecki's theory of the political business cycle (1971) and Keynes' analysis of how persistent high unemployment affects power struggles and the stability of a capitalist system (1936, Chapter 24). In Kalecki's theory, conflict is a natural outcome of a social order that combines capitalism with full political democracy, because of the tensions between the political demands flowing from universal suffrage and the distributional rewards generated by the market system. Kalecki believed that in the long run, full employment capitalism and full political democracy were incompatible. To survive, capital had to retain a minimum amount of power, and prolonged periods of full employment denied them this critical minimum. However, having the upper hand in both the market and the political arena, capital could alter the terms of the conflict and the degree of labour militancy by varying the distribution of political power, i.e. more or less democracy, and the distribution of economic power, i.e. more or less unemployment. The political business cycle was the result of capital manipulating the unemployment rate.

Writing in the middle of the Great Depression, when unemployment was near its historical high and totalitarian movements were growing in strength, Keynes saw the effects of unemployment in a different light. Rather than being the means of reducing tensions and conflict, prolonged high unemployment was a source of economic and political power struggles that could lead to the destruction of capitalism or of democracy. One danger, an economic consequence of democracy, was socialism. Militant labour, in the interests of distributional fairness, would demand replacement of the existing capitalist system. The other danger was the political consequence of capitalism in the form of the disenfranchisement of the citizenry. Sensing an imminent attempt by labour to replace the existing economic order, capitalists would pre-empt this move by installing a fascist political order. Full employment was considered necessary to avoid either outcome.

From the perspective of the Golden Age, Keynes' analysis and remedy for capitalism seemed correct and Kalecki's views wrong. Democracy and capitalism prevailed during a long period of full employment and historically high relative power of labour. From today's perspective, things are less clear; the Golden Age has been succeeded by a long period of high unemployment and a marked shift in the distribution of economic and political power from labour to capital without the destruction of either capitalism or democracy. In this chapter we argue that Kalecki and Keynes uncovered different features of an evolving capitalist system which, when considered together, offer insights into the post-World War II performance of the developed capitalist economies.[1] They do so by clarifying the determinants and role of power during capitalism's finest hour and in the more recent period of macroeconomic malfunction. Following some preliminary remarks on power, we proceed to an historical explanation of the shifts in power and their impact on institutions, i.e. the rules, laws and customs that govern behaviour, and on economic performance. The chapter concludes with an evaluation of Kalecki's and Keynes' views and the outlook in the near future for globalization, the distribution of power, and full employment.

Power

Some Concepts

Although a vast literature exists describing strongly asserted but differing views of the 'true' meaning of power, we find it sufficient to use a simple two-part definition proposed by Wartenberg (1990, pp. 17–27). Power refers both to the ability to do something and to the ability to control or command others, i.e. the ability of dominant individuals or groups in economic relationships to make subordinate individuals or groups act in the former's interest.

Although our main interest lies in the relation between power and the economy, it is useful to categorize two types of power. We distinguish between economic and political power in terms of the means that enable individuals or groups to exercise power, and not for what particular purpose power is used. For example, economic power is involved when labour succeeds through collective bargaining in altering rules governing safety conditions in the workplace. The exercise of political power is illustrated by labour's ability to induce their political representatives to pass legislation with the same purpose. The connection between political and economic power is very close. In general, when private groups are dissatisfied with market-determined outcomes, they will organize against the market and redress their grievances through political channels (Hibbs, 1987). These are cases where the economic power of private agents is insufficient to secure their objectives. Resort to political action can influence laws and government regulations, i.e. formal institutions, enabling them to achieve what was previously unachievable. In many instances, this amounts to harnessing political power to increase economic power.

Following the lead of social scientists outside economics, we focus attention on the power of organized interest groups, the factors influencing their relative power and the institutional goals they pursue.[2] We also find it useful to adopt Kalecki's and Keynes' terminology and speak in terms of two broad categories of organized interest groups, such as capital or business and labour or workers, in explaining the distribution of power and the way in which the distribution of power affects the economy.[3]

Our approach is made clearer by a summary of the party control theory of economic policy (Alesina and Roubini, 1997, Chapter 3; Hibbs, 1987, 1994; Tufte, 1978). This power theory focuses on the exercise of political power as the origin of formal institutional change, e.g. the enactment of laws that foster low unemployment or low inflation. One basic premise of the theory is that the distribution of political power and the way power influences institutions and macro performance derive from the underlying economic and social divisions of society. Another is that labour places greater weight on full employment than capital and therefore always chooses policy points on a negatively-sloped Phillips curve further down and to the right. For example, if the labour movement is powerful, being organized in a centralized union confederation, this will be reflected in strong left-of-centre political parties and laws and regulations reflecting labour's interests and strength, e.g. full employment policies and an extended welfare state. A natural extension of this approach is to consider the use of economic power to alter institutions, e.g. the introduction of 'fairness' considerations in wage settlements (Hicks, 1974) or 'restructuring' the workplace (Kalecki, 1971).

Capital's Special Function

A weakness of the party control theory, in addition to the fact that it deals only with political power, is that it assumes the distribution of political power and its impact on institutions and economic performance to be primarily determined by electoral success. This shortcoming is made clearer by a summary of Lindblom's analysis of the sources of capital's power. According to Lindblom (1977, Chapters 13 and 14), even if business did not participate in politics, under capitalism it will always be accorded special privileges and powers because of the special functions it performs. For example, the decisions of business leaders determine the technology to be used, the way in which work is organized, the location of industry, the allocation of resources and the structure of markets. Economic security and living standards depend upon these decisions. Consequently business is not simply one of many interest groups pursuing its agenda with government. In practical terms it is part of government – not elected, but clearly governing economic performance.

Also, electoral fortunes are tied to economic performance, and this alone would predispose governments to extend to business leaders the privileges and powers that induce them to perform their economic functions successfully. But business does participate in politics and, according to Lindblom, more effectively than other organized groups, for two reasons: it has greater financial resources at its disposal to sell its agenda and it has the organization already in place to persuade voters to accept this agenda.

This does not mean that the power of business is uncontested or that it is uniform among economies or over time, or that the electoral strength of labour should be given no weight. Capitalism takes many forms, and the strength and type of power that business exercises are among the causes of differences. To examine how the distribution of power is determined and how it affects institutions and performance, we allow that business holds the preferred position that Lindblom assumes, but that its power is limited by opposing interests. These limits depend, for example, on the strength of the trade union movement and the political parties supporting its causes, and the tightness of the labour markets. They also depend on the institutions that determine the extent to which elected officials take responsibility for regulating the economy, or in Kalecki's terminology, on the 'fullness' of political democracy.

Having made these preliminary points, we take up an historical account of the factors leading to a marked shift in the distribution of power and the role of this shift in power on institutions and the unemployment record over the past half century. This era spans two periods – the Golden Age and the ensuing episode of mass unemployment. We begin with the Golden Age and describe the institutional features that made it possible. We refer to these institutions collectively as a social bargain regime, and argue that such regimes reconcile full employment with other domestic and external macroeconomic goals.

The Origins of the Social Bargain Regimes

Reconciling Domestic Macroeconomic Goals

By the early 1950s, most of the OECD economies had entered a period of near full employment; capital was still in control of production, socialism had been avoided and democracy saved, but a new capitalism had emerged in which labour's power was at its greatest. The question is how such an episode could arise from an immediate past that included the rise of Soviet communism, the Great Depression and World War II. We have argued that business is not like other pressure groups, but holds a unique position in a capitalist system, and has special powers and privileges. Other things being equal, business will resist efforts to reduce its economic and political power. Yet the Golden Age was a period in which capital in most of the OECD was willing to enter into cooperative arrangements with government and labour that led to a reduction in its relative power. A very clear exception is the USA, which pursued a different domestic path.

The radicalization of labour and its early post-war success in electing governments friendly to its cause appeared to present a democratic challenge to the longstanding influence of business in political and economic affairs. The challenge from labour at the end of World War II was aimed directly at the essential control function of business. The nationalization and economic planning labour demanded would shift decision-making power from business to governments. These demands flowed from four main sources: the political ideologies of the left-wing parties labour sponsored and supported; the experience of wartime planning and the high incomes and full employment it delivered; the impact of the *General Theory* on labour's support of government intervention; and the widespread public hostility to capitalists depicted (with more or less accuracy) as fascists, fascist collaborators, war criminals or war profiteers. Public condemnation of wartime activities and the demonstrated responsiveness of governments to public pressure for state ownership were manifestations of the new power relationships that had emerged. The various combinations of state ownership, control and planning introduced were not merely retaliatory, but were integral components of government policies for economic reconstruction outside the USA. The shift in political power to labour that lay behind these government initiatives carried the threat of further restrictions should business fail to cooperate.

At the same time, fundamental institutional changes in their labour markets were evolving in the new economic systems; this carried dangers that Keynes had not fully explored. Full employment might well be enough to fend off socialism, but it would greatly increase the economic and political power of labour. Yet in spite of this new threat to the stability of capitalism, there were over two decades of low unemployment and low inflation. The social bargains established in the early post-war years made the simultaneous realization of these two economic goals possible.[4] To understand how the Golden Age came about therefore requires an understanding of how this compromise between capital and labour was achieved and the key role of government in the process.

In the political climate of the time, in Western Europe, the UK and Japan the competing demands of labour and capital may have appeared irreconcilable. However, these differences co-existed with a common desire for rapid reconstruction and return to normal peacetime life, providing an environment conducive to compromise. Governments sought political and economic stability, and the restoration of national prestige and economic power. Labour wanted employment, decent incomes and security in times of misfortune. Business recognized the opportunity for profitable enterprise, but labour's strength and radicalism led to fears about socialism. The compromises that were reached differed in detail and emphasis among countries, but had features in common that would meet the priorities of all parties. First, most governments accepted full employment as a goal and took steps to ensure that labour's rights were clear and conditions of employment fair.[5] Social safety nets were improved, both regarding the numbers covered and the benefits that could be claimed. In return, labour was required to agree to wage restraint and cooperation. That labour agreed to wage restraint is an indication of the relative preference for security of workers who remembered the Depression all too clearly. Labour had gained a political presence that yielded many of the economic benefits it had long sought, and more were promised as productivity and incomes rose. Finally, labour's agreement gave capital reason to expect economic stability and orderly industrial relations, reducing the risk for the large investments they were to make.

In summary, governments laid the groundwork for the rise in the relative power of labour, creating a potential inconsistency or conflict of domestic goals that stood in the way of a Golden Age. That potential conflict was the desire to simultaneously achieve full employment, politically acceptable rates of inflation and unrestricted collective bargaining. This internal inconsistency was resolved in most economies by labour foregoing unrestricted collective bargaining and accepting wage targets consistent with acceptable rates of inflation and international competitiveness as part of the social bargain regime.

Reconciling External Goals

These domestic institutional changes were to play a very large part in subsequent events. But international political developments also played a decisive role. Particularly important was the international policy of the USA, now emerging as the economic and political hegemon. It had declared itself early in World War II as a proponent of a multilateral system of liberalized trade.[6] With the largest economy, a strong trade surplus, and holding the bulk of the world's foreign reserves, American views on the post-war international order dominated the Bretton Woods conference and subsequent international agreements in the 1940s. There was broad recognition of the need for a system of multilateral trade and payments designed to discourage the competitive devaluations and controls that had blighted trade in the inter-war period. The basis of the international monetary system would be fixed but adjustable exchange rates and controls on private international capital flows. As Keynes pointed out, only in this way could external balance and full employment be achieved simultaneously.

In sharp contrast to the economic strength of the USA, Japan and the countries of Western Europe faced post-war reconstruction with large trade deficits and dwindling foreign reserves (Armstrong, Glyn and Harrison, 1984, pp. 107–10). In the absence of other sources of finance for reconstruction, by early 1947 there was a growing belief that continued recovery depended upon support from the USA. For

Japan and the European countries, the impending dollar shortage confirmed fears about competitiveness and the trade balance, increasing their resistance to abandoning controls. Consequently, the Bretton Woods institutions (the IMF and the World Bank) as well as the General Agreement on Tariffs and Trade were the outcome of compromise between the American objective of trade liberalization and the deficit countries' strong preferences for managed trade and protectionism.[7] These agreements embodied the long-term commitment to the trade and payments liberalization sought by the USA, but permitted trade and capital controls in the shorter term with some American assistance for payments deficits. Although the USA believed that the transition period would be brief, controls persisted and implementation of policies to liberalize trade was delayed until the 1960s.

The commitment of the USA to unregulated markets was not confined to international trade and payments, but included an ideal vision of a united Europe modelled after itself, both politically and economically, i.e. a non-interventionist, market power regime. In particular, the USA promoted the view that unfettered free enterprise capitalism and an American-style industrial relations system would deliver the productivity growth and rising living standards that would resolve social conflict.[8] However, in the UK and Europe, the USA faced governments responding to the views of highly politicized labour movements. Nationalized industries and the welfare state were central to the social bargains. Economic management was viewed as essential to reconstruction and to the full employment most governments had promised. Political stability precluded any backing away from these measures, thus confirming the welfare state and mixed capitalism as part of the new order (Hobsbawm, 1994, Chapter 9).

In the event, these governments were to receive the assistance they needed, without relinquishing the welfare state or protection from international competition. This was ensured by the emergence of the Cold War. American Cold War policy hinged upon alignment with a strong and stable Europe; political stability was essential, and required economic stability. Restoration of German industrial power became central to the USA vision of a united Europe. A similar position was adopted towards Japan, as part of a general policy of strengthening the 'free world'.

Thus, although the USA was clearly the dominant economy at the end of the war, it was not able to promote the market power regime, nor even to achieve quickly the international objectives agreed upon at

Bretton Woods. Instead, outside the USA the international political–economic system that eventually arose has been termed 'embedded liberalism' (Keohane,1984); it is characterized by governments that pursue interventionist domestic policies and liberal international economic policies. This system did not arise spontaneously, but was engineered by the USA. It provided the groundwork for the social bargain regimes that would deliver the Golden Age.

Self-Reinforcing Tendencies

The success of the social welfare capitalism that was established to meet labour's demands depended ultimately upon there being full employment. A necessary condition for full employment is the absence of constraints on aggregate demand (AD). In most countries, the new labour market institutions were designed to avoid inflation, to maintain international competitiveness, and to minimize industrial strife, thus encouraging the investment needed for modernization and growth. For reasons already discussed, capital was in no position to insist upon restricting AD in order to reduce labour's power, as labour had achieved political ascendancy by the early 1950s.

Events of the two succeeding decades were to reinforce the terms of the social bargain regime. The ever-present threat of communism sustained American interest in economic and political stability throughout the 'free world'. Through American aid and technology transfer, together with a strong investment effort, productivity growth accelerated everywhere. This and full employment not only provided the source of growing real wages, but also financed the expansion of a welfare state favoured by labour. Together these benefits reinforced labour's original decision to agree to a social bargain and helped sustain labour's growing power. For capital, productivity growth and expanding markets were sources of growing profits.

The Origins of the Market Power Regimes

The new episode in capitalist development that followed the Golden Age and continues to the present has been marked by mass unemployment, greatly reduced growth in productivity and per capita incomes, growing inequality of incomes and increasing poverty. These events are interrelated with a redistribution of power towards capital.

The Golden Age is generally considered to have ended in the early to mid 1970s. In hindsight, it is clear that by this time the transition from a period of high growth and full employment to another of slow growth and high unemployment was well under way. Early signs of its demise were the explosion of wages and various shocks generating accelerating rates of inflation in the late 1960s to early 1970s, the period of the Great Inflation, and the breakdown of Bretton Woods in the early 1970s. Continued strong inflation in the first half of the 1970s, coupled with payments problems in many economies in 1973–74, were met by the implementation of restrictive AD policies.[9] These policies achieved a reduction in inflation rates beginning in 1975, although they remained double their Golden Age rates up to the second oil shock in 1979. The main impact was on unemployment, which increased throughout the second half of the 1970s, reaching rates twice those of the 1960s. In the 1980s, governments redoubled their efforts to stabilize inflation at low rates, using very restrictive policies. By the end of the decade, inflation was controlled, but unemployment was about three times the Golden Age rates. In spite of partial recovery in unemployment rates in the 1990s in some economies, conditions of mass unemployment have remained. In the OECD economies considered in this chapter, unemployment had risen from 8.8 million in 1973 to an average of approximately 26 million in the period 1994–97 (OECD, *Labour Force Statistics*, various issues).

In our view, the explosion of wages was the dominant force fuelling the Great Inflation and reflected critical institutional changes in the labour market. Because it arose out of changes in the institutional framework, the Great Inflation played a crucial role in ending the Golden Age. It led to the introduction of restrictive AD policies whose overall stance remained restrictive long after the Great Inflation came to an end. These institutional changes and those initiated by the collapse of the Bretton Woods system set the stage for the advent of market power regimes now in their third decade, regimes of reduced government intervention, deregulation of markets, cutbacks in the welfare state, reduced labour power and the sacrifice of full employment for price stability. They also signalled the beginning of the current period of mass unemployment.

Institutional Changes in the Labour Market

As stated earlier, in the Golden Age the goals of full employment and politically acceptable rates of inflation were achieved simultaneously by removing unrestricted collective bargaining from the list of desired domestic macroeconomic goals. Wage targets were part of the social bargain. The wage explosions of the late 1960s reflected the breakdown of these bargains.[10] Labour unrest and wage explosions now led to the belief that labour had become too powerful, and was responsible for inflation. The reputation of business rose as labour's fell. The bad reputation earned in World War II, which had caused capital to exercise restraint in its use of power, was all but forgotten. A second motive for capital to temper its use of power was removed with the collapse of the Soviet Union in the late 1980s. This relieved both government and business of their fears of socialism. These events led to a greater assertion of power by business and reduced its interest in social bargains.

Without a 'second generation' of social bargains, either the goal of full employment or acceptable rates of inflation had to be sacrificed. Throughout the OECD, the decision was made to sacrifice the full employment goal and to contain inflation through restricting AD and letting unemployment rise. Collective bargaining outcomes could be left to the market. The fact that little – if any – attempt was made to establish a 'second generation' of social bargains, thereby preventing a constraint on AD, suggests the lack of 'political will' or desire to re-establish social bargain regimes. The adopted restrictive AD policy responses and the upward trend in unemployment rates beginning in the mid-1970s marked a major shift of economic power to business.[11]

Globalization and Locking in the Market Power Regimes

In a parallel post-golden age trend, self-imposed constraints have limited governments' power to manage their economies. These constraints take several forms: laws and regulations limiting government's use of discretionary AD policies, e.g. balanced budget resolutions and greater independence for central banks; international agreements binding the signatories to abide by regulations limiting their use of discretionary AD policies, e.g. Maastricht criteria; international agreements deregulating capital movements that in effect become constraints on stimulative AD policies; and trade regulations preventing the use of import restrictions to combat sectoral rises in unemployment.

All of these legal constraints reinforce the effects that previously adopted restrictive AD policies had on the distribution of economic power by moving the full employment goal beyond the reach of democracy. Governments have voluntarily curtailed their own power to intervene, providing support for the market power regime. Some of the international developments set in motion by the breakdown of Bretton Woods and the expansion of free trade agreements to include a number of NICs deserve special consideration. Often subsumed under the heading of increased globalization, these developments reinforced the terms of the new regime by entrenching international markets beyond the reach of popular democracy. In varying degrees, elected representatives in nation states were relieved of their power to enact independent policies. Instead, international organizations, largely under the control of the USA, were empowered to interpret the terms of the agreements.

In this chapter, globalization refers to the integration of economies through free trade and deregulated international capital markets. The forms that greater globalization have taken in the recent period have done much to reinforce labour's weakened economic position and to make more difficult any radical improvement in unemployment in the near future. We will concentrate on two examples. The trend in free trade agreements has been the expansion of the number of NICs able to compete freely with the developed economies for market shares of merchandise trade. Taking advantage of technology transfer opportunities, their rapid industrialization has been aided by the introduction of advanced (but standardized) technologies that result in labour costs substantially below those in similar industries in the developed economies. This in itself would contribute to the surge in exports from the NICs to the developed economies. However this overlooks the importance of outsourcing, the disintegration of the production process whereby production activities done abroad are combined with those done at home. In cases where this is technically possible, the cost advantage of the NICs will probably apply to component parts of production processes, leading to outsourcing by the developed economies. Indeed in the current period the large growth in merchandise trade relative to merchandise production in the OECD economies can be attributed both to the increased number of NICs exporting final goods to the developed economies, and also to growth of the latter's outsourcing (Feenstra, 1998; Irwin, 1996).

Both developments act to reduce the bargaining power of labour, especially union labour (Feenstra, 1998). When rules limit direct investment and outsourcing, both producers and labour want enforcement of labour standards abroad to maintain competitiveness for their product. Once the rules are relaxed, the interests of producers and consumers diverge, as low wages and lax labour standards make foreign production more profitable. The threat to move all or part of production abroad can be used at home to exact reductions in labour compensation (wages plus benefits). Moreover, the threat of significant job losses allows large firms to demand changes to labour legislation that further weaken labour. In addition to endangering jobs, wages, labour standards and union powers, globalization also hastens the decline of social safety nets. Citing international competitiveness, business has been able to shift the tax burden to labour. But job losses and low wages will erode this tax base, reducing governments' ability to finance welfare programmes (Rodrik, 1997). Globalization thus undermines labour strength, reinforcing the impact of higher levels of overall unemployment on capital's ability to control the workplace in the developed economies.

The deregulation of financial capital movements is a second example of globalization's negative effect on labour power and the prospects of improved employment. This it accomplishes by creating an additional barrier to stimulative AD policies. Under an international monetary regime of deregulated financial capital and flexible exchange rates, the inflation costs are immediately increased in any economy attempting to pursue a full employment goal unilaterally. In these circumstances, stimulative AD policies generate fears of accelerating inflation and a depreciating currency. Managers of large, mobile capital funds respond to unilateral stimulative policies by withdrawing funds from the country, causing depreciation of the currency and higher expected and actual rates of inflation. The more 'credible' and persistent is the stimulative AD policy, the greater and more prolonged will be the speculation against the currency because of the effects on expected and actual rates of inflation. Governments are soon forced to reverse their policies in order to protect the exchange rate. Simplifying slightly, without coordinated expansionary policies, the deregulation of capital flows under a flexible exchange rate system has locked the OECD economies in a high unemployment equilibrium trap by ruling out stimulative AD policy as an instrument of reducing unemployment rates.[12]

Globalization and the Role of the Hegemon

In this historical account of shifts in power, changing institutions and the advent of mass unemployment, we have said little about the role of the USA in a period of increased globalization or about the unique form of American capitalism. Unlike the majority of the capitalist economies discussed in this chapter, a social bargain regime was never established in the USA. Given a weak labour movement, the acceptance of a relatively free rein for capital and a tradition of limited intervention by government on behalf of labour, this is understandable. Indeed as early as the beginning of the twentieth century, the political and economic structure of a non-interventionist, market power regime in domestic markets was in place and remains intact.

As detailed earlier, following World War II attempts to impose this kind of market-dominated, non-interventionist regime on the 'free world' failed. In the face of the Soviet danger and strong foreign demands for a new kind of capitalism, the USA compromised by accepting embedded liberalism, a social bargain regime embedded in a liberal international order. What is emerging following the end of social bargains and the introduction of altered international monetary institutions is a trend toward the kind of order the USA wanted to impose following World War II.

Today any leadership role for the USA cannot be based on unchallenged economic and military superiority as it had been following World War II; the new strength of the other OECD economies and the end of the Cold War have seen to that. However there is one residual hegemonic role that the USA desires to play and is best positioned to play, given its longstanding support of unregulated capitalism. This is leadership in a globalization process in which market forces replace domestic interventionist policies. There is, of course, American leadership in removing controls on international capital movements, but it has another dimension. In the Golden Age, other governments in the advanced capitalist world committed themselves to full employment policies, and tight labour markets encouraged business loyalty to employees. In addition these governments enacted laws that governed lay-offs and dismissals, further protecting workers. In the USA there has been no serious commitment to full employment, business has retained almost total freedom to hire and fire, and strong business loyalty to employees has been the exception. Without ties to location and employees, American business is footloose, free to move production to exploit low labour costs or adopting a 'take it or leave it' attitude in wage settlements. Indeed in a free trade world, in the face of competition from an increasing number of NICs, it has felt compelled to do so. Firms in other developed economies can only follow the American lead and, by adopting the same behaviour, join the race to the bottom.

Conclusions

In concluding, we offer some remarks on the views of Kalecki and Keynes cited at the beginning of this chapter, and the outlook for globalization, the distribution of power, and full employment. The two post-war episodes were shaped by their institutions: the Golden Age by the institutions of a social bargain regime and the mass unemployment episode by the institutions of a market power regime. With respect to whether unemployment is destabilizing (as Keynes argued) or stabilizing (as maintained by Kalecki), it must be emphasized that the Golden Age was an episode in which full employment was achieved in most of the OECD economies and for a prolonged period of time. It stands as testimony to Keynes' diagnosis of the importance of full employment in ensuring political and economic stability. It should also be noted that the Golden Age emerged from an institutional framework in which labour's power was at an historical high. Under these circumstances full employment capitalism flourished.

However, viewed from the perspective of the entire post-war era, the relationship between unemployment and economic and political stability is ambiguous. Beginning in the mid-1970s, a succession of policies were introduced leading to the mass unemployment now in its third decade, yet the economic and political instability that many foresaw under earlier similar circumstances has not occurred. Indeed, the Golden Age episode of low unemployment followed by the current period of high unemployment outlines a sequence very much like that of Kalecki's political business cycle. In both cases the downturn in economic activity was a policy response to increased labour militancy, taking the form of measures to reduce labour's economic and political power. However, in at least two ways the historical record differs from Kalecki's theory. First, the historical sequence we have outlined is a long run sequence lasting half a century; Kalecki's cyclical theory has a shorter time horizon.[13] Second, in the first phase of the historical sequence, the Golden Age, a relatively equal distribution of economic and political power between capital and labour arose out of a process of consultation, compromise and cooperation. In Kalecki's scheme changes in the distribution of power are initiated and carried out by capital, and whatever the phase of the political cycle, capital never relinquishes its dominating power position.

The question arises: are we on the verge of a second Golden Age in which unemployment rates will again fall to low if not full employment levels? The question can be more appropriately reformulated – is an episode of consultation, compromise and cooperation between capital, labour and government, one reflecting a more equal distribution of power between capital and labour, likely to emerge in the near future? Unlike the immediate post-World War II period, there is a noticeable lack of conditions forcing capital to relinquish power and accept a social bargain regime.

Moreover, the continuous, radical reorganization of the workplace that globalization forces on business and the important role that loose labour markets play in providing this flexibility are strong incentives for capital and government to condone current labour market conditions. As long as deregulated international capital markets and the formal constraints on AD cited earlier prevail, they provide additional reasons to anticipate a continuation of the current high unemployment.

This leaves the possibility that the reduction of labour's power and further strengthening of market power regimes will create an environment conducive for the private sector to generate a return to Golden Age unemployment rates without relinquishing control of the workplace or unacceptable inflationary conditions. The record of the American economy in the late 1990s is often cited as support for such a possibility. Our response is that in the short run it may be possible for unemployment rates to fall to Golden Age levels but that extended periods of such low unemployment rates, *if permitted by governments*, will lead to an acceleration of inflation rates and a growing labour militancy that will be politically unacceptable.

Notes

1. In this chapter we refer to the long-standing members of the OECD, excluding the less developed and small countries such as Iceland and Luxembourg, as simply the OECD economies or the developed capitalist economies.
2. The exercise of power is assumed to be sanctioned or legitimized by institutions, because we do not deal with illegitimate power.
3. This is to be contrasted with Public Choice Theory where collective decision-making is the result of competition between individuals rather than organized groups. See (Cornwall, 1994, pp. 72–73)
4. High rates of growth of productivity and incomes also resulted, but we would argue that these were very much related to prolonged low unemployment.
5. This commitment varied widely in its practical aspects. For example, it was an integral part of the British Labour Party's platform, to be achieved by fiscal measures as Keynes had prescribed, and was enshrined in the French Constitution; in West Germany it was made only in the late 1950s; the

public commitment in Italy was sacrificed in private to achieve greater productivity; and in the USA it was reduced to a responsibility of the President, who had no power to achieve it.

6. Article VII of the 1941 Lend–Lease Agreement required Britain to eliminate its system of imperial trade preferences.
7. For a concise account of these compromises, see Brett (1985, Chapter 3).
8. Maier (1987) refers to this as the 'ideology of productivism'.
9. Austria, Japan, Norway, Sweden and Switzerland were able to avert the use of strong restrictive AD policies until the late 1980s or early 1990s.
10. See Cornwall (1994, Chapter 9) for detail.
11. Restrictions on union activities and cutbacks in public safety nets also point to the shift in power.
12. Possible exceptions are a country whose currency serves as the international reserve currency or a country assessed by the financial community to have a strong payments position based on such 'fundamentals' as strong export possibilities, e.g. Norway.
13. Phelps Brown (1971, 1975) was the first to explain postwar movements in unemployment in this manner.

References

Alesina, A. and Roubini, N. with Cohen, G. D. (1997) *Political Cycles and the Macroeconomy*, Cambridge and London, MIT Press.

Armstrong, P., Glyn, A. and Harrison, J. (1984) *Capitalism Since World War II*, London, Fontana Paperbacks.

Brett, E. A. (1985) *The World Economy Since the War: The Politics of Uneven Development*, London, Macmillan.

Cornwall, J. (1994) *Economic Breakdown & Recovery: Theory and Policy*, Armonk NY, M. E. Sharpe.

Feenstra, R. (1998) 'Integration of Trade and Disintegration of Production in the Global Economy', *The Journal of Economic Perspectives*, Fall.

Hibbs, D. (1987) *The Political Economy of Industrial Democracies*, Cambridge MA, Harvard University Press.

Hibbs, D. (1994) 'The partisan model of macroeconomic cycles: more theory and evidence for the United States', *Econ. Politics* 6(1).

Hicks, J. (1974) *The Crisis in Keynesian Economics*, New York, Basic Books.

Hobsbawm, E. (1994) *Age of Extremes: The Short Twentieth Century, 1914–1991*, London, Michael Joseph.

Irwin, D. (1996) 'The United States in New World Economy? A Century's Perspective'. *American Economic Review*, May.

Kalecki, M. (ed.) (1971) 'Political aspects of full employment', in *Selected Essays on the Dynamics of the Capitalist Economy*, Cambridge, Cambridge University Press, pp. 138–45.

Keohane, R. O. (1984) 'The world political economy and the crisis of embedded liberalism', in J. Goldthorpe (ed.) *Order and Conflict in Contemporary Capitalism*, Oxford, Oxford University Press, pp. 15–38.

Keynes, J. M. (1936) *The General Theory of Employment Interest and Money*, London, Macmillan.

Lindblom, C. E. (1977) *Politics and Markets*, New York, Basic Books.

Maier, C. S. (ed.) (1987) 'The politics of productivity: foundations of American international economic policy after the war', in *In Search of Stability: Explorations in Historical Political Economy*, Cambridge, Cambridge University Press, pp. 121–52.

OECD, *Labour Force Statistics*, Paris, various issues.

Phelps Brown, E. H. (1971) 'The analysis of wage movements under full employment', *Scottish Journal of Political Economy*, November.

Phelps Brown, E. H. (1975) 'A non-monetarist view of the pay explosion', *Three Banks Review*, March.

Rodrik, D. (1997) *Has Globalization Gone Too Far?* Washington, DC, Institute for International Economics.

Tufte, E. (1978) *Political Control of the Economy*, Princeton, NJ, Princeton University Press.

Wartenberg, T. (1990) *The Forms of Power*, Philadelphia, Temple University Press.

7

Competition Policy, Development, and Developing Countries

*Ajit Singh and Rahule Dhumale**

WTO, Competition Policy and Development

The Declaration of the WTO Ministerial Conference held in Singapore in December 1996 stated in paragraph 20:

'. . . we also agree to:

. . . establish a working group to study issues raised by Members relating to the interaction between trade and competition policy, including anti-competitive practices, in order to identify any areas that may merit further consideration in the WTO framework.

In the conduct of the work of the working group[s], we encourage cooperation . . . to make the best use of available resources and to ensure that the development dimension is taken fully into account. . . It is clearly understood that future negotiations, if any, regarding multilateral disciplines in these areas, will take place only after an explicit consensus decision is taken among WTO Members regarding such negotiations.[1]

The General Council of the WTO established a Working Group in April 1997 on the Interaction Between Trade and Competition Policy under the chairmanship of Professor Frédéric Jenny, a French expert on industrial organization. The non-paper by the chair, 'Checklist of Issues Suggested for Study', called for particular attention to the 'development dimension' in the Working Group's discussion on these issues: 'It was widely recognized that the Working Group's work programme

---

* This chapter was originally published by the South Centre, Geneva, as Working Paper 7, November 1999.

should be open, non-prejudicial and capable of evolution as the work proceeds. It was also emphasized that all elements should be permeated by the development dimension.'[2]

Although the WTO Working Group has made notable progress on its mandate, and there has been much useful work carried out at UNCTAD and other fora, it is, to put it mildly, rather anomalous that it is precisely the developmental dimension that is missing from the interim documentation released by the international agencies.'[3] A serious policy analysis of competition policy and economic development, it will be argued here, requires fresh concepts and new definitions. An analysis of these issues, which are of vital importance to developing countries, within the traditional WTO framework, will be highly prejudicial to the South's development needs.

The order of discussion of the various topics in this chapter and the construction of its central argument is as follows:

Firstly, it is suggested here that although many developing countries may not have needed a competition policy[4] before, most require it today, regardless of whether or not the subject is discussed at the next or future WTO ministerial meetings. This is in part due to the potential welfare-reducing effects of the current merger wave that is sweeping the world economy. Further significant structural changes within developing countries themselves also underline the need for competition policy.

Secondly, it is argued that many developing countries cannot aspire to have the kind of competition policies implemented by advanced countries. More importantly, it is suggested that it is not, in any case, in the interest of developing countries to do so. Competition policies for advanced countries are shown not to be appropriate for the stage of development of most developing countries.

Thirdly, the chapter outlines the kind of competition policies that would best serve the interests of developing countries. Policies will be required both at the national and the international level. It will be suggested that the formulation of national competition policies in developing countries requires rather different economic concepts than those that are normally applied in advanced countries.

Fourthly, it will be argued that these new economic concepts are thoroughly grounded in modern economic analysis, as well as being supported by a large body of empirical evidence. It will however be suggested that many of these concepts are 'new' only in relation to the current studies and discussions on the subject at WTO, UNCTAD and other international fora; indeed some of them are implicit in the existing WTO Agreements.

Finally, the chapter sets out the implications of the above analysis for developing countries.

The Global Merger Wave

One of the most important reasons why some kind of competition policy for developing countries has become imperative is the gigantic merger wave that has gripped the world economy in the 1990s. As Fig. 7.1 shows, between 1990 and 1998 the value of worldwide mergers and acquisitions rose nearly five-fold. Most of this merger activity took place within the USA. Data reported in the Financial Times (25 October 1999, not reproduced here) suggests that of the total worldwide merger activity of nearly US$2.5 trillion, almost US$1.6 trillion represented takeovers and mergers within the USA; much of the remaining activity occurred in other industrial countries.

A significant characteristic of the present merger wave is the large number of cross-border takeovers and mergers. This type of merger activity has become increasingly important with the further integration of the world financial markets over the last two decades.[5] However, most of the cross-border amalgamations also take place among the industrial countries themselves. Nevertheless, during this decade, a considerable proportion of foreign direct investment (FDI) by industrial country firms in developing countries has taken the form of acquisition of existing enterprises rather than greenfield investment. UNCTAD (1999) data suggests that if China (which among developing countries has not only

Figure 7.1: Worldwide mergers and acquisitions

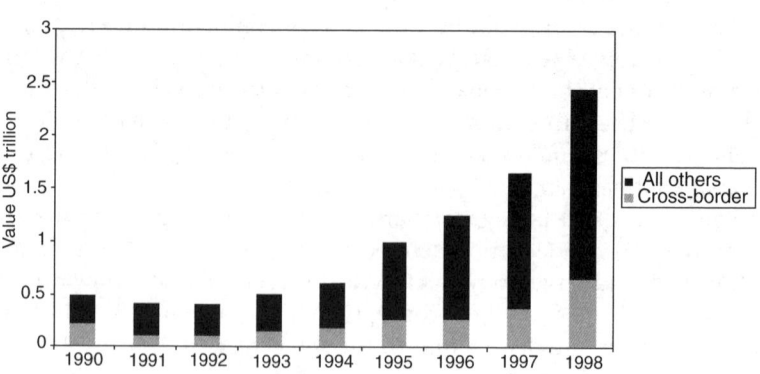

Source: *Economist*, January 1999.

been the largest recipient of FDI, but most of this investment has also been greenfield) is excluded, the share of mergers and acquisitions in the accumulated FDI rises from 22 per cent during 1988 to 1991 to an average of 72 per cent between 1992 and 1997.

Periodic waves of mergers have been an integral part of the capitalist development since its inception.[6] Mergers and acquisitions represent an important mechanism for reorganization and restructuring of a market economy.[7] Many of the leading corporations in the world today are the products of mergers that happened in previous merger waves. Economic theory suggests that mergers can have both positive and negative effects on welfare. At the simplest level, the former may take the form of synergy among the amalgamating firms, and/or economies of scale that improve efficiency and reduce costs of production; the latter may arise from increased monopoly power of the merged firms, which may be welfarereducing.[8]

Both in the USA and the UK one of the most important and the largest merger movements occurred over a hundred years ago, during the 1890s. Although rigorous empirical work has not yet been done on the subject, back-of-the-envelope calculations suggest that the merger boom of the 1990s, taking into account the effects of factors such as the growth in the size of the economy and the rate of inflation, may be the biggest ever recorded, notably in the USA.[9] This wave has already resulted in increased concentration in a wide range of industries including aerospace, defence equipment, power equipment, home machinery, automobile and automobile components, pharmaceuticals, soft drinks, snack foods, chemical fertilizers, retailing, accountancy and financial services (Nolan, 1998).[10]

The merger boom of the 1990s is of course not entirely an exogenous or autonomous event. As indicated earlier, it is in part caused by liberalization and globalization, closer integration of world markets through finance and trade, and the creation of the European single market, among other factors. Firms are jockeying for strategic advantages in the new environment through mergers, acquisitions, and other kinds of tie-ups.[11] However, once some large takeovers have occurred in a particular industry, this creates an oligopolistic disequilibrium in the sense that the market shares of leading firms are disturbed. As a consequence, other giants are obliged to follow in order to maintain their share in the world market. In this sense, evidence suggests many mergers in the present wave are defensive, but that does not stop their overall effect in a number of cases from being welfare-reducing due to potential reduction in competition as outlined above.

Competition Policy Implications for Developing Countries

Whether the mergers take place in the USA or Europe or through cross-border takeovers in developing countries themselves, there are serious competition policy concerns for developing countries. If the largest producers in, say, the US automobile industry merge, this may not only lead to anti-competitive behaviour in the USA, but also similar or worse behaviour in developing countries (e.g. cartelization of markets, increased barriers to entry). The USA has long had a competition policy which provides it with a defence against such welfare-reducing consequences of mergers.

In the famous example of the Boeing–McDonnell Douglas takeover case, although both companies were located in the USA, the European Community objected to the merger on account of its potentially competition-reducing effects in Europe.[12] The Community was able to extract important concessions from Boeing before the merger was approved. It is also now commonplace for jurisdictions in other industrial countries to scrutinize separately all large proposed mergers for their effects on competition, even if they occur abroad.[13]

Leaving aside perhaps China, India, Brazil, and the small number of relatively advanced newly industrializing countries (NICs), the vast majority of developing countries will find it difficult to stop anti-competitive behaviour by the local subsidiaries of merging large corporations in industrial countries. These corporations may behave competitively within industrial countries because of the effective competition regulations of the latter but may indulge in anti-competitive practices in developing countries. A Ghana or a Tanzania is likely to find it difficult to prove, let alone punish, predation or collusive pricing by large industrial country corporations.

Recently, US anti-trust authorities imposed a fine of US$700 million on the leading European producers of vitamins for creating a cartel to charge high prices to consumers. If such cartels can operate in the USA, with all its regulatory machinery and its extra-territorial reach, the task of adequately policing such abuses is likely to be beyond the capacity of most developing countries' competition authorities. These considerations suggest that the huge current international merger movement, even though it is largely occurring in advanced countries, has potentially serious adverse implications for developing countries. Therefore, the latter not only need competition policies in their own countries but also international and South–South cooperation. They need to involve the international community in cooperative action against potentially anti-competitive practices of the mammoth corporations emerging in industrial countries as a consequence of the current merger wave.

Level Playing Fields

Analysis of the international merger wave also suggests another area of concern for the more advanced developing countries. This relates to the question of unequal competition between large multinational and big domestic corporations in these countries. Even the largest developing country corporations tend to be much smaller than the industrial country multinationals. The large merger wave of the 1990s is likely to make this disparity even bigger. By means of worldwide mergers and tie-ups, the advanced country corporations are able to integrate their international operations. This may be a source of genuine technical economies of scale, but evidence indicates that in most industries average cost curves are L-shaped, i.e. after a threshold size that is relatively small and which most of these giant corporations would have achieved even before mergers, costs do not fall as the size of the firm increases. The economies which nevertheless the multinationals are able to achieve through integration are those relating to bulk buying of inputs, reduced cost of capital due to large size as well as economies achieved in advertising and other marketing activities on a large scale. To the extent that these economies depend on the market power of the multinational in relation to inputs, the cost saving measures are not necessarily welfare-enhancing, furthermore, these 'pecuniary economies' create barriers to entry that make the markets less contestable.[14]

During the last 50 years, Japan, and many NICs in Asia and Latin America, have been able to foster the development of big businesses to the advantage of these countries' overall economic development. This has usually been achieved through various kinds of state support. These large domestic corporations, which are privately owned, have often been the leaders in the diffusion of new technologies and the adaptation of imported technologies to domestic circumstances.[15] However, in the current, new international economic environment these firms are likely to be handicapped in three significant ways:

1. through the limiting of state aid as part of WTO disciplines;
2. through the increased size and market power both in the product and input markets of large multinationals;
3. through increased barriers to entry and contestability which the merger boom creates.

In these circumstances, it will be much more difficult than before for large developing country corporations to become even national let alone international players.

It is normal for multinationals to complain that there is not a level playing field between themselves and national corporations that are government supported; hence, the multinationals' demand for 'national treatment'. However, the actual situation is often quite the opposite: the playing fields are tilted in favour of multinationals who invariably have considerable market power. Liberalization and globalization, together with the international merger movement, are making these fields more unequal even from the perspective of *large* developing country corporations.

Privatization, Deregulation and Competition Policy

Many of the same ideological, political and economic forces of liberalization and globalization which have led to the current gigantic merger wave in the industrial countries have also been responsible for fundamental changes in the organization of economic activity in developing countries around the world. In the 1980s, and particularly during the 1990s, many developing countries underwent far-reaching market-oriented reforms, leading to considerable diminution in the direct role of the state in economic activity. This has resulted in widespread privatization, deregulation, and internal and external financial liberalization.

The timing and extent of these liberalization measures has varied between countries. In relation specifically to privatization, the pattern was set by the programme of privatization of larger state-owned enterprises (SOEs) beginning in the 1980s in the UK under the conservative government led by Mrs Thatcher. This was followed not only by many advanced countries, but also by the vast majority of developing countries. Leaving aside transition economies where there has been mass privatization, the leading developing countries each with privatization proceeds worth more than US$1 billion between 1990 and 1997 were Argentina (proceeds of US$27.9 billion), Brazil (US$34.3 billion), Colombia (US$5 billion), India (US$7.1 billion), Indonesia (US$5.2 billion), Malaysia (US$10 billion), Mexico (US$30.5 billion), Pakistan (US$2 billion), Peru (US$7.5 billion), Singapore (US$1.9 billion), South Africa (US$2.5 billion), Turkey (US$3.6 billion), Thailand (US$3.6 billion) and Venezuela (US$5.9 billion).[16]

Considerable privatization also took place in African countries. However, in view of the smaller size of their economies and their lower level of development, in absolute terms the proceeds from privatization during the same period were substantially lower for these countries, other than South Africa. Nevertheless, privatization proceeds amounted to US$864 million in Ghana, US$227 million in Kenya, US$197 million in Zimbabwe, US$140 million in Tanzania, US$730 million in Nigeria, and US$412 million in Zambia. In general, according to *WDR* (1999), the lower the level of per capita income, the lower the extent of privatization.

Privatization was ostensibly undertaken for a number of reasons, including improving economic efficiency, reducing the drain on government resources caused by public sector losses, raising revenues for the government and to help pay off the foreign debt by raising foreign exchange through the sale of public assets to foreign multinationals. In most developing countries, privatizations were strongly encouraged, if not required, under structural adjustment programmes of the international financial institutions. It is generally recognized that, rather than efficiency reasons, the main motive for privatization in many countries was to achieve a relaxation of the hard budget constraints that the international financial institutions enforced as part of their conditionality. There have been few studies of the effects of privatization on economic efficiency in developing countries. However, a number of studies have been carried out for developed countries, particularly the UK, which indicate that it is not ownership *per se* which is the main determinant of economic performance, but rather the degree of competition in the market.

In this overall context, it is not difficult to see why the need for competition policy becomes crucial. Further, many of the privatized companies were natural monopolies under state ownership. Privatizing them does not necessarily lead to greater social welfare because it simply involves replacing the public monopoly with a private one. The former may in fact be preferable to the latter from a social welfare perspective, as there may be some consideration given to the public purpose in the former's activities. The presence of a large state sector is probably an important reason why many developing countries have not until now felt it necessary to have a competition policy. However, in the new privatized domestic economic environment, competition and regulatory policies become essential. Moreover, as Stiglitz points out, external liberalization cannot substitute for a competition policy if liberalized imports and exports become subject to domestic monopolistic restrictions (Stiglitz, 1999).

Khemani calls attention to another aspect of privatization via foreign takeovers that affects many developing countries. He reports cases where foreign acquiring firms, normally multinational enterprises, demand that governments erect barriers to entry or permit certain pricing practices. He notes: 'Often developing and emerging market economies facing hard budget constraints or rising deficits, and/or are in desperate need of foreign investment, may have no choice but to cave in to such demands' (Khemani, 1999, p. 105).

Competition Policies in Advanced Economies: a Model for Developing Countries?

The argument so far has suggested that the new internal and external environment facing developing countries makes it necessary for them to have competition policies. The important question, and the one which is central to this chapter is what kind of policies would be appropriate for developing countries. Should developing countries simply follow the advanced countries in their competition policies and enact legislation accordingly? To answer this question it is necessary first to consider what kind of competition policy the advanced countries follow. Here, the significant point is that there are major differences among them in the policies that they pursue, their underlying philosophies, their legislative practices, and their modes of implementation.[17]

The USA, which has long experience in competition policy – the first US legislation was passed nearly a hundred years ago in response to the merger movement at the turn of the nineteenth century (referred to earlier) – takes a so-called structural approach to this issue. Competition is regarded as being a good thing in itself and anti-trust laws (including Federal Trade Commission (FTC) rulings and Supreme Court judgements) attempt to discourage anti-competitive practices. The spirit of this view is well captured in the epigram: the purpose of competition policy is to advance the competitive process rather than to protect the competitors. The WTO report notes, 'A guiding principle that is often referred to by competition agencies and tribunals or courts is that "competition law protects competition, not competitors" ' (WTO, 1997, p. 44).

Competition policy in the UK and in Western Europe has traditionally been based on a rather different philosophy. It does not regard competition as an end in itself, but a means to an end. This leads to a trade-off approach – encroachments on competition are acceptable if they are adequately counterbalanced by benefits to the community. Thus, in the simplest case, i.e. mergers between two large firms in the same industry – which by the traditional US anti-trust policy would be ruled out *per se* – may be permitted under traditional UK competition laws, if it can be shown that the welfare-reducing effect of increased market power resulting from the merger is more than matched by gains to society, as a consequence of reduced costs of production because of economies of scale and/or because of synergy.

This leads in practice to a case-by-case approach to mergers rather than the promulgation of *per se* structural rules as has historically been the case in the USA. Singh (1993) noted that there was some convergence of competition policies in the USA and the UK in the 1980s and the 1990s. The US authorities, partly due to increased international competition, started to give greater importance to the so-called 'economies of scale defence' for mergers than they used to do before. Regulators in the UK, on the other hand, have started giving much greater weight to the effects of mergers or of other kinds of corporate behaviour on competition *per se* than to other considerations (such as regional impact) in the calculation of net social gain.

Among industrial countries, Japan has its own approach to competition policy questions. Following the end of World War II, the US occupation authorities in Japan enacted US-type anti-trust laws in part to punish the large Japanese firms – the *zaibatsu* – who were thought to have been responsible for aiding and abetting Japan's aggression and war effort. However, as Professor Richard Caves of Harvard University and Professor Uekusa of Tokyo University, leading students of Japanese industrial organization, point out, the US-imposed laws had no domestic constituency in the country (Caves and Uekusa, 1976). The laws therefore soon fell into disuse for this as well as other strategic Cold war-related considerations. Although the *zaibatsu* disbanded, they soon re-emerged in the form of a looser association of companies called *keiretsu*. Moreover, competition policy in Japan became subservient to the country's vigorous industrial policy. Professor Okimoto explains the philosophy behind the Japanese approach to the subject:

. . . the Japanese government takes a more pragmatic approach to anti-trust enforcement, one that makes allowances for national goals such as industrial catch-up. It takes into account other collective values and extenuating circumstances in weighing enforcement decisions against the letter and spirit of anti-trust laws. Included here are such considerations as economies of scale, enhanced efficiency, optimal use of scarce resources, international competitiveness, heightened productivity, business cycle stabilization, industrial orderliness, price stabilization and economic security.

(Okimoto, 1989, pp. 12–13)

Competition policy in Japan has thus evolved over time, as indeed has industrial policy (see Singh, 1998; Tsuru, 1993; Johnson, Tyson and Zysman, 1989). This has been particularly true since Japan joined the OECD and began to implement trade and financial liberalization measures. The evolution of Japanese competition policy in the 1970s and the 1980s is interesting but not as relevant to developing countries as the competition policy practised by Japan between 1950 and 1973. This is because, at the beginning of the period, Japan was very much like a developing country with low levels of industrialization and economic development. Indeed, its industrialization prospects at the time were thought to be altogether precarious (World Bank, 1991). How Japan, starting from such low levels, caught up with the West is clearly a story of great interest to developing countries. As seen below, the theory and practice of competition policy during the Japanese catch-up process in the 1950s and 1960s is particularly instructive for such economies.

To sum up, this brief review of the different approaches to competition policy in the USA, UK and Japan suggests that the most appropriate model from the perspective of economic development may be that of Japan during 1950–73. This period will therefore be examined more closely below.

Economic Theory, Competition Policy and Development

Before moving to the discussion of Japan's competition policy in the period 1950–73, it is useful to consider what insights are provided by economic theory to the question of competition policies for countries at different levels of development.

Recent advances in economic theory, particularly agency theory, transaction cost theory and information theory, have greatly enriched our understanding of how competition and competition policy may work in various spheres of an economy and in different economies. Thus, a leading authority on the theory of industrial organization recently observed:

> Competition is an unambiguously good thing in the first-best world of economists. That world assumes large numbers of participants in all markets, no public goods, no externalities, no information asymmetries, no natural monopolies, complete markets, fully rational economic agents, a benevolent court system to enforce contracts, and a benevolent government providing lump sum transfers to

achieve any desirable redistribution. *Because developing countries are so far from this ideal world, it is not always the case that competition should be encouraged in these countries.* (italics added)

[Laffont, 1998, p. 237]

Laffont provides a number of examples to support his contention. All of these involve what economists call the theory of the 'second best', which asserts that, if any one of the assumptions required for the validity of the fundamental theorems of welfare economics cannot be met, restricted rather than unrestricted competition may be a superior strategy. Laffont draws particular attention to the 'demonization' by many economists (including those at the World Bank) of cross-subsidization of different groups by large public utilities. However, he points out that in developing countries, where, in practice, taxes cannot be collected from the wealthy for redistribution, it may be a good strategy for the government to require public utilities in these countries to subsidize poor consumers in the countryside at the expense of richer residents in the city.

Laffont suggests that even if competition policy of the kind followed by advanced countries such as the USA or the UK were appropriate for poor African countries, they are a long way from having the institutional capacity to implement such policies. The implementation of a comprehensive competition policy requires a strong state, which many developing countries at low levels of industrialization do not have. Therefore, at the very least, for such countries there will need to be far fewer and simpler competition rules which are capable of being enforced. Clearly it would be unfair, if not absurd, to subject a Sierra Leone to the same competition policy disciplines as the USA.

We now turn to consideration of the case of the semi-industrial countries, many of which are now fairly advanced in industrial development, e.g. Korea, India, Brazil, Mexico. These countries have reasonably strong states with competent government machinery. However, economic theory suggests that, even for these economies, the US and UK types of competition policies may be inappropriate. A very important reason for this conclusion is that the essential focus of competition policy in advanced countries such as the USA is the promotion of allocative efficiency and reduced prices for consumers (WTO, 1997). However, from the standpoint of economic development, this perspective is too narrow and static. In order to raise their people's standard of living, a central objective of developing countries must necessarily be the promotion of long-term growth of productivity. The pursuit of this objective of dynamic rather than static efficiency requires, among other things, high rates of investment. In a private enterprise economy, this necessitates encouragement of entrepreneurs' propensity to invest. However, the private sector's 'animal spirits' are likely to be dampened if, as a result of competition, profits became too low, even if only temporarily.

This suggests that unfettered competition may not be appropriate for a developing economy. Economic theory – as well as experience – indicate that, in the real world of incomplete and missing markets, unfettered competition may lead to price wars and ruinous rivalry and therefore may be inimical to future investment: from this perspective, too much competition can be as harmful as too little. What is required by developing economies is an optimal degree of competition which would entail sufficient rivalry to reduce inefficiency in the corporate use of resources at the microeconomic level, but not so much competition that it would deter the propensity to invest. This central analytical point is altogether ignored in competition policy discourse in countries such as the USA, where the concept of optimal degree of competition is simply assumed to be maximum competition, that is, the more competition the better.[18]

It is useful in this context to reflect on the operation of competition policy in Japan in the period 1950–73. The Japanese economy achieved historically unprecedented growth during this time: its manufacturing production rose at a phenomenal rate of about 13 per cent a year, GDP at 10 per cent a year, and its share in world exports of manufacture rose by a huge 10 percentage points (Singh, 1998). A central role in this spectacular economic advance was played by the very high rates of savings and investment in the Japanese economy. As noted earlier, the competition policy was subordinated to industrial policy, an essential concern of which was to maintain the private sector's high propensity to invest. For this purpose, the Japanese government's Ministry of International Trade and Industry (MITI) frequently imposed restrictions on product market competition. Amsden and Singh (1994) note: 'It [MITI] encouraged a variety of cartel arrangements in a wide range of industries – export and import cartels, cartels to combat depression or excessive competition, rationalization cartels, etc. Similarly, believing that large scale enterprises were required for promotion of technical change and for Japanese firms to compete effectively with their western counterparts, MITI encouraged mergers between leading firms in key industries' (Amsden and Singh, 1994, p. 944).

The Korean government broadly followed the Japanese strategy of economic development. It also had a strong industrial policy which, as in the case of Japan, dominated competition policy. The government helped create the mammoth corporations, the *chaebol*, which went on to capture world markets. Korea was unequivocally an industrially backward country in the 1950s. Its per capita manufacturing output in 1955 was US$8 compared to US$7 in India and US$56 in Mexico. During the last four decades Korea has managed to transform itself into an industrial and technologically sophisticated economy. It is the world's leading country in electronic memory chip (DRAM) technology. Until the recent financial crisis, it was expected to become the fourth largest producer of automobiles in the world by the year 2000.

As a result of lax enforcement of competition policy, Korea has one of the highest levels of industrial concentration in the world. However, the giant conglomerates compete with each other fiercely. A significant part of the competition has been of the non-market variety, in which the *chaebol* have competed for government support. The latter has been given in return for meeting specified performance targets for exports, new product development, and technological change. In the market place, the *chaebol* competed for market share, as that determined their subsequent investment allocations in a particular industry. As in Japan between 1950 and 1973, the Korean government until recently has purposefully coordinated industrial investments by competing *chaebol*, so as to prevent overcapacity and too much competition (Chang, 1994).

The policies adopted by these East Asian countries find endorsement in the new developments in economic theory. Essentially, modern economic theory suggests that dynamic efficiency is best promoted by a combination of cooperation and competition between firms rather than by maximum or unfettered competition (Graham and Richardson, 1997).

It has been suggested by some scholars and high US government officials that the recent financial crisis in Asia demonstrates the failure of state-directed capitalism of the Asian countries. However, a careful analysis of these issues indicates that the crisis was caused not by too much state direction but rather by too little. Overinvestment by the *chaebol* in Korea or the property bubble in Thailand were caused essentially by the fact that these countries were pursuing capital account liberalization in the immediate period before the crisis. Korea had become a member of the OECD in the early 1990s and in fact had abolished its planning agency. Neither industrial overinvestment by the *chaebol* nor excessive investment in the property sector in Thailand would have occurred had the governments coordinated investment activity as before.[19]

Analytical Conclusions and Implications

Analytical Conclusions

The main analytical conclusions for developing countries emerging from the theoretical and empirical analysis of competition policy and economic development, as well as from the earlier discussion of the new developments in the international economy and their implications for competition policy, may be summarized as follows:

1. Developing countries need a competition policy in the wake of the international merger movement and because of the privatization, deregulation and liberalization that has occurred in their domestic economies.
2. In examining this issue, a distinction was made between countries at low levels of development and with meagre institutional capacity and semi-industrial countries with greater institutional capabilities. In neither case were the US and UK types of competition policy found to be appropriate.
3. To address seriously the concerns of developing countries with respect to competition policy, this chapter has suggested new economic concepts in place of those used in the current WTO discourse on the subject. Specifically, we have called attention to the following points:
   - the need to emphasize dynamic rather than static efficiency as the main purpose of competition policy from the perspective of economic development;
   - the concept of 'optimal degree of competition' (as opposed to maximum competition) to promote long-term growth of productivity;
   - the related concept of optimal combination of competition and cooperation to achieve fast long-term economic growth;
   - the critical significance of maintaining the private sector's propensity to invest at high levels and hence the need for a steady growth of profits; the latter in turn necessitates government coordination of investment decisions so as to prevent overcapacity and falling profits;
   - the concept of simulated competition, i.e. contests, for state support that can be as powerful as real market competition;

• the crucial importance of industrial policy to achieve the structural changes required for economic development; this in turn requires coherence between industrial and competition policies.

It is clear from this analysis that, in order to give effect to the stated desire in the Singapore WTO Ministerial Declaration of December 1996, 'to ensure that the development dimension is fully taken into account', it would not be enough to simply suggest that all that developing countries need is a longer time frame to be able to implement the US or UK type of competition policy. The special and different circumstances of developing countries and their developmental needs require a creative application of the new concepts above to competition policy questions.

The concepts introduced in this chapter are not only relevant to competition policy in relation to economic development but also have important developmental implications for a number of different areas of the WTO Agreements, including those on TRIPs, TRIMs, and on Subsidies and Countervailing Measures. However, in view of their complexity, each of these subjects merits a full chapter. Further, because a number of these topics are being dealt with in other parts of the work programme of the South Centre, these are not discussed here in any detail. Nevertheless, some brief remarks need to be made on some of the topics to indicate the wider application of the analysis presented in this chapter.

First of all, it is important to appreciate that the concepts outlined above are only 'new' in relation to the present WTO, UNCTAD and OECD studies and working groups on the subject: at another level, the validity of the concepts is not only accepted by modern economics but also implicitly recognized in various parts of the WTO Agreements themselves. For example, the underlying economic justification for the TRIPs Agreement is to be found in the concept of dynamic efficiency. Restrictions on competition are accepted under the Agreement in order to promote technical change and long-term economic growth. However, because most patents are held by advanced country corporations and individuals, the Agreement promotes the dynamic efficiency of developed rather than developing countries.[20]

Similarly, the notion of industrial policy is implicit in the Agreement on Subsidies and Countervailing Measures which does not prohibit government grants to private firms to promote R&D, or subsidies granted to disadvantaged regions, or those relating to new environmental laws. This rule again favours industrial policy requirements of advanced countries; many of the subsidies of interest from the perspective of industrial policy in developing countries are ruled out, for example, prohibited subsidies include those contingent on export performance, or those given for the use of domestic in preference to imported products.[21]

Thus, those who are uncomfortable with new concepts may wish to note that essentially what this chapter has done is to make explicit certain economic principles which are already implicit in WTO Agreements. These have been used in the Agreements to the advantage of advanced countries but they can be applied just as well to the question of competition policy from the perspective of developing countries.

The broad analytical framework of this chapter also has implications for some other important areas of WTO Agreements to which it may be useful to draw attention. To take first the question of anti-dumping and countervailing duties, these have been used by advanced countries as a straightforward protectionist device, as is increasingly recognized (Stiglitz, 1999). A recent study of US anti-dumping cases suggests that, if these had been subject to the equivalent US competition policy standard of predation, more than 90 per cent of them would have failed (reported in Stiglitz, 1999).

Should developing countries favour the abolition of anti-dumping measures because these are often used unfairly against their products? The answer to this question is not simple, as is indicated by the fact that a number of developing countries are also using this device, often against the products of other developing countries. In the past, under GATT, developing countries were able to use the balance of payments clause to support their infant industry policies. Under the WTO, however, there has been considerable erosion of this 'balance of payments defence'. In view of the fact that developing countries will require, for some considerable period, protection for their successive new industries as they expand their industrial base, they may have to resort to anti-dumping and countervailing measures for this purpose. Section C, Article XVIII of GATT, permitted developing countries to impose restrictions and protect infant industries. However, because the use of this provision required payment of compensation, since 1967 no developing country has invoked this article. Instead many developing countries used Section B (protection for balance of payments reasons), which did not require compensation, to achieve in effect the same result. Therefore, unless developing countries are provided with an alternative instrument for protection, it will not be in their developmental interest to seek the abolition of anti-dumping and countervailing measures.

Turning to the Agreement on TRIMs, the analysis in this chapter suggests that it deprives developing countries of important industrial policy instruments that have proved useful for economic development. Some of these on the prohibited list, such as local content requirements, have been widely used by the highly successful East Asian countries during the last three decades. Further Correa (1999) suggests that some TRIMs were also used to control horizontal as well as vertical restrictive business practices of multinational corporations. He criticizes the prohibition of such measures under the TRIMs Agreement as this withholds from developing countries important instruments to counteract anti-competitive practices. Developing countries should therefore seek to revise this Agreement when it comes up for review as part of the in-built WTO agenda.

Implications for Developing Countries

There is an immediate difficulty in discussing the implications for developing countries of these analytical conclusions. Because the experience of many developing countries is that even a seemingly non-prejudicial discussion of a sensitive subject such as competition policy can subsequently, under advanced country pressure, lead to full-blown negotiations, in practice many countries will quite rightly take a tactical approach to this question. They may therefore simply wish to terminate discussions on the subject altogether in the WTO and other fora in order to maintain their freedom of manoeuvre.

These tactical and practical considerations are fully understandable and so will not be commented upon here. These are matters of judgement for those directly involved in WTO diplomatic activities.

However, in any substantive discussion of competition policy, either in the WTO or in other fora, it would be useful to draw attention to the implications of the foregoing analysis, which to some may seem obvious. Firstly, developing country representatives should point out that the issue of competition policy has hardly received any serious attention from the perspective of economic development in any of the fora where these issues are being considered. Secondly, for this purpose, the need to examine these matters in terms of new concepts of the kind outlined here should be stressed. This in turn requires developing country representatives to themselves gain an understanding of why the discourse on competition policy entirely in terms of the traditional WTO framework of market access, national treatment, transparency, etc. is prejudicial to their developmental interests.

To provide a simple illustration, it may be perfectly legitimate for a developing country competition authority to allow large domestic firms to merge so that they can go some way toward competing on more equal terms with multinationals from abroad. Even if the amalgamating national firms are on the horizontal part of the L-shaped static cost curve, bigger size may still promote dynamic efficiency for the reason that firms need to achieve a minimum threshold size to finance their own R&D activities. The competition authority may therefore quite reasonably deny national treatment to the multinationals and prohibit their merger activity (because they are already large enough to achieve either static or dynamic economies of scale in this sense). In these circumstances, a violation of the doctrine of national treatment is likely to be beneficial both to economic development and to competition.[22]

Thirdly, a clear message of this chapter is that developing countries require special treatment in the sense of being allowed to pursue competition policies which are appropriate to their stage of development. There should certainly be no multilateral disciplines of the WTO type obliging developing countries to have universal competition policies or indeed any competition policy at all if they do not think that the cost/benefit analysis of such a policy is worth their while. As indicated by the analysis in this chapter, it would be advisable for most developing countries to institute a competition policy appropriate to their needs. However, as suggested earlier, enforcement of the competition policy does require a strong state, which many developing countries may not have. In these circumstances, a competition policy could simply lead to more corruption and rent-seeking.[23]

Fourthly, even with appropriate domestic competition policies that meet the development test, developing countries would still require international cooperation to cope with the anti-competitive consequences of large international mergers, cartels, etc. The best solution would be the establishment of an international competition authority, having proper representation of the South in its governance and not dominated by the North. The international competition authority would be charged with maintaining fair competition in the world economy and keeping the markets contestable by ensuring that the barriers to entry to late industrializers are kept at low levels. It would have the authority to scrutinize mega-mergers, to prohibit them if necessary and, in any case, to deter the mega firms from abusing their dominant positions. For good administrative and practical reasons, references to the competition authority would only be permissible in case of anti-competitive behaviour by corporations above a certain size. The size criterion would normally keep even most large developing country corporations outside the direct purview of the competition authority, but, nevertheless, the latter would recognize the special needs of developing countries, as indicated in this chapter.

However, such a legally enforceable international agreement will take some time to construct in view of the differences between developed and developing countries and significantly between the developed countries themselves on this subject. This is not to deny that there has been some useful international cooperation in this area between different groups of countries during the last two decades, but it has been quite limited. Following discussions of restrictive business practices by large multinationals in developing countries at UNCTAD II, New Delhi, 1968, and UNCTAD IV, Nairobi, 1976, the UN General Assembly in December 1980 adopted by Resolution 35/63 a 'Set of Multilaterally Agreed Equitable Principles and Rules for the Control of Restrictive Business Practices'. The 'Set' is fairly comprehensive in scope and covers a wide range of restrictive business practices by multinationals, including the abuse of their dominant positions whether achieved through mergers and acquisitions or joint ventures. However, the Set is not legally binding and has therefore not been helpful to developing countries (see Correa, 1999.)[24]

What is being suggested here is a legally binding rather than a voluntary international agreement for a global competition policy authority. Until such time as an agreement materializes, developing countries, especially small ones, would do well to begin to cooperate with each other through regional pacts and other arrangements, in order to restrain these restrictive business practices and influence the outcome of merger activities in advanced countries.

Notes

1. The full text of paragraph 20 of the Singapore Ministerial Declaration (INT/MIN(96)/DEC) is contained in Annex I of WTO (1999).
2. WTO (1998, Annex I, p. 51).
3. WTO (1999). The final report of the WTO working group not only provides information on the activities of this group itself but also reports on the work that has been carried out in relation to competition policy for developing countries at UNCTAD, OECD and the World Bank.
4. For the purposes of this chapter, competition policy is defined as a body of laws, administrative rules and case law that are employed to deter restrictive

business practices so as to maintain fair competition. Competition policy also includes rules and regulations governing mergers and acquisitions.

5. For comparison with previous merger waves, see the discussions in Singh (1993), Hughes (1992) and Hughes and Singh (1980).

6. Evidence suggests that mergers are not randomly distributed over time but occur in waves. See, for example, Golbe and White (1988).

7. For the differences between mergers and acquisitions (or takeovers) and their implications, see Singh (1971).

8. It is important, however, to remember that not all mergers necessarily lead to increased monopoly power, and even when they do, they are not always welfare-reducing. Some of these points will be elaborated in the following sections. See also Scherer and Ross (1990); Singh (1992, 1993).

9. For an analysis of the relative magnitude of previous merger waves, see Golbe and White (1988); Singh (1993); Hughes and Singh (1980).

10. The above discussion has been concerned only with mergers, but other kinds of tie-ups and cooperative arrangements between firms can have similar anti-competitive effects. Often a case-by-case investigation is needed to determine the size of such effects. However, the observations in note 8 remain relevant.

11. Cooperation between firms can take various forms, with mergers and acquisitions representing one end of the spectrum in which two or more firms are amalgamated into a single entity. Other kinds of inter-firm cooperation may involve joint ventures, technology-sharing agreements, and outright cartels. Some forms of cooperation may be benign, e.g. technology sharing, while others (e.g. cartels) are not, and may reduce social welfare more than full-scale mergers between firms.

12. See also Khemani (1999); WTO (1997).

13. See also Jenny (1999); Fox (1999).

14. For a comprehensive discussion of the economies of scale and of scope, and of multiplant economies of scale, see Scherer and Ross (1990).

15. See also Amsden (1989); Singh (1995a).

16. *World Development Indicators* (1999).

17. For a more in-depth discussion of competition policy in advanced countries see Scherer (1994); Hughes (1992); Waverman *et al.* (1997); Amsden and Singh (1994). For the section on competition policy in Japan, this chapter draws on Amsden and Singh (1994).

18. See earlier discussion of philosophy of US competition policy which finds virtue in competition itself rather than to examine its effects.

19. For various interpretations of the Asian financial crisis see Singh (1999a,b); Singh and Weisse (1999); Radelet and Sachs (1998); US Council of Economic Advisors (1999); IMF (1998); World Bank (1999).

20. For a more in-depth discussion of competition policy in relation to the TRIPs Agreement see Dumont and Holmes (1999); Correa (1999).

21. The Agreement does recognize the interests of developing countries to some extent by allowing an extension of the time period for its implementation by different groups of countries. For example, least developed countries and other WTO members with GNP per capita of less than US$1000 are exempted from the prohibitions on certain subsidies (such as export subsidies) until export competitiveness is achieved (defined as

the attainment of a share of 3.25 per cent of world trade in a product for two consecutive years). Other prohibited subsidies must, however, be eliminated by these countries within a period of five years (eight years for LDCs) from the entry into the force of the WTO Agreement (see Singh, 1996).

22. As far as we are aware, there are no agreements as yet that specify national treatment of firms in relation to merger activity. What is being suggested here is that developing countries should resist any moves in that direction.

23. In practice, however, most countries do have some form of a competition policy, although this may be implicit rather than explicit. Without some generally accepted rules governing fair competition, economies and societies will experience a number of difficulties (see Graham and Richardson, 1997).

24. Similarly in 1986, the OECD, the organization of developed countries, issued guidelines concerning restrictive business practices by multinationals. Under the guidelines, which again were advisory rather than legally enforceable, multinational enterprises were enjoined to refrain from a wide range of anti-competitive activities including abuses of intellectual property rights, predatory behaviour, competition-reducing acquisitions, etc. (see OECD, 1986; Scherer, 1984).

References

Amsden, A. H. (1989) *Asia's Next Giant: South Korea and Late Industrialization,* New York, Oxford University Press.

Amsden, A. and Singh, A. (1994) The optimal degree of competition and dynamic efficiency in Japan and Korea. In *European Economic Review*, Vol. 38, Nos. 3/4, p. 940–951.

Baumol, W. and Ordover, J. (1992) 'Antitrust: source of dynamic and static inefficiencies', in T. Jorde and D. Teece (eds) *Antitrust, Innovation and Competitiveness,* New York, Oxford University Press, pp. 82–97.

Caves, R. E. and Uekusa, M. (1976) *Industrial Organization in Japan,* Washington, DC, The Brookings Institution.

Chang, H. J. (1994) *The Political Economy of Industrial Policy,* New York, St Martins Press.

Correa, C. (1999) *Competition Law and Development Policies.* Paper presented at Zurich Seminar on Issues of International Competition Law.

Dumont, B. and Holmes, P. (1999) The breadth of intellectual property rights and their interface with competition law and policy: divergent paths to the same goal. In *International Conference: Innovation, Appropriation Strategies, and Economic Policy, Paris.* Financial Times, October 25, 1999.

Economist, January 5–12, 1999.

Fox, E. (1999) Can we control Merger control? – An experiment. *Policy Directions for Global Merger Review in Global Competition Review.*

Golbe, D. and White, L. (1988) 'A time series analysis of mergers and acquisitions in the U.S. economy', in A. Auerbach (ed.) *Corporate Takeovers: Causes and Consequences,* Chicago, University of Chicago Press pp. 265–302.

Graham, E. and Richardson, J. (1997) *Competition Policies for the Global Economy*, Washington, Institute for International Economics.

Howes, C. and Singh, A. (eds) (2000) *Competitiveness Matters: Industry and Economic Performance in the US*, Ann Arbor, MI, University of Michigan Press.

Hughes, A. (1992) Competition Policy and the competitive process: Europe in the 1990s. In *Metroeconomica*, Vol. 43, No. 1–2, p. 1–50.

Hughes, A. and Singh, A. (1980) 'Mergers, concentration and competition in advanced capitalist economies: An international perspective' in D. Mueller (ed.) *The Determinants and Effects of Mergers: An International Comparison*, Cambridge, MA, Oelgeschlager, Gunn and Hain, pp. 1–26.

International Monetary Fund (1998) *World Economic Outlook*, October 1998.

Jenny, F. (1999) International Merger Control. In *Policy Directions for Global Merger Review in Global Competition Review*.

Johnson, C., Tyson, L. and Zysman, J. (1989) *Politics and Productivity: How Japan's Development Strategy Works*, New York, Harper Business.

Jorde, T. and Teece D. (eds) (1992) *Antitrust, Innovation and Competitiveness*, New York, Oxford University Press.

Khemani, S. (1999) International Mergers Activity: Some Concerns for Developing and Emerging Economies. In *Policy Directions for Global Merger Review in Global Competition Review*.

Khemani, S. and Schone, R. (1998) International Competition Conflict Resolution. In *PSD Occasional Paper No. 33*, World Bank: Washington.

Laffont, J. (1998) Competition, Information, and Development. In *Annual World Bank Conference on Development Economics*, World Bank, Washington.

Nolan, P. (1998) *Globalization, Big Business, and Industrial Policy in Developing Countries*, Cambridge, Judge Institute of Management Studies.

OECD (1986) *The OECD Guidelines for Multinational Enterprises*, Paris, OECD.

Okimoto, D. I. (1989) *Between the MITI and the Market*, Stanford, Stanford University Press.

Radelet, S. and Sachs, J. (1998) *The East Asian Financial Crisis: Diagnosis, Remedies, and Prospects*, Massachusetts, HIID.

Scherer, F. (1994) *Competition Policy for an Integrated World Economy*, Washington, DC, Brookings Institution.

Scherer, F. and Ross, D. (1990) *Industrial Market Structure and Economic Performance*, Boston, Houghton Mifflin.

Singh, A. (1971) *Takeovers: Their Relevance to the Stock Market and the Theory of the Firm*, Cambridge, Cambridge University Press.

Singh, A. (1992) 'Corporate takeovers' in J. Eatwell, M. Milgate and P. Newman (eds) *The New Palgrave Dictionary of Money and Finance*, London and New York, Macmillan, pp. 480–6.

Singh, A. (1993) 'Regulation of mergers: A new agenda' in R. Sugden (ed.) *Industrial Economic Regulation: A Framework and an Exploration*, London, Routledge, pp. 141–60.

Singh, A. (1995a) *Corporate Financial Patterns in Industrialising Economies: A Comparative International Study*. IFC Technical Paper No. 2, World Bank, Washington, DC., ISBN 0–8213–3231–7.

Singh, A. (1995b) Institutional requirements for full employment in advanced economies. In *International Labour Review*, Vol. 135, No. 4–5.

Singh, A. (1996) *Expansion of Trading Opportunities to the Year 2000 for Asia-Pacific Developing Countries: Implications of the Uruguay Round and Adaptation of Export Strategies*, New York, Geneva, UNCTAD.

Singh, A. (1998) Savings, investment and the corporation in the East Asian miracle. *Journal of Development Studies*, Vol. 34, No. 6, pp. 112–137.

Singh, A. (1999a) 'Global unemployment, long-run economic growth and labour market rigidities: A commentary' special contribution in B. Dibroy (ed.) *Perspectives on Globalization and Employment*, Office of Development Studies Discussion Paper Series, New York, United Nations Development Programme, pp. 50–69.

Singh, A. (1999b) 'Asian capitalism and the financial crisis' in J. Grieve-Smith and J. Michie (eds) *Global Instability and World Economic Governance*, London, Routledge pp. 9–36.

Singh, A. and Weisse, B. (1999) The Asian model: A crisis foretold? In *International Social Science Journal*, No. 160, p. 203–215.

Stiglitz, J. (1999) *Two principles for the next round, or how to bring developing countries in from the cold*. Speech, Geneva, September 1999.

Tsuru, S. (1993) *Japan's Capitalism: Creative Defeat and Beyond*, Cambridge, Cambridge University Press.

UNCTAD (1995) *Trade and Development Report*, New York, Geneva, United Nations.

UNCTAD (1999) *Trade and Development Report*, New York, Geneva, United Nations.

US Council of Economic Advisors (1999) *Economic Report of the President*.

Waverman, L., Comanor, W. and Goto, A. (1997) *Competition Policy in the Global Economy: Modalities for Co-operation*, Routledge Studies in the Modern World Economy, London, Routledge.

World Bank (1991) *The Challenge of Development: World Development Report*, Washington, DC, World Bank.

World Bank (1998) *Global Economic Prospects*, Washington, DC, World Bank.

World Trade Organization (1997) *Annual Report*, Geneva, WTO.

World Trade Organization (1998) *Report of the Working Group on the Interaction Between Trade and Competition Policy to the General Council*, Geneva, WTO.

World Trade Organization (1999) *Report of the Working Group on the Interaction Between Trade and Competition Policy to the General Council (WT/WGTCP/3)*, Geneva, WTO.

8
A Brazilian-Style 'Ponzi': How to Create a Financial Crisis by Trying to Avoid One

Gabriel Palma

Introduction

In the last two decades there have been four major financial crises in the Third World: the 1982 debt crisis (affecting mainly Latin America, with the Chilean economy the worst hit in the region); the 1994 Mexican crisis (and its repercussions throughout Latin America, particularly in Argentina, commonly known as the 'Tequila effect'); the 1997 East Asian crisis, and the 1999 Brazilian one. The main characteristic of all these financial crises is that the economies most affected were those that had previously undertaken comprehensive processes of economic reform, particularly financial liberalization. Furthermore, these countries had not only liberalized their capital accounts and domestic financial sectors, but had done so at times of both high liquidity in international financial markets, and slow growth in most OECD economies, i.e. at times when a large, volatile and under-regulated international liquidity was anxiously seeking new high-yield investment opportunities.

These recurrent financial crises, which repeatedly took most business and academic observers by surprise, have generated a heated debate on fundamental issues of economics, finance, and economic policy-making in general. In fact, the only issue on which almost everybody seems to agree is that before these crises, international and domestic financial institutions had over-lent, and that in these countries the government, corporations and/or households had over-borrowed. In both instances, 'over' refers to the fact that lenders and borrowers ended up clearly accumulating more risk than was privately (let alone socially) efficient.

However, there are several related issues regarding these financial crises, which are among the most controversial topics in (real-world) economics today. The most important one is whether the fact that borrowers and lenders accumulated excessive amounts of risk was due to **exogenous** market interference that distorted otherwise efficient financial markets, or whether it was the result of **endogenous** market failures. In other words, whether the incentive mechanisms and resource allocation dynamics of financial markets were distorted because of outside interference, or because of inside market failures proper.

Those who argue that it was exogenous destabilizing mechanisms which led agents to lose their capacity to assess and price risk properly have placed their emphasis on both the **moral hazards** created by government deposit insurance and bail-outs by international institutions, and the **cronyism** which affected the mechanisms that determine the access to finance.[1]

Those who emphasize the existence of endogenous market failures in financial markets are concerned with at least three related issues. First, if these crises were in fact the result of market failures proper, were these failures the consequences of endogenous mechanisms that are set in motion only when financial markets work under certain specific circumstances (e.g. the role of excess liquidity in Kindleberger's cycle of mania, panic and crash)? Or are financial markets intrinsically unstable and unable to allocate resources efficiently (Minsky)?

Secondly, were there special factors that intensified the endogenous market failures in these crises? (Some commonly mentioned ones are the presence of inexperienced financial players working in recently deregulated domestic financial markets, and international financial institutions that got heavily involved in emerging markets before being able to grasp the institutional dynamics of these economies).

Thirdly, if these crises were essentially the result of endogenous market failures, were the over-lending and over-borrowing set in motion by relatively independent mechanisms that interacted because of special circumstances? Or were both of them in fact part of the same market failure (i.e. the result of a single interrelated process with a clear direction of causality)?

This chapter attempts to answer some of these questions regarding the Brazilian financial crisis, mainly from a 'Kindlebergian' endogenous-failure perspective. It argues that the general mechanisms leading to this financial crisis were in essence endogenous to the workings of financial markets when they are characterized by excess liquidity; and that the behaviour of lenders and borrowers was interconnected in a particular way – leading to a general macro–micro dynamics that ultimately rendered both lenders and borrowers unable to assess and price their risks properly, and to accumulate more risk than was privately efficient. However, this chapter will also argue that within this general framework, there are specific 'Minskian' features to the Brazilian crisis, which made it different from other financial crises. In Brazil, the absorption of this liquidity and the dynamic that it generated were uniquely conditioned by an environment characterized by particularly high and unstable interest rates – these were mainly due to the way in which the Brazilian government tried to defend the economy, and its economic strategy, from continuous external shocks, especially those of the Mexican, East Asian and Russian crises. These high and unstable interest rates, and the peculiar way in which the government dealt with the continuous domestic financial crises that they created, meant that in Brazil it was the public sector that sleepwalked into a 'Minskian' 'ponzi'.[2]

From this perspective, the Brazilian financial crisis seems to contradict one of the key propositions of the moral hazard literature. As is well known, this literature basically cites artificially low interest rates as the main reason why lenders and borrowers ended up accumulating excessive amounts of risk. It is not that international and domestic lenders are unable to assess and price their risk properly; it is that moral hazard takes away the incentive to do so. In short, if only moral hazard had not existed, interest rates would have been higher, the over-lending (and over-borrowing) would not have taken place, and the financial crisis would have been averted. What the case of Brazil shows is the dangers of the opposite situation: artificially high interest rates can equally lead to financial crisis, in particular because of the problems it creates in the domestic financial system (especially banking assets). Thus, as will be discussed in detail below, Brazil shows that what the moral hazard literature seems crucially to forget is the fact that financial liberalization in emerging markets – when done in a context of high, volatile and unregulated international liquidity – creates speculative activity of the sort that generates 'damned-if-you-do, damned-if-you-don't' choices in relation to interest rates.

This chapter concentrates on the period between the beginning of the Brazilian experiment with financial liberalization and economic reform proper and the outbreak of the financial crisis, i.e. between the Cardoso 'Real Plan' of mid-1994 and the financial crisis of January 1999. However, some attention will also be given to the period between the 1990 'Collor Plan' and the 1994 'Real Plan', because it was with the 'Collor Plan' (or 'New Brazil' programme) that the reforms first began to be implemented. Throughout the chapter, this period will be compared and contrasted with similar Latin American and East Asian financial crises, in particular the cases of Chile (1975–82), Mexico (1988–94), and Korea, Malaysia and Thailand (1988–97).

Financial Liberalization and Economic Reform in Latin America

Brazil, like the rest of Latin America, was badly affected by a series of negative external shocks at the end of the 1970s and the beginning of the 1980s, which found the region in a particularly vulnerable position due to its large deficits on the current account and its enormous stock of foreign debt. There are four main reasons for this. First, international interest rates began to rise rapidly in 1979 (following Paul Volcker's tightening of monetary policy at the Federal Reserve). Secondly, the terms of trade of most countries in the region began to decline from 1980 onwards. Thirdly, with Mexico's default in 1982, voluntary lending to Latin America stopped abruptly in the second half of that year. Finally, recession and growing protectionism in most of the North complicated even further the economic environment within which the Latin American economies had to regain their internal and external macro-equilibriums during the 1980s.

As had happened in the 1930s, a massive and continuous external shock that found Latin America in an extremely vulnerable position not only brought about the need for a very painful internal and external macroeconomic adjustment, but also laid the foundations for a radical and widespread change in economic thinking. The resulting ideological transformation eventually led to a generalized change in the economic paradigm of the region. In this case, it was characterized by an extreme move towards trade and financial liberalization, wholesale privatization and market deregulation, along the lines begun in Chile in 1973. In this way, a key element to understanding these reforms, particularly the 'fundamentalist' way in which they were implemented throughout the region, is that they were carried out as a result of the substantial economic weaknesses of these economies, and not because of their perceived strengths. In other words, they were a desperate attempt to reverse capital flight, reduce runaway inflation and bring the economies out of recession. This fact also helps to explain the different degrees of intensity with which the reforms were implemented in Latin America, as opposed to East Asia.

As I have argued elsewhere (Palma, 1998), it is not that East Asia did not implement its economic reforms partly out of necessity (and also because of mounting external political and financial pressure to do so); but its economic weaknesses were very different in nature and intensity from those in Latin America. As is well known, the East Asian economies had integrated their economies into the increasingly complex world division of labour in a very different way to that of Latin America. Instead of accepting their static, exogenously-given comparative advantages, they struggled to gain a different type of endogenously created comparative advantage, mainly via a 'flying geese' pattern of production and upgrading. Following Japan's example, this was achieved through an increasing export penetration of OECD markets for manufactured goods, within a process of the regionalization of production. The extraordinary success of the East Asian economies was based on several factors – mainly the openness of OECD markets, especially the USA, to their manufactured exports (this openness was clearly not extended to Latin America, and especially not to Brazil); their fast rate of expansion of international trade in these goods; their ability to produce manufactured goods that could compete globally; the continuous upgrading of their exports through the above-mentioned 'flying geese' path (which helped them to remain competitive as wage levels began to increase); their being able to generate the high levels of savings and investment required for this upgrading; and their achieving an effective coordination of this investment through different forms of industrial policy.

However, problems for the East Asian economies emerged in the late 1980s and early 1990s. One of the most significant was a result of their own success: some of their most important exports, particularly electronics, began to experience excess supply and rapidly falling prices. In part this was also the result of the increased standardization (or 'commoditization') of inputs to the electronics industry, in which many of these economies had concentrated their exports. As a response to this, their corporate sector massively expanded investment in new productive capacity, trying to turn falling prices to their advantage via increased market shares. In fact, the combined result was to exacerbate the global excess supply and to put further downward pressure on prices.[3] An obvious casualty of this increased struggle for market shares was profitability. This declining profitability led to a changing composition of the finance for investment, away from internally-generated profits and towards (domestic and foreign) debt. This was clearly reflected in rising debt/equity ratios, which particularly in Korea were reaching heights that even for this part of the world should have produced feelings of vertigo. This necessity to have access to an ever-growing amount of finance was clearly one of the key domestic pressures behind the drive towards external and domestic financial liberalization.

Another problem was that in the same period China became a formidable competitor in many of the markets that were crucial to the second-tier East Asian NICs, a process that also affected their profitability and led to an increased need for finance. At the same time, given the changing international division of labour, some of these economies, particularly Thailand and Malaysia, were reaching a point where further upgrading of exports to higher value added products was becoming increasingly difficult. In particular, it was becoming more and more complicated to break away from a 'sub-contracting' type of industrialization, and to advance further along the path towards the form of industrial development that characterized the first-tier NICs. So, in a pragmatic way, they increasingly looked towards financial liberalization as a way to **continue** and accelerate their ambitious growth strategy.

In Latin America, however, the economic environment in which the reforms were being implemented was very different. It was one characterized by an attitude of 'throwing in the towel' *vis-à-vis* their previous growth strategy of import-substituting industrialization. As a result, a widespread 'born-again' type of neo-liberalism emerged, which sought totally to reverse almost every aspect of the growth strategy previously followed by the region. This new 'fundamentalist' framework, for example, not only took for granted that trade and financial liberalization would switch the engine of growth towards **domestically** financed private investment in **tradable** production, but also assumed that budgetary balance and unregulated market signals would be **sufficient** conditions for macroeconomic equilibrium and microeconomic efficiency. At the macro level it was believed that fiscal balance would inevitably release private savings for more productive uses in the private sector; and, at the micro level, market deregulation and trade liberalization would not only stimulate tradable production but would also significantly increase private investment, while higher interest rates would increase domestic savings and reverse capital flight.

So far, as the Brazilian crisis yet again showed, this process of reform has turned out to be far more complex than predicted, and its results more mixed. The main achievement of the new policies in the period between liberalization and the subsequent respective financial crisis was the relaxation of the external financial constraint. This led to extraordinary reductions in inflation and increases in growth (in Brazil the latter turned out to be short-lived). There was also a welcome inflow of foreign direct investment, often directed (as in Brazil) to the privatization of utilities, leading in some cases to important gains in efficiency. Exports of many primary commodities increased significantly and, except for Brazil, there were sharp reductions in public deficits.

However, these reforms also had many negative effects. In particular, financial liberalization not only greatly increased the likelihood of shocks, but (mainly because it was implemented with the wrong 'sequencing', i.e. together with drastic stabilization programmes) also altered the fundamentals in a way that threw the export-led growth strategy off-course. In particular, those countries that shifted their domestic imbalances into the external sector by using the nominal exchange rate as a price 'anchor' have been the ones where the positive results of this process of adjustment and policy reform proved to be less sustainable. Their exchange rate policy produced a substantial appreciation of their currencies, which distorted the whole of the export-led growth strategy – switching the engine of growth away from domestically financed private investment in tradable production, and towards private consumption and externally financed private invest-ment in non-tradable production and services (see Palma, 1998). This switch, coupled with over-optimistic expectations of future perform-ance (set in motion mainly by easy access to credit and the massive 'spin' put on the economic reforms), had many serious negative effects, particularly on the balance of payments, national savings, non-residen-tial investment and employment – and, uniquely in Brazil, also in the public sector accounts. As a result, the Latin American economies in general, and Brazil's in particular, have ended up being more vulnera-ble to domestic and external shocks than at any time since the 1920s.

The Brazilian Reforms

Brazil turned decisively towards industrialization after the depression of the 1930s made its economic and political elite finally lose faith in the growth potential of its coffee-based export sector. For six decades thereafter, governments of all kinds pursued a fairly successful state-led industrial development through often unorthodox interventionist poli-cies. As a result, Brazil emerged as a major industrial power in the Third World (e.g. by the end of the 1970s Brazil was already producing one million vehicles per year), and by the late 1980s it had become the tenth largest economy in the world. In fact, according to a study by Maddison, between 1900 and 1987 Brazil's economy grew more rapidly than any other in the world (for a discussion of this data, see Palma (1999)).

Despite bouts of selective economic nationalism, foreign capital was generally welcomed into the manufacturing sector, beginning in particular in the 1950s. However, the state frequently insisted upon stringent requirements relating to the source of capital, the transfer of technology, and joint ventures (often with state, rather than private, capital). One of the key stated aims of the reforms was to reverse this pattern of state-led development in favour of deregulation of the economy, financial and trade liberalization, and the integration with Argentina, Paraguay and Uruguay into a regional common market, Mercosul (Mercado Comum do Sul or, more familiarly in Spanish, Mercosur – Southern Common Market).

A striking feature of state-led development was a massive building of productive capacity, particularly in the areas of energy, heavy industry and capital goods. As a consequence of this, and of Brazil's large internal market and abundant and varied natural resources, the country experienced rapid (though markedly cyclical) growth after World War II. Between 1947 and 1980, an average compound rate of growth of real GDP of 7 per cent per year was achieved; this puts Brazil more in the East Asian than in the Latin American league. As a result, domestic output increased nearly ten-fold in this 33-year period. However, after the 1982 debt crisis the country experienced a severe recession, made more acute by inexorably rising inflation and a heavy debt burden. Thus, between 1981 and 1983, Brazil's real GDP declined by nearly 6 per cent, but then it expanded again by 27 per cent between 1984 and 1987. Subsequently, with the exception of 1990, there were small increases in the economy until the beginning of the reforms, when growth accelerated rapidly, reaching 10.4 per cent in the first quarter of 1995. The main growth stimulus was the massive reduction of the 'inflationary tax' that followed the implementation of the 'Real Plan'. (see Fig. 8.1).

However, as growth accelerated, the balance of payments deteriorated rapidly; at the same time the 'Tequila effect', which followed the Mexican crisis of December 1994, began to bite. This forced the government to rapidly curtail aggregate demand, and measures were taken to ensure a sharp decline in output growth. This fell by nearly 12 percentage points between the first quarters of 1995 and 1996. As

Figure 8.1: Brazil: Quarterly GDP growth, 1993–2000

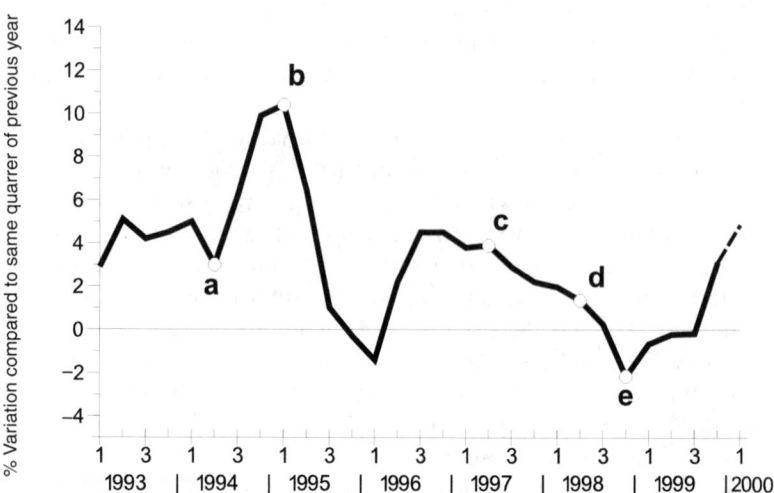

a = Beginning of the 'Real Plan'; b = Mexican crisis; c = East Asian crisis;
d = Russian crisis; and e = State of Minas Gerais' default.
Source: Macrometrica (January 2000). [4] First quarter of 2000 is Macrometrica's
forecast.

monetary and fiscal conditions eased afterwards, growth began to
recover again in the second quarter of 1996, but after the East Asian
crisis both had to be tightened again and growth fell once more. This
fall accelerated in 1998 as a result of the repercussions of both the
Russian devaluation and default, and the political crisis following the
default declared by the Minas Gerais State Governor (former president
Itamar Franco) on the state debts with the Central Government.

   Thus, one of the most important peculiarities of the January 1999
Brazilian crisis is that repeated external and internal shocks brought
down the growth rate long before the financial crisis. In fact, this crisis
is unique (among those studied here) not only in that it took place
during a period of recession, but also in that growth actually picked up
immediately after the crisis.[5] As will be discussed below, the continuous external shocks and the resulting different growth trajectory of
Brazil are directly related to the other peculiarities of Brazil's experiment with economic reform and liberalization, especially with its
much higher interest rates, its growing public sector deficit and, in particular, its 'ponzi' finance.

Throughout the period of Brazil's industrial expansion, state investment was a crucial component of total investment. Therefore, the reductions in state spending from the mid-1980s (to balance the budget) had a substantial effect on the rate of expansion of productive capacity and the economy as a whole. Gross domestic investment fell from 32.2 per cent of GDP in 1980 (current prices), to 22.9 per cent in 1985, 21.8 per cent in 1990, and 20.8 per cent in 1994, to remain at just under 20 per cent until 1998. Estimates for 1999 show a further reduction. A key element in this fall was the squeeze on public investment, which fell steadily from 1982 onwards (from over 8 per cent of GDP to just 4.4 per cent before the 'Real Plan' in 1993, to under 3 per cent of GDP throughout the period of the Plan). This policy not only had an obvious negative impact on growth on the expenditure side, but also on the supply-side of the economy (due to problems such as the rapid deterioration of the infrastructure of the country).[6]

The finance of investment also changed significantly after 1980. In that year gross national savings financed 88 per cent of investment, while foreign savings financed the remaining 12 per cent. However, as foreign savings became more difficult to obtain following the 1982 debt crisis, until 1994 investment had to be fully financed by national savings. In fact, in several years foreign savings were actually negative. This picture changed abruptly with financial liberalization: the inflow of foreign savings increased from 0.3 per cent of GDP in 1994, to 4 per cent of GDP in 1995, 6.8 per cent in 1996, and 8.5 per cent in 1997. Furthermore, the figure for the first half of 1998 shows an even higher level, which collapsed after the Russian devaluation. In terms of net resource transfers, in 1991 Brazil had a net outflow of US$8.6 billion (an amount equivalent to 25 per cent of exports). This negative transfer was reduced to US$0.7 billion in 1994, the year of the beginning of the 'Real Plan'. In 1995 this net transfer not only became positive, but an amount equal to 42 per cent of exports (US$20 billion); a similar level was reached in 1996. This situation contrasted markedly with the rest of Latin America, which had an overall negative transfer that year.[7] External shocks brought net transfers into Brazil down to US$9.5 billion in 1997, and US$4.8 billion in 1998. Estimates for 1999 actually show a negative figure for the year.

As in the rest of Latin America, in Brazil increased foreign savings became a substitute for, instead of a complement to, national savings. These decreased sharply, from 21.2 per cent of GDP in 1993, to 17 per cent in 1996, and just 14.7 per cent in 1997. The figures for 1998 and 1999 are estimated to be at an even lower level. This is in sharp contrast with the previous period of inflow of foreign capital, before 1982, when it occurred with only partial financial liberalization, when internal and external savings complemented rather than substituted each other.

Despite its other failures, the Collor government did achieve a budget surplus in 1990 equivalent to 1.4 per cent of GDP. This was due to a mixture of tax increases, expenditure reductions and privatization. This surplus changed to a deficit of 0.2 per cent in 1991 and 1.8 per cent in 1992. The 'Real Plan' again achieved a budget surplus in 1994 (equivalent to 1.1 per cent of GDP), but by 1995 this had already turned into a massive deficit of 4.9 per cent. In part this was the result of the Federal Government and Central Bank absorbing bad debt from state governments and private and public banks, in part due to the increase in interest rate necessary to fight the 'Tequila effect' (see Fig. 8.8 on p. 169). This deficit increased in 1996 to 5.9 per cent of GDP, and (with the new jump in interest rates that followed the East Asian Crisis and new bad-debt absorption) increased again to 6.1 per cent in 1997. The same, but augmented, cycle followed the Russian devaluation in mid-August, and the 1998 deficit reached 8 per cent of GDP.

Thus, **net** public debt (that is, total debt minus international reserves and assets associated with the public debt) increased at a very rapid pace during the 'Real Plan' – from well under US$200 billion in 1994, to US$215 billion in 1995, US$259 billion in 1996, US$276 billion in 1997, and about US$320 billion at the end of 1998. As a share of GDP, it nearly doubled between 1994 and 1999, from 28.5 per cent to 50.0 per cent. This amount, although not excessively large as a share of GDP compared with other countries, became unmanageable because of the constant need to increase interest rates after each external or domestic shock. Over 80 per cent of this net debt was domestic and the rest was foreign debt. Practically all the growth of the net public debt is accounted for the component of the Federal Government and Central Bank: as a share of GDP, this debt grew from 1.8 per cent of GDP in 1993 to 21.1 per cent in 1998 (see Fig. 8.9, p. 169). As the 'primary' accounts of the Federal Government and Central Bank were either in surplus (1994), in balance (1995, 1996 and 1998), or with a very small deficit (1997, see Fig. 8.8, p. 169), this large increase was not the result of rapid growth in ordinary public expenditure, but of the public sector having repeatedly to rescue the domestic financial system by absorbing large amounts of its bad debt, and having to borrow at recurrent extraordinarily high interest rates in the domestic market to do this. This was the way through which the Brazilian authorities sleepwalked into their 'ponzi' (see Figs 8.10 and 8.11 on pp. 172–3).

With the exception of Cardoso's Real Plan, attempts to halt periodically rampant inflation since the 1982 debt crisis experienced only brief success. With the rate of increase in consumer prices at over 200 per cent per year when the military left power in 1985, it was then held at close to zero for nine months, from February 1986, by President José Sarney's 'Cruzado Plan'. Under this Plan the cruzeiro was replaced by a new currency, the cruzado, which was equivalent to 1000 units of the old currency, and a briefly successful price 'freeze' was instigated. Inflation resumed late in the year, however, and the average annual rate of increase accelerated, to reach 1863 per cent by 1989. In March 1990, with an annual rate of inflation threatening to reach 5000 per cent, the new president, Fernando Collor de Mello, introduced his 'New Brazil Programme' or 'Collor Plan'. This restored the cruzeiro as the currency, froze US$110 billion worth of financial assets, and reduced price rises to a monthly rate of around 10 per cent within six months. Inflation was held to 2938 per cent for the year as a whole, then fell to 473 per cent in 1991, but increased again thereafter, to reach 2477 per cent in 1993. Following the implementation of the 'Real Plan' in mid-1994, the rate of inflation decreased sharply (from a monthly rate of nearly 50 per cent in June 1994, to one of approximately 2 per cent), reaching 22.4 per cent in 1995, 9.5 per cent in 1996 and 5.6 per cent in 1997. Finally, in 1998 inflation was estimated at only 0.8 per cent. With the large January devaluation, inflation in 1999 increased again, but only to 12.3 per cent for the year.

Needing to generate massive external resources to maintain payments on external debt after the 1982 debt crisis, Brazil produced large trade surpluses after 1983, reaching a peak of US$16.2 billion in 1988 (while imports remained stagnant, exports rose sharply to US$36.1 billion). This surplus stood at US$15.2 billion in 1992, when some parts of the reforms slowly began to be implemented; and when the reforms began in earnest in 1994, the surplus was still at US$10.5 billion. After that, it rapidly collapsed to a deficit of US$3.4 billion in 1995, and US$5.6 billion in 1996. Early projections for 1997 (based on data for the first quarter) expected this deficit to jump to more than US$16 billion, but as a result of turmoil in international financial markets following the East Asian crisis of mid-1997, the economic authorities were forced to implement drastic policies to reduce this deficit in the second half of 1997.

As a result, the trade deficit for the whole year ended up at only US$8.4 billion. The deterioration of the trade balance until 1997 was the result of a rapid increase in the value of merchandise imports that followed the process of import liberalization and the overvaluation of the currency. These trebled between 1992 and 1997, to reach US$61.4 billion. Exports also increased in the same period, but not at the same rate (to US$53 billion). Thus, while imports grew at an average annual rate of 25 per cent in these five years, exports did so at only 8.2 per cent.

In 1998, a new adjustment following Russia's devaluation left the deficit at US$5.9 billion. However, given that international financial markets went into 'panic station' after Yeltsin's announcement, their new emerging market paranoia made even this reduced deficit unsustainable, mainly due to the still huge financial requirements of the current account and the capital flight stampede. Eventually, this led to the January 1999 financial crisis and forced devaluation. Not unexpectedly, a key conditionality of the IMF rescue package that followed was to turn this trade deficit into a surplus; preliminary data for 1999 show that this aim was nearly achieved, as the trade deficit only reached US$1.2 billion.

Despite the trade surpluses between 1983 and 1994, heavy debt obligations still produced deficits in the current account of the balance of payments in seven years of this period. The improvement in external conditions contributed to a surplus in the current account in 1988 (US$4.2 billion), and in 1992 (US$6.1 billion). As trade and financial liberalization led to a rapid deterioration of the trade balance and the service of the growing foreign debt was mounting, the current account went into a deficit of US$1.7 billion in 1994, US$18 billion in 1995, US$23 billion in 1996, US$31 billion in 1997, and US$34 billion in 1998 (equivalent to 4.5 per cent of GDP, and 70 per cent of merchandise exports). Preliminary data for 1999 show that despite the near equilibrium in the trade balance, the current account was still in a deficit of US$25 billion for the year – indicating the difficulty of the task ahead of bringing the balance of payments back into a sustainable equilibrium.

Large as these deficits were, until the Russian devaluation capital inflows into the country for most of the 1990s were even larger, increasing the level of foreign reserves. These increased from US$35 billion in December 1994 to US$50 billion in 1995. Reserves continued to increase in 1996, reaching US$59 billion, but decreased in 1997, to US$53 billion by December. As capital inflows increased to a record amount at the beginning of 1998, the level of reserves at the end of May reached a peak of US$72 billion, a level US$15 billion higher than at the beginning of the East Asian crisis in mid-1997. The huge financial requirements of the current account came from Brazil's ever-growing foreign debt. In February 1987, with a debt-service ratio equivalent to about 80 per cent of exports, the country declared a moratorium on payments on its medium- and long-term debt of more than US$120 billion. Early in 1992 President Collor de Mello negotiated a partial rescheduling with the IMF, by which time total foreign debt was US$136 billion. However, foreign debt continued to increase, reaching US$180 billion by 1996. In that year the service of the long- and medium-term debt reached US$27 billion, or 57 per cent of exports. In 1997, this foreign debt broke the US$200 billion barrier, and in 1998 it increased again to US$225 billion (38 per cent of which was public and 62 per cent private). According to IMF statistics, in 1998 about 60 per cent of this debt was short-term, up from under 20 per cent in 1994.

Thus, as the events of the 1980s placed the model of state-led development under considerable strain, in March 1990 the incoming President, Collor de Mello, announced the first reform measures in his 'New Brazil' Programme: the removal of subsidies for exports, and phased reductions in tariffs. Also, a privatization programme was begun in 1991, the fuel market was deregulated (ending years of state support for ethanol production), and the dissolution of the coffee and sugar trading boards was announced. The most contentious measure was the temporary freezing of virtually all financial assets (with limits of US$1000 on bank and savings account withdrawals), but, by the middle of the year, this was subject to increasing evasion and was subsequently abandoned.

Despite the political weakness of Collor de Mello's short presidency, its unsure handling of macroeconomic policy, and the humiliating way in which he was thrown out of office, the initiatives he launched radically changed the direction of Brazilian economic development. Tariffs were set to halve in three years, with no tariff exceeding 35 per cent by the end of that period. Of equal moment was the commitment to remove the cumbersome system of import licensing. This system was partly responsible for Brazil being named, in 1989, under the 'Super 301' provisions of the 1988 US Trade Act.

The programme of privatization was initially intended to raise US$18 billion from the disposal of 27 state companies. Privatization eventually began in October 1991, with the sale of the USIMINAS steel mill, after delays arising from a legal challenge. Although the sale raised US$1.2 billion, more than the US$1 billion reserve price, it was a rather odd privatization in that only 6 per cent of the shares on offer were taken by foreign investors, while the rival state firm of CVRD (Companhia Vale do Rio Doce, SA) and the pension fund of the state-owned Banco do Brasil took large stakes. Over the following months further privatizations took place in smaller concerns, but receipts tended to fall far short of the target. Privatization receipts totalled US$1.6 billion in 1991, US$2.6 billion in 1993 and only US$0.9 billion in 1995. From that year the government of President Fernando Henrique Cardoso gave another impetus to privatization, which resulted in receipts quadrupling in 1996 to US$3.7 billion; and in the first half of 1997 alone, just two privatizations produced receipts twice the whole of the 1996 figure. These were the sale of 40 per cent of CVRD for US$3.2 billion, and the sale of the concessions for cellular telephones for about US$4 billion. This process continued in the second half of 1997, and increased rapidly in 1998, particularly due to the sale of about 20 per cent of TELEBRAS stock for US$19 billion (a rather well-timed privatization, as it took place just days before the emerging market paranoia brought about by the Russian devaluation).

A related trade policy initiative of the Collor government was the creation in March 1991 of Mercosur. Trade between Brazil and Argentina grew by 45 per cent in the first year alone. Exports to Argentina grew 4.5-fold between 1991 and 1998, and imports from Argentina by 5-fold. In 1998, 17 per cent of exports (and about one-quarter of manufactured exports) and 16 per cent of imports were with Mercosur countries. However, the continuing economic problems of Brazil and Argentina, made significantly worse by the Russian devaluation, raised doubts as to whether harmonization of tariffs and economic integration could continue on schedule.

In 1992 escalating corruption charges and several extraordinarily bizarre private scandals (even by Brazilian standards) led to the resignation of President Collor de Mello. His deputy, Itamar Franco, became acting president in September and president in December. Economic policy continued very much unchanged during the first year of President Franco's government, with its principal objectives being the liberalization of most prices, control over public expenditure and a strict monetary policy through high interest rates (the average real lending interest rate for the year reached 197 per cent). However, political and economic uncertainty continued after the change of president and inflation increased in late 1992, and in 1993 it reached 2489 per cent.

In May 1993, after several changes of finance minister, President Franco appointed senator (and world-famous sociologist) Fernando Henrique Cardoso to the position. Together with a group of highly skilled economists, including Edgar Bacha and Pedro Malan, Cardoso devised an all-encompassing stabilization plan, which began operations on 1 July 1994 (the 'Real Plan', which took its name from the new currency, which it introduced, the real). The main characteristic of this new plan was that, as opposed to most of its predecessors, it intended to avoid 'shock treatments', price freezes or surprise announcements. The Plan took a long time to be prepared and was announced in all of its details several months in advance of its implementation. It was an attempt to reduce prices gradually by reducing inflationary expectations (through the real being 'pegged' to the US dollar at a rate around one real to US$1), and inflationary 'inertia' (indexation), together with the aim of a progressive achievement of internal and external macroeconomic equilibrium. One of the main strengths of this new Plan was the fact that it succeeded in gathering an overwhelming degree of consensus and public support. Its initial successes in mid-1994 significantly helped Cardoso's campaign for the presidency.

As mentioned above, the main peculiarity of the 'Real Plan' is that it was implemented during a period when Brazil had three major external shocks, which had severe implications for its external accounts (and fiscal position). The Mexican crisis meant that 1995 did not begin well for Brazil. As a direct result of the 'Tequila effect', which followed the sudden devaluation of the Mexican peso, there was a reduction in the inflow of foreign capital into Brazil. Also, the stock exchange suffered a similar problem – in the first three months there was a net outflow of US$2 billion. The figure for the same period in 1994 had been a net inflow of US$5 billion. Foreign reserves also fell by US$7 billion in early 1995.

However, these problems did not last long, and from the second quarter of 1995 there was a rapid return of private foreign capital. This continued in 1996, aided by changes in legislation regulating foreign investment, as well as the planned and actual ending of state monopolies (such as in the petroleum and telecommunications sectors) and the privatization of public assets (particularly in the electricity sector). In this year, foreign direct investment nearly trebled, to US$9.1 billion. As is often the case, however, inflows of foreign capital of this magnitude have a double-edged effect: together with its positive effects, they tend to 'crowd out' national savings (as discussed above), and lead to a sharp revaluation of the currency. This problem was exacerbated by the economic authorities' use of the nominal rate of exchange as one of their main anti-inflationary mechanisms. The real exchange rate (nominal exchange rate deflated by the consumer price index and adjusted by the US consumer price index) fell by about one-half between mid-1992 and mid-1996. In 1997 and 1998 this trend began to be reversed, but at a rate that eventually proved to be too little, too late.

In 1997, the new upheaval in international financial markets owing to the crisis in many of the Asian economies brought the net quarterly inflow into Brazil down from US$10 billion (third quarter of 1997) to just over US$0.7 billion (fourth quarter). However, the foreign direct investment component of these inflows continued to increase, reaching US$14.5 billion for the year (60 per cent higher than in 1996). The sharp fall in net inflows at the end of 1997 was drastically reversed in the first quarter of 1998, when total net inflows reached US$22.5 billion (a figure equivalent to 86 per cent of net inflows for the whole of 1997). This was followed by another large net inflow in the second quarter of 1998, US$10.6 billion, but then, due to the impact of events in Russia, the figure for the third quarter dipped to a massive outflow of US$15.9 billion, followed by another net outflow in the fourth quarter. As these net outflows proved unsustainable, the government had no option but to devalue the real in January 1999. Thus, 1998 posted both the all-time record for net inflows of foreign capital into Brazil (first quarter), and for net outflows (third quarter). This exemplifies the difficulties confronted by economic authorities in the implementation of their macro-policies when they operate with a liberalized capital account in a world of highly volatile flows. Chile's experience with controlling short-term capital flows seems to be one of the few options open to policy-makers wishing to escape from this kind of instability.

The Brazilian authorities reacted swiftly to the East Asian crisis, increasing deposit interest rates to an extraordinarily annualized level of 43 per cent, raising some import tariffs significantly, and taking measures to facilitate the inflow of foreign capital. However, a clear danger of complacency followed this short-term success. By mid-1998, particularly due to the massive inflow of foreign capital in the first half of the year, the East Asian crisis appeared to have been forgotten – and so was the large cost for the public sector of having to rescue yet again the domestic financial sector. Nevertheless, there remained the real possibility that another external crisis could affect the world economy, particularly international financial markets, in a way that could seriously damage the Brazilian economy again. As it was, even before the Russian devaluation, Brazil already needed to borrow at a higher interest rate than some other Latin American countries, pay a higher price for its huge debt, and cope with reduced demand for its exports from Asia and Argentina. Its public sector accounts were also already out of control. Furthermore, 1998 was a year of presidential, state government and municipal elections. Not surprisingly, little was done, especially in relation to sorting out the public accounts. This may have helped Cardoso's re-election, but did little to strengthen the Brazilian economy; as a result, the Russian crisis of mid-1998 hit the Brazilian economy very badly. In particular, once again it became evident that no matter how large the levels of reserves are, they never seem to be large enough to withstand a sudden collapse in confidence and withdrawal of funds by international financial markets. By January 1999, the Central Bank had lost half its reserves, and had little option but to devalue. To contain the subsequent crisis, the government not only had to increase deposit interest rates yet again, to 45 per cent, but this time it had to look serious about its determination to begin to sort out the public sector accounts. A large IMF rescue plan made this, and the reversal of the trade deficit, its central conditionality.

Preliminary estimates show that by November 1999 the public sector deficit had shrunk to 3 per cent of GDP (calculated with interest payments in real terms). This was the result of a substantial improvement in the 'primary' accounts (from a surplus of 0.01 per cent of GDP in 1998 to one of 3.6 per cent), but little change in interest payments on the public debt (these only declined from 7.6 per cent of GDP in 1998 to 6.6 per cent). Once in a 'ponzi'-type of finance, it is very difficult to come out of it.

How to Sleepwalk into a (Public Sector) 'Ponzi' Finance

If a comparison is made of the four financial crises mentioned above, what distinguishes the Brazilian period between financial liberalization and financial crisis most in terms of economic policy is its high interest rates, both deposit and lending rates (see Figs 8.2 and 8.3).

Undoubtedly, the Brazilian authorities used these particularly high interest rates as their main policy tool both to defend their economic strategy from the continuous external shocks that they were experiencing, and to avoid the worst excesses that had characterized other

Figure 8.2: Latin America and East Asia: Domestic real deposit rates between the beginning of financial liberalization and respective financial crises

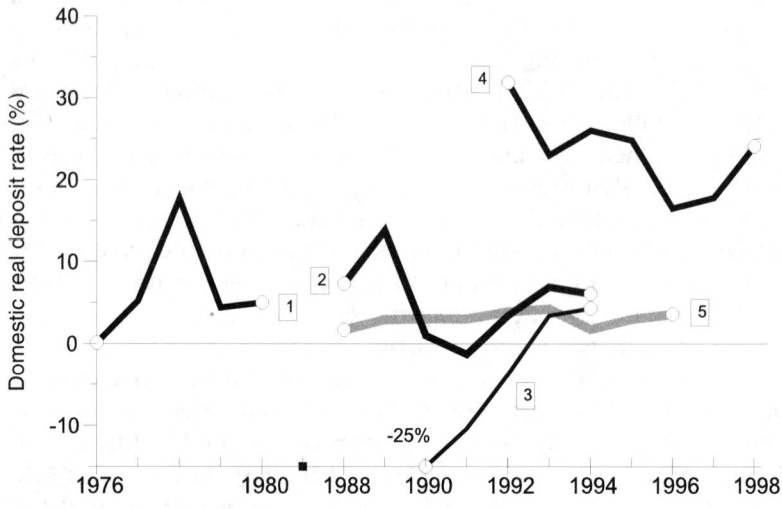

☐1 = Chile; ☐2 = Mexico; ☐3 = Argentina; ☐4 = Brazil; and ☐5 = average of Korea, Malaysia and Thailand.

Figure 8.3: Latin America and East Asia: Domestic real lending rates between the beginning of financial liberalization and respective financial crises

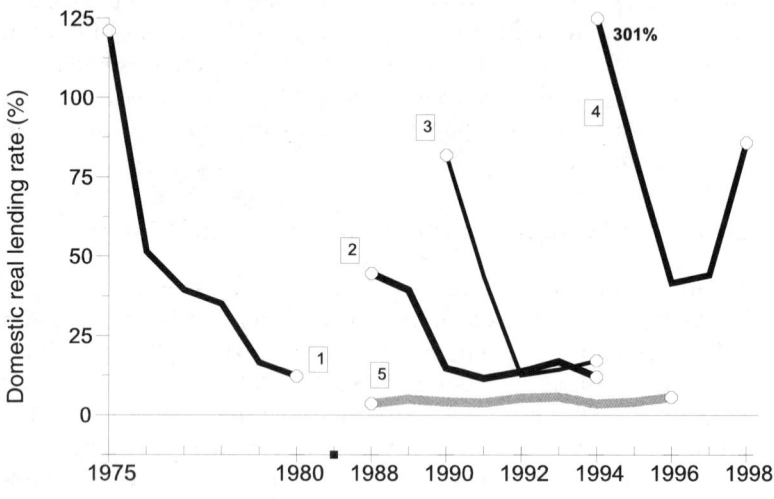

☐1 = Chile; ☐2 = Mexico; ☐3 = Argentina; ☐4 = Brazil; and ☐5 = average of Korea, Malaysia and Thailand.

experiences of financial liberalization, particularly in Chile (before 1982), and Mexico and Argentina (before 1994).

In short, in these countries financial liberalization and economic reforms had attracted massive amounts of foreign capital, the absorption of which had led (mainly via increasing expectations, declining interest rates and currency appreciation) to a Kindlebergian mania-type credit expansion, and an unsustainable consumption and property boom.[8] Figure 8.4 (p. 166) shows how successful the Brazilian authorities were in averting that their massive flow of foreign capital transformed itself into a private credit boom. In fact, according to World Bank statistics, in relative terms to GDP, credit to the private sector in Brazil actually fell by nearly half between the beginning of the 'Real Plan' and its financial crisis.

The control of credit expansion (and a more moderate trade liberalization policy) also succeeded in restraining the rate of growth of imports of consumer goods (see Fig. 8.5, p. 166).

Also, in Brazil high interest rates avoided a Kuznets-type of cycle: in the other crisis countries large inflows of foreign capital, the liberalization of domestic finance, and the appreciation of the real rate of exchange did set in motion a construction mania, led by a real estate boom (see Fig. 8.6, p. 167).

So far, the Brazilian experience of liberalization and reform with high interest rates seem to support at least part of the McKinnon and Pill-type of moral hazard argument. Although the Brazilian government did give deposit insurance, and everybody expected that the IMF and the US government would bail out big international institutional investors in case of a crisis, at least high interest rates were able to check the development of a Kindlebergian-mania (via credit expansion leading to a consumption and construction boom, which characterized in particular other neo-liberal experiments in Latin America).

However, high interest rates did not prevent recurrent problems in the domestic financial system, and the public sector accounts. On the one hand, they may have helped to reduce the quantity of the credit exposure to the private sector of the financial system, but they certainly did not help to improve the quality of this exposure. On the other hand, they were at the core of the worsening public sector finance.

While all the other crisis countries did manage to improve their public accounts significantly, ending in either equilibrium or in surplus before their financial crisis, Brazil alone shows a growing deficit (see Fig. 8.7).

Figure 8.4: Latin America and East Asia: Credit to private sector between the beginning of financial liberalization and respective financial crises

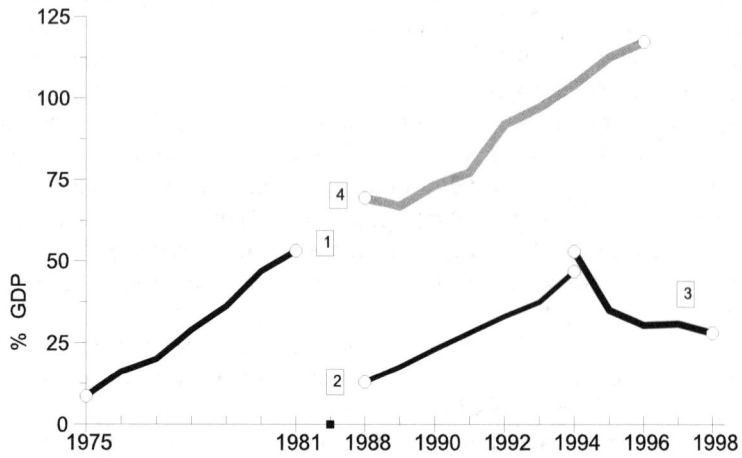

☐ = Chile; ② = Mexico; ③ = Brazil; and ④ = average of Korea, Malaysia and Thailand.

Figure 8.5: Latin America and East Asia: Imports of consumer goods between the beginning of financial liberalization and respective financial crises

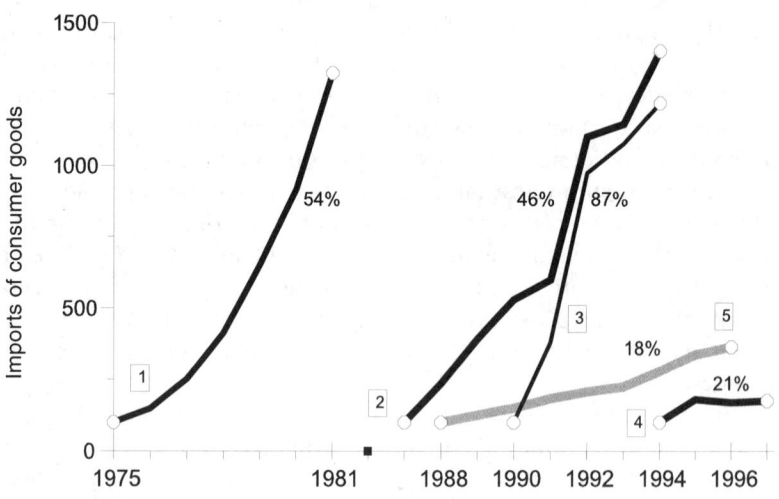

Base year: 100 in each case, constant US$ values
☐ = Chile; ② = Mexico; ③ = Argentina; ④ = Brazil; and ⑤ = average of Korea, Malaysia and Thailand. Percentages are average **annual** rates of growth.

Figure 8.6: Latin America and East Asia: Real estate price indices between the beginning of financial liberalization and respective financial crises

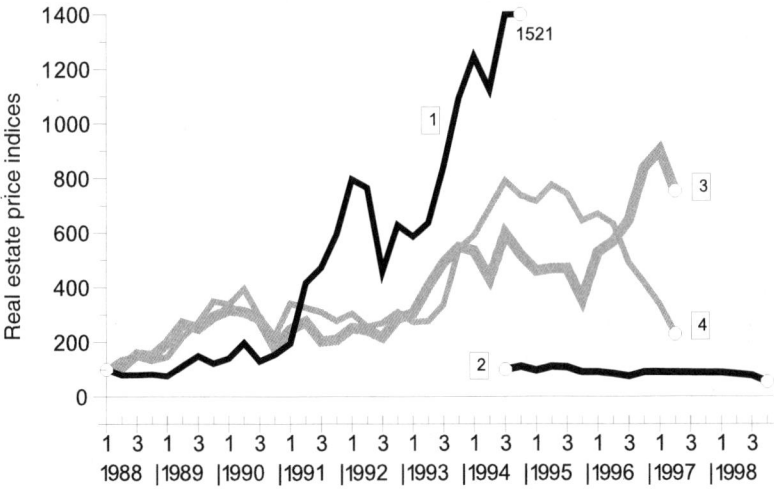

Local currencies, base year = 100 in each case
① = Mexico; ② = Brazil; ③ = Malaysia; and ④ = Thailand.
Source: Datastream. This source does not have data on Chile between 1975 and 1982. However, Chilean Central Bank statistics show an increase even larger than that of Mexico (an analysis of this data can be found in Palma, 2000).

Figure 8.7: Latin America and East Asia: Public sector deficit between the beginning of financial liberalization and respective financial crises

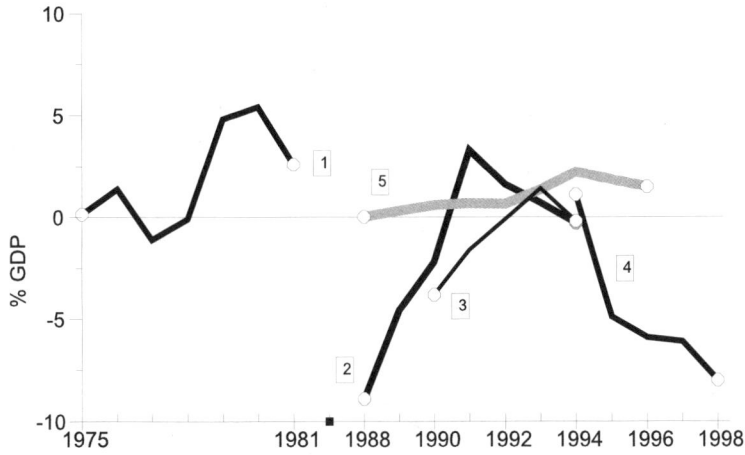

① = Chile; ② = Mexico; ③ = Argentina; ④ = Brazil; ⑤ = average of Korea, Malaysia and Thailand.

Obviously, the key question in Brazil's case is whether what was happening in the private and the public sector finances were interrelated phenomena, or whether the growing imbalance in the public sector was simply the result of a weak, populist government unable or unwilling to keep its house in order.

One of the difficulties that those working under the 'Washington Consensus' paradigm have had in explaining previous financial crises is that crisis countries, particularly in Latin America, had both opened up their economies and implemented economic reform more or less by the book, and their public sector had kept their accounts in order. Under these conditions it was not easy to explain why the private sector had run wild, creating such large macroeconomic imbalances, and accumulated so much financial risk – as to make a financial crisis almost inevitable. Fanciful theories of the 'rational' bubbles-type had little explanatory power and credibility. As a result they seem to have had little option but to fall back into well-rehearsed arguments of exogenous market interference by governments and international institutions, thus switching the whole debate towards issues such as moral hazards and 'cronyism'.

Brazil's financial crisis, however, seems to be the exception; apparently, a crisis easy to explain – the growing public sector deficit provided a familiar way out. Under these conditions reforms are not credible; either governments understand that they have to be serious about the way in which they implement their reforms, and make the necessary efforts to do so, or there is little chance of success.[9] 'Populist' governments are easy to dismiss, and are not an attractive subject to write about.[10]

Nevertheless, the obvious issue that so far is missing is precisely the dynamics that led to this growing public deficit, and its relationship to the economic policies that kept the private sector relatively under control. The first point to note is that the growing public deficit was entirely the result of interest payments on the public debt (see Fig. 8.8).

Other than for a small deficit in 1997, Fig. 8.8 shows that the 'primary' accounts of the public sector were in surplus throughout the period, and that it was the growing interest payments that brought the public sector into deficit. This seems to be the other side of the high interest rates coin. However, the problem is far more complex than that.

First, in the Brazilian case it is the service of the internal debt that accounts for most of these interest payments. Thus, while the external net debt of the government fell by more than half between 1993 and 1998 (from 14.4 per cent of GDP to 6.3 per cent), the internal debt

Figure 8.8: Brazil: Financial requirements of the public sector, 1992–99

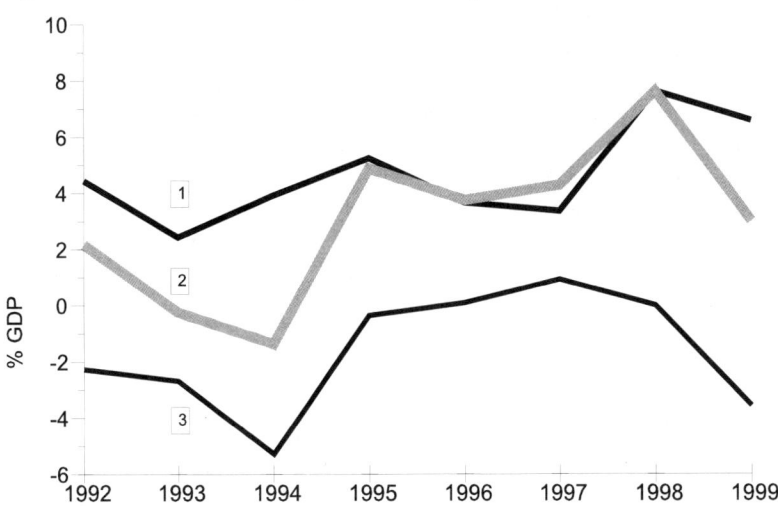

[1] = Interest payments; [2] = public sector deficit/surplus; and [3] = 'primary' deficit/surplus. A positive figure is a deficit, a negative is a surplus.

Figure 8.9: Brazil: Net internal debt of the Federal Government and Central Bank, and state governments, municipalities and public corporations, 1992–99

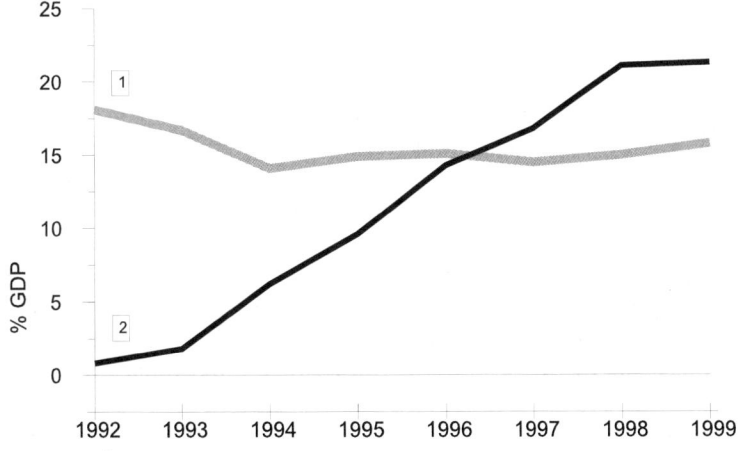

[1] = State government, municipalities and public corporations; and [2] = Federal Government and Central Bank.

doubled (from 18.5 to 36.1 per cent). Secondly, within the internal net debt, it was the Federal Government and Central Bank component of this debt that was booming (see Fig. 8.9).

Now, the reasons for the growth of the net debt of the Central Government and Central Bank are not at all obvious. There was no 'primary' deficit that required to be financed; and it is difficult to immediately blame high interest rates for this extraordinary growth, as this sector had practically no stock of debt to start with.

Obviously, in order to get into a 'ponzi' one needs to have debts in the first place. This is the crucial issue that needs to be explained: where did the stock of debt of the Federal Government and Central Bank come from? (Because this is from where the 'ponzi' took off.) Was this 'primary' stock of debt related to the effects of high interest rates policy in the rest of the economy?

The answer to the first question is that the Federal Government and the Central Bank ended up constantly having to rescue the domestic financial system both private and public (and State Governments) from collapse by absorbing their bad debts; and to the second is that the difficulties of the domestic financial system (and other sectors of the economy), which led to the 'primary' stock of debt of the Federal Government and Central Bank, certainly had a lot to do with the high interest rates policy of the government.

The key issue is that in a financially liberalized economy, the government constantly has to face 'damned-if-you-do, damned-if-you-don't' type choices in relation to interest rates. As in Brazil, if they start with a high interest policy to begin with, this tends to overvalue the currency; then, so long as this overvaluation is expected to continue (commitment to a 'peg'), this becomes an incentive to substitute borrowing in domestic currency with borrowing in foreign currency. Soon, there are domestic exposures that require interest rates to come down, but there are also external exposures that require that the currency remain overvalued (i.e. interest rates need to stay up). In other words, from the point of view of the domestic financial system, interest rates are soon stuck between the needs of banks' foreign currency liabilities, and those of the banks' domestic assets. In the case of Brazil, policy-makers opted for avoiding bankruptcies on banks' foreign exchange exposures, at the cost of bankruptcies on banks' domestic assets exposures – and then they opted to foot the bill for the latter. The problem is the choice of the one type of bankruptcy against the other; one type of government rescue operation against the other. Either way, the public sector debt would swell and, given the character of the present international financial market, from there on the economy is just one step away from speculative activity of the partly self-fulfilling, partly truth-telling type that tends to end in a financial crisis (see Kuczynski, 1999).

In summary, a financial liberalization with low interest rates seems to unleash a private sector credit explosion, leading to an unsustainable consumption and construction boom; another that tries to avoid this via high interest rates seems to destabilize the domestic financial system in a way that leaves the government having to choose between a rock (absorbing large amounts of bad debt created by underperforming banking assets) and a hard place (allow the collapse of the domestic financial system because of its foreign exchange exposures). The Brazilian government chose the route of high interest rates, and high financial sector bad debt absorption due to problems on its assets side.[11]

Added to this, of course, there is another crucial factor fuelling the financial fragility: in Brazil, financial liberalization was implemented with a particularly grossly inadequate system of regulation and supervision of the domestic financial sector. Furthermore, the Federal Government deliberately exacerbated this problem by overlooking and covering up cases of wrongdoing and corruption in financial institutions, particularly when they were owned by political *caudilhos*, which were crucial for the survival of its weak political coalition.

Once the stock of debt of the Federal Government and Central Bank began to swell, the high interest rate-related 'ponzi' finance took over (see Fig. 8.10).

Two crucial phenomena of the public sector 'ponzi' finance are evident in Fig. 8.10. First, the violation of one of the most important financial 'golden rules': interest rates paid on public debt were systematically higher than the growth of public revenues. Second, each external and internal shock led to a sudden rise in this interest rate. This led to a similar (but augmented) phenomenon in lending rates (Fig. 8.3), which (in 'Minskian' terminology) turned some private sector finance from 'hedge' into 'speculative', and some 'speculative' into 'ponzi'.[12] Not surprisingly, banking assets under-performed, and each of these increases led to a banking crisis and to a government rescue.

Finally, Fig. 8.11 shows the third side of the public sector 'ponzi' finance. Again, until the January 1999 crisis, interest payments on liabilities (sterilization of huge foreign inflows) were systematically higher than revenues from related assets (foreign exchange reserves).

Figure 8.10: Brazil: Interest rates paid for internal public debt and growth of public revenues, 1994–99 (domestic currency)

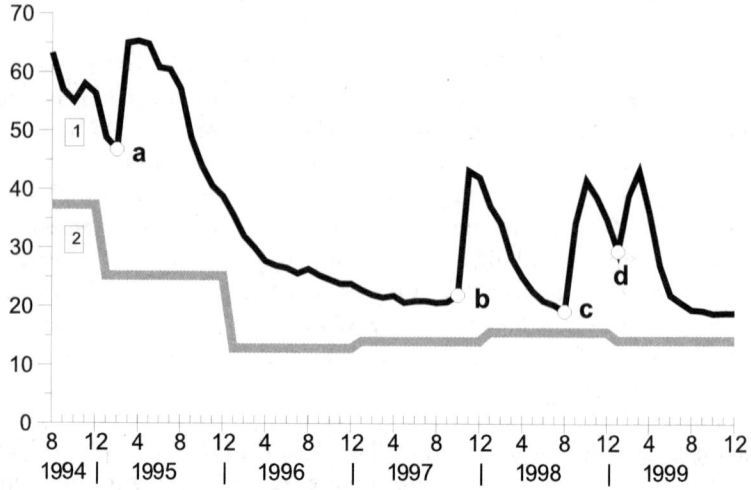

☐ = Interest rate paid by the government on its domestic paper (annualized monthly rates); and ☑ = growth of public revenues (annual rates).
a = Interest rate increase due to the Mexican crisis; b = due to the East Asian crisis; c = due to the Russian crisis, and d = due to the State of Minas Gerais' default.

To sum up, high interest rates led to domestic financial crises mainly via problems in banking assets. This led to an increase in the stock of public debt via government rescue activities. This debt exploded because of the same high interest rates. In the meantime, the real economy imploded because of these rates, which also affected the growth of public revenues. However, these interest rates were necessary to defend the 'peg' in order both to avoid further domestic banking crises due to foreign exchange banking liabilities and a stampede by restless international fund managers – the 'ponzi' finance in the public sector ballooned out of control.[13]

Conclusions

The legacy left by the military regimes to their civilian successors was a complex one. The Brazil of 1985 was very different from that of 1964. Brazil's economy had improved significantly, but the lot of its people certainly had not. The Sarney Government proved unable either to

Figure 8.11: Brazil: Interest rates paid for internal public debt and received for foreign exchange reserves, 1994–99 (annualized monthly rates, domestic currency)

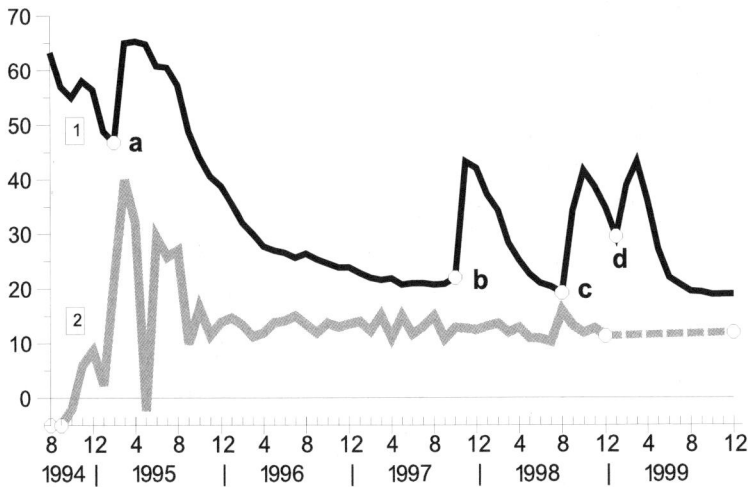

☐ = Interest rate paid by the government on its domestic paper and ☐ = interest rate received for foreign exchange reserves (1999 is not included due to large monthly variations caused by sharp exchange rate changes).
a = Interest rate increase due to the Mexican crisis; b = due to the East Asian crisis; c = due to the Russian crisis, and d = due to the State of Minas Gerais' default.

alleviate even the worst of the social problems afflicting rural and urban areas or to deal with the pressing problems of debt, inflation and recession. President Collor de Mello's attempt to bring about a significant shift in the character of the economy and its external relations, and to put a gradual end to over 50 years of state-led development failed. Short-term economic problems and the emergence of massive corruption and bizarre private scandals as major issues in 1992 revealed the fragility of his political base. This threatened not only his liberalization programme, but also the survival of the administration itself. After his forced resignation, his successor also proved unable to deal with Brazil's major political and economic problems, but achieved some recognition in the last year of his government with the appointment of Fernando Henrique Cardoso as his finance minister. President Franco allowed Cardoso and his team to freely devise and implement what seemed to be the best planned and most ambitious stabilization programme in

Latin America since the 1982 debt crisis. The 'Real Plan' succeeded in dramatically reducing inflation and resulted in the election of Cardoso to the presidency (just for ex-President Franco, now elected governor of the state of Minas Gerais, to become his worst enemy; as mentioned above, the detonator of the January 1999 devaluation was Governor Franco's default on his state debt with the Federal Government).

Although by the end of 1998 the stabilization plan had hitherto succeeded in its inflation objective, it was at a growing cost. The exchange rate was massively overvalued; there was a fast-growing deficit in the current account of the balance of payments; foreign and domestic debt was increasing at an accelerating pace; domestic interest rates were high and volatile; unemployment remained high; and levels of public investment were absurdly low. Finally, Brazil had an ever-growing public sector deficit, which the government seemed unable to sort out.

One of the strengths of the Brazilian economy in the past was that its economic authorities (of different political persuasions) did not allow its domestic inflation, interest rates, exchange rate and external balance to become a constraint on economic growth. As this policy ended in the 1980s in 'hyper-stagflation', the present economic authorities reversed it into a new policy in which interest rates, external balance and economic growth were not allowed to become a constraint in the fight for exchange rate and price stability. Although inflation has so far been successfully controlled (even after the huge January devaluation, the 1999 consumer price index increased by only 8.6 per cent – so much for nominal exchange rates having to be a necessary price 'anchor' in an economy like Brazil), this created major economic problems, not least the 'ponzi' finance of the public sector.

A domestic deregulated but badly supervised financial market, closely linked to a highly liquid, under-regulated and unstable international financial market, coupled with a domestic economy characterized by large imbalances, a weak state, and an even weaker government coalition, made a sudden collapse of confidence and withdrawal of funds a real possibility. As soon as inflation was conquered, by the end of 1995 or beginning of 1996, a tight regulation and supervision of the domestic banking system, some exchange controls on short-term flows, a managed real devaluation, a decrease in interest rates, and an increase in public revenues were the only sensible options. However, as often happens in politics, risk-averting inertia takes over. A successful set of economic policies that brings inflation down from four to single digits in a few months (the 'Real Plan') is kept in place after it has accomplished its objectives and has run its full course. As a result, the same policies that were the solution to the previous problem (hyperinflation) begin to be a problem in the new cycle; and the longer they are kept, the more difficult becomes their change. When in 1998 the Brazilian policy-makers finally realized that some drastic policy changes were necessary, it was unfortunately an election year – not the most propitious time to take a major risk. Also, and very importantly, at that time the Cardoso government still benefited from the Brazilian people's disillusionment with previous development and economic policies. Although this had been the ultimate condition required for the success of the 'Real Plan' in its initial stages (i.e. for a radical change in a [relatively] democratic society), by 1998 the government still hoped that it was political capital from which they could continue endlessly to depreciate. Some of the worst populists are those disguised as 'technocrats'.

Acknowledgements

An earlier version of this chapter was presented at the workshop 'The New World Financial Authority', organized by the Center for Economic Policy, The New School for Social Research, New York, 6–7 July 1999. I would like to thank the Center for its financial support and permission to use the material from the original paper. I would also like to thank the participants at the workshop, especially Lance Taylor and Jose Antonio Ocampo, and the participants at the conference on 'Globalization', Cambridge, 9–11 October 1999, especially John McCombie and Paul Davidson, for their helpful comments.

Notes

1. Of the large amount of literature on the role of moral hazards in financial crises, probably the best exposition is that of McKinnon and Pill (1997). Part of this literature can be found on the web site http://www.stern.nyu.edu/~nroubini/asia/AsiaHomepage.html
2. According to Minsky, an agent runs into 'ponzi' finance when it is forced to borrow to keep up with payments on its existing debt obligations; i.e this agent has to capitalize interest and thereby add to its total debt (Minsky, 1982).
3. For example, in 1996, in part as a result of new investment in Taiwan, the price of a 16-megabyte memory chip fell to about one-fifth of its 1995 price; Korea was particularly affected because a significant amount of its exports consisted of this type of microchip.
4. Unless otherwise stated, all the data in this chapter is sourced from the monthly bulletins of Macrometrica, those of the Central Bank, Datastream,

the Statistical Division of ECLAC, or the data banks of the IMF and the World Bank.

5. In the other crises the opposite was the case – in the year before its financial crisis (1981) Chile was growing at 4.8 per cent, Mexico at 4.6 per cent (1994), Argentina at 8.5 per cent (1994), and in 1996 Korea grew at 7.1 per cent, Malaysia at 8.0 per cent and Thailand at 6.4 per cent; and in all these countries output fell massively after their financial crises.

6. During the 'Real Plan', public expenditure on health and education also fell significantly relatively to GDP, from (an already reduced) 7.0 per cent of GDP in 1993, to just 5.1 per cent in 1998.

7. In particular, Mexico posted a negative figure of US$10.4 billion.

8. For an analysis of this cycle, see Kindleberger (1996), and Palma (1998).

9. See, for example, World Economic Outlook (May, 1999).

10. Although there is an over-abundance of literature on other financial crises, especially on those of Mexican and East Asia, there is very little on the Brazilian neo-liberal experiment. See the relevant sections on the web site http://w.w.w.stern.nyu.edu/~nroubini/asia/AsiaHomepage.html

11. For a chronology of the Brazilian government absorption of the domestic financial sector bad debt, see ECLAC (1999).

12. According to Minsky (1982), a firm is engaged in 'hedge' finance if the expectation is that gross profits after taxes, for each and every period contemplated, will exceed gross payments on debts. The liability structure is fully covered by receipts that will occur in the normal course of producing goods and services. The larger the equity in a firm relative to its debt, the greater the likelihood that the firm is engaged in 'hedge' finance. In turn, a firm is engaged in 'speculative' finance if the expectation is that, in the long term, gross profits after taxes will exceed by a margin of safety the sum of total payment commitments; and that on a year-by-year basis, gross profits after taxes will exceed the interest portion of payments coming due; but that, in the near term, total payment commitments for principal and interest will exceed cash flows. In the near term this firm and its bankers expect payment commitments to be fulfilled by borrowing. The viability of a 'speculative' financing structure depends, of course, upon the continued well-behaved functioning of particular financial markets.

13. There were obviously further problems with the banking sector and public finance, which we cannot expand here due to lack of space. The most important ones were the effect of rapid price stabilisation on banking profitability and public finance, and the delicate political balance between Central and State Governments' finance. Regarding the first, as Brazilian hyperinflation lasted for a long time, the banking and public sectors had adjusted to it in a way that made them vulnerable to a sudden decline in the rate of inflation – the first via declining spreads, the second via loss of an asymmetric indexation between revenues and expenditure. Regarding the second, part of the increase in the Central Government stock debt was due to a complex process of renegotiations and rescheduling of State Government debts.

14. A good example of this, and of the political 'mania' so often brought about by power, is the extraordinary statement made by President Cardoso, more than a year into his first mandate (and while he was already sleepwalking through his 'ponzi'): 'Brazil is such an easy country to govern'.

References

ECLAC (1999) 'La Economia Brasilera ante el Plan Real y su Crisis' (paper written by P. Sainz and A. Calcagno). *Serie Temas de Coyuntura* No. 4.

Kindleberger, C. (1996) *Manias, Panics, and Crashes: a History of Financial Crises*, New York, Chichester, John Wiley & Sons.

Kuczynski, M. (1999) *How Asian has the Asian crisis been?*, mimeo, Adenauer Stiftung December.

McKinnon, R. and Pill, H. (1997) 'Credible economic liberalizations and over-borrowing', *American Economic Review*, 87(2).

Minsky, H. (1982) 'The financial instability hypothesis: capitalist processes and the behaviour of the economy' in C. Kindleberger and J. P. Laffargue (eds) *Financial Crises: Theory, History and Policy*, Cambridge, Cambridge University Press, pp. 13–39.

Palma, J. G. (1998) 'Three and a half cycles of "mania, panic and [asymmetric] crash": East Asia and Latin America Compared', *Cambridge Journal of Economics*, November.

Palma, J. G. (1999) 'An overview of Brazil's economy and the January 1999 crisis', in *Regional Surveys of the World: South America, Central America and the Caribbean*, 8th Edition, Europa Publications Ltd.

Palma, J. G. (2000) The economics of financial crises: East Asia and Latin America Compared, mimeo, Cambridge.

9
Technology and Growth: Between Regionalization and Globalization

Pascal Petit

Introduction

The process of internationalization, by changing regulations and practices, is eroding the institutional fabric, which has determined past national growth patterns. Because this process takes place within a whole set of partner countries, it might be thought that all development paths would be affected in the same way. It might be further considered that growth rates are now, as a consequence, converging towards a similar pattern, best described by a single model of a new more open economic environment. However, this view rules out any alternative approach to modelling the effect of globalization and is thus greatly oversimplified and prevents the formulation of alternative realistic policy targets. We may identify two major shortcomings of this monocausal approach.

First, it neglects the fact that national institutional fabrics do, in fact, change with their environment, but in specific ways that take advantage of complementarities and synergies existing within their own institutional context. This has been the case not only at the various stages of internationalization that have occurred in the past, but also when there have been major changes in technological systems.

Secondly, the monocausal approach underestimates the length of time necessary for these institutional changes to be completed, and consequently leaves some room for manoeuvre in national policy-making.

A major question is how effectively national policy-making can be redesigned to take account of the new situation, as it is unrealistic to assume that policies can now only be implemented at the world level. International bodies, even if they are able to change and learn in the new environment (see, for example, the slow evolution of the World Bank away from the Washington Consensus of the 1980s), are not yet in position to be the main instruments of the necessary institutional change and policy-making that globalization requires.

The lack of effectiveness of the international bodies means that an important role still remains for policy-making at the national level, even though this is constrained by the changing circumstances. Two polar views may be identified with respect to the present scope for policy-making.

One view is that the internationalization and opening of markets lead to a convergence towards a unique model of the free market economy. National policies are seen as having to facilitate a rapid liberalization of markets in order for a country to gain the advantage of being one of the first to develop into a fully-fledged open market economy.

The other, contrary, view is that internationalization is not fundamentally changing the way national economies function. This is because the current process of internationalization is not unprecedented. Moreover, regional cooperation can eventually reduce the degree of exposure of economies to external competition. By this means, structural economic policy should be able to help recreate the conditions for standard macroeconomic Keynesian policies to be effective again.

An assessment of the nature of the present phase of internationalization is thus crucial to assess the validity of these two positions. However, *both* views are flawed as they underestimate the diversity of the models of capitalism. They also fail to appreciate the length of time necessary for the institutional changes, set in motion by a process of economic integration at various geographical and functional levels, to occur.

European integration is a good example of why this argument is deficient, because it should have led to substantial cooperation between the European countries. These countries, despite the widespread impression that they share a common ideal of a social contract, present a wide range of different types of capitalism. This greatly complicates international cooperation between these countries in the setting of economic policies. This is the lesson of the past three decades, when European countries failed to abolish mass unemployment, in spite of making substantial progress towards greater economic integration. This is notwithstanding the fact that the countries were reiterating in the early 1990s their past commitment to full employment. The gap between the market-oriented economies and those that took a more corporatist or statist stance reduced to a minimum the possibility of coordination of macroeconomic policies.

Clearly, the process of integration affected the old national structures and their internal cohesion in very different ways. The degree of institutional convergence between the European countries remains limited. Countries may have found new lines of internal cohesion in this transformation, but it is doubtful that it has fostered complementarities and synergies at the European level, which could have supported a revival of Keynesian policy-making. There are two reasons for this.

The first is that, even if it made theoretical sense, in practice there were severe constraints that prevented any revival of Keynesian policies at a larger geographical level. The second reason is that the institutional changes are lengthy evolutionary processes. Such changes are reminiscent of the concept of path dependency, which has been developed in the more recent economic growth literature. The path of transition is just as important as the long-term outcome. The last decade has shown that the endogenous nature of economic growth could have many origins, but it is obviously conditioned by a whole set of facilitating factors.

An important example of this is the pre-eminent role that national systems of innovations play in economic growth. At the same time as the pre-eminence of coherent specific subsets of national institutions is reasserted as a vector of economic growth, the process of internationalization seems to erode most of these national characteristics. It leaves rather uncertain the way in which the dynamics of innovation will henceforth foster economic growth.

The purpose of this chapter is to discuss to what extent this reconstruction can take place within the framework of regional integration and to what extent the diversity of a region can be turned into a factor that positively affects the growth of itself and its partner countries. The answer is not straightforward and we shall only attempt to set up an analytical framework here. This will identify some crucial issues concerning the development of advantageous complementarities and synergies at a regional level.

We begin with a discussion of the contemporary phase of internationalization and consider the extent to which it is unprecedented. This section also illustrates how the effects of internationalization differ between countries (in other words, it shows that these economies are not in the final phase of internationalization and convergence). The next section considers the extent to which this new form of internationalization conforms to the standard scheme of cumulative growth (used to explain the 'fordist' growth trajectories of the 1950s and 1960s). We then elaborate the substantial changes which the structural forms are presently undergoing and sketch the different resulting patterns of internationalization. The following section returns to the initial question of the relevance of regional levels for developing positive externalities and we conclude with some observations on the importance of such externalities and how to internalize them for the benefit of the regional partners.

Our proposals in this chapter take advantage of the processes of regional integration to develop a stepwise approach to the construction of a more global development policy.

What is New About the Present Phase of Internationalization?

The debate concerning this issue on the one hand forces those who think that the present phase of internationalization is unprecedented to argue that the major changes are due to the intensification and diversification of intangible flows of information and knowledge. On the other hand, the basic argument of those who stress that the present phase of internationalization is not unprecedented is two-fold. In the first place, they stress that trade flows and foreign direct investment (FDI) as a proportion of GDP have barely increased in the last two decades. Moreover, the levels now reached are not unique; they were experienced in the period 1870–1913 by countries such as the UK, the Netherlands and Japan (see Bairoch and Kozul-Wright, 1998; Kleinknecht and Wengel, 1998). In the second place, they point out that FDI flows are mainly intra-regional and that globalization is really a process of regional integration (see Hirst and Thompson, 1996).

There are a number of shortcomings to this argument. The large number of countries involved today, as well as the wide-ranging nature of trade and FDI flows, is sufficient to undermine this position.[1] The development of horizontal (different varieties of a particular product) and vertical (different qualities of a similar product) intra-regional trade also shows the greater extent of the differentiation of markets and integration of production processes than in the past (see Fontagné, Freudenberg and Péridy (1997) and OECD (1999, section 7.4)).

But the major difference with this present phase of internationalization, compared with earlier ones, is concerned with intangibles. These relate to the new flows of information and knowledge and to institutional changes which allow a much broader range of economic agents to interact faster across borders and to execute a wider range of international economic transactions than ever before. This is the result of the accumulation of knowledge and the continuous institutional changes that are now occurring, and are due to the rapid development of information and communication technologies.

We can cite four kinds of development to substantiate this argument:

1. The extensive deregulation of trade, investment flows, and the many intermediate services that are central to the organization of markets and transactions.
2. The formalized (and publicly announced) international cooperation and agreements between firms that are now occurring.
3. The increase in the free exchange of information and knowledge in the academic world and the media more generally.
4. The changes in international relations in the business world, mainly through the activities of internationalized business services, but also through personal contacts and cultural links.

We shall consider these points in rather more detail. The move towards deregulation gained momentum in the late 1970s as stringent regulatory frameworks which were set up for most of the intermediary services (banking, transport and communication) in the late 1930s and in the early post-war period began slowly, but surely, to unravel. The trend to trade and investment liberalization started much earlier, but gained a new momentum over the last two decades as regional agreements flourished and developing countries liberalized their economies. The combined effect of both these changes has greatly affected international transaction costs.

The development of alliances and formal agreements between firms is also a new feature. They developed rapidly during the 1980s and the 1990s (from 100 in 1980 to 700 in the mid-1990s).[2] Forty-five per cent of these agreements concern production organization, 25 per cent marketing, and 30 per cent development and innovation. They are found in all industries, although they are mostly concentrated in the high-tech sectors and international alliances normally involve firms outside the region.[3]

The rapid increase in the extent of the exchange of information and knowledge has been primarily due to the increasing importance of the foreign capital resulting from mergers and acquisitions, and the internationalization of R&D expenditure by the multinational corporations.[4,5] The diffusion of information and knowledge through academic activities (scientific meetings, publications, etc.) and the media (the press, either general or specialized, as well as TV, radio, etc.) has accelerated the innovation of technology transfers. Universities and public research centres are pre-eminent in the globalization of innovation (as stressed, for example, in the taxonomy of Archibugi and Michie, 1995). There has been a marked rise in international cooperation between researchers. Between 1985 and 1995, the percentage of papers with international co-authors nearly doubled to reach a good third of all publications[6] (see also OECD, 1999, section 9.4, for figures on the share of scientific papers and patents with a foreign co-author in 1995). Forthcoming statistics on the effect of the Internet are likely to support the above assessment and to confirm that the cooperation of researchers is a global effect.[7] The media are also an important international source of information and knowledge, not only through TV, but also through the technical press and international profession events, such as seminars and fairs. The latter rank high in the European Community Innovation Survey (CIS) as a means of technology transfer between firms.

The role of a now significant group of professionals working in business and finance services and who set the norms of international transactions will be our final illustration of the greater global spread of the decisions of individual agents. Behind the small number of managers of pension funds there are numerous experts and special authorities, operating in the areas of insurance, law, finance and accountancy. Strange (1996) reports that the six largest accountancy firms audit 494 of the Fortune 500 companies with worldwide fees that total US$30 billion (equivalent to the GDP of Ireland). Their influence extends even further than simply over the large MNEs and they have developed a culture and norms which are diffusing freely and widely around the world (O'Shea and Madigan, 1997). Even if these influences are subject to fads and contradictions, they are still leading to varied and changing strategies of internationalization in the business world. The rapid development of highly qualified business services (which was one of the fastest growing sectors in terms of employment in the 1990s, and is expected to nearly double between 1996 and 2006 in the USA, for example – see Hecker, 1999) suggests the growing importance of these 'symbolic workers' who are well attuned with this phase of 'globalization' (to quote Reich, 1991).

These qualitative and structural changes resulting from the growth of the intangible flows of information and knowledge are also consistent with similar changes in the structure of trade and FDI flows. In the 1980s and 1990s, international transactions of real services (i.e. excluding incomes from factors) developed more rapidly than did trade in goods. This is in contrast to the position in the 1970s. Trade in real services was finally equivalent to about one-third of the trade in goods in the mid-1990s. Of this, business and financial services[8] had the highest growth rates, increasing from 4.8 per cent of world exports in 1981 to 7.5 per cent in 1993.

Transfers of factor incomes also expanded rapidly: they represented up to 15 per cent of world exports in 1993 compared with only 7.9 per cent in 1975. Similar support for the argument comes from the structure of FDI. The high-tech sectors, where intra-firm trade is important, are attracting substantial FDI flows. Over the last two decades, two-thirds of FDI has been in services, mostly in the areas of distribution, finance and real estate. This reflects the growing importance of the need to gain access to markets.

Finally, to complete this picture, we should note that trade and FDI flows are dwarfed by the huge volumes of financial flows. In the OECD countries, cross-border trade in bonds and equities increased from 10 per cent of GDP in 1980 to between 150 and 250 per cent of GDP in 1995. At the same time, the worldwide value of foreign exchange trading has increased to a turnover of more than US$1200 billion per day (Chesnais, 1997).

We can draw two main conclusions from this discussion about the present internationalization in the advanced countries. First, the forms of competition are being drastically transformed. Access to knowledge and information, i.e. the ability to make the most of the present conditions, are a key factor affecting the competitiveness of nations, together with the more traditional ability to produce at lower prices and to acquire advanced technology by purchasing equipment goods.

Secondly, these changes in transactions and organizational phenomena, which are characteristic of this new phase of internationalization, are bound to be deeply influenced by country specificities. This is shown by the way nations have set up progressively more specific national systems of innovation and organized their specialized services. Even if there is a later trend towards some harmonization, the shift towards services has already influenced the growth of nations in country-specific ways. Let us now turn to the consequences of such changes on the growth regimes of nations.

How does Internationalization Affect the Growth Regimes of Nations?

The fact that economies are more open and that agents have greater international reach has changed the dynamics of economic growth. This does not stem so much from the increase of trade or FDI flows as a proportion GDP, but more from the qualitative change that increasing openness has brought in the forms of competition prevailing in the various economies. To illustrate the effect of this on the growth paths of the market economies, we shall develop a very general growth model similar to the cumulative causation model of Kaldor. A growth process is defined by the ways in which productivity gains are generated, how these gains are distributed, how they affect the various components of demand and, finally, how in turn these changes in demand generate further productivity gains. At this level of generality, the process may not be cumulative at all if the feedback effects are weak or non-existent.

The various 'ways', mentioned above, in which productivity gains are induced refer to the institutional fabric that governs the determination of wages, the working of labour markets, the type of competition in product markets, the rôle of money, and the rôle of the state, together with economic relations with other economies. The fact that we explicitly acknowledge that we are dealing with open market economies demonstrates that the generation of productivity gains and the composition of the growth of demand have an international dimension. It is therefore necessary to assess the external as well as the internal factors affecting economic change.

The easiest approach is to start with a brief assessment of an ideal type of growth pattern, which is supposed to have prevailed in the past. For the sake of clarity, we shall not deal with the wide variety of capitalist economies that presently exist, but will simply concentrate on the basic elements of a fordist growth regime in an open economy. In such a world, productivity gains are generated through the extension of the Taylorian organization of work. These gains are dependent on economies of scale and the mechanization of work, both of which are fuelled by an extension of home and overseas markets. The growth of both these markets will clearly benefit from the distribution of the productivity gains between wages and (relative) prices. For these reasons the wage labour nexus can be considered as the central structural form in a fordist growth regime (Petit, 1999b). In open economies it is complemented by a 'contained' rôle for external factors: external competition is basically determined by price differentials and is imperfect (given that price elasticities are low). Price differentials are themselves related to differences in levels of development. There is a catching-up process where countries lagging behind in their level of development can benefit from lower wages and unit costs. They are therefore more competitive in terms of price and this leads to both an increasing share of world demand for their goods and services and a greater opportunity to invest in new equipment, leading to a catch-up in terms of development and technology. The international consequences of the fordist growth regime are limited by the existence of a fixed exchange rate agreement (Bretton Woods) as well as by restrictions on the mobility of financial capital and the prevalence of price competition .

The changes of the last two decades have greatly transformed the above process in both its internal and external context. As argued in Petit (1999b), the central institutional nexus now revolves around the different types of competition. Forms of competition, as a structural phenomenon, have to be understood in a comprehensive way to include all the institutions, conventions, rules and practices which are reorganizing and extending the sphere of market activities. Forms of competition will be defined by characteristics of the product (such as its price and quality), as well as by those factors affecting its provision (e.g. communications, transport, distribution and finance), all of which involve tangible and intangible infrastructures.

A distinction between price and non-price competitiveness, and their relative importance, is necessary for some forms of competition. Changes in the other structural forms that Regulation Theory identifies to account for the whole institutional nexus on which economies rely (see Fig. 9.1), are greatly conditioned by changes in these forms of competition. Changes in financial markets have very obvious effects on the wage labour nexus and a marked impact on the structure of incomes. A great deal of re-regulation of activities with strong social externalities (from large service networks to health and education systems) will be necessary. But this will also be accompanied by a substantial transformation in international relations.

A large proportion of the flows of information and knowledge considered above are congruent with this general change in the functioning of product markets, which is leading to more sophisticated markets and differentiated products.

Part of the answer to the questions raised in the introduction to this chapter lies in clarifying how changes in the form of competition

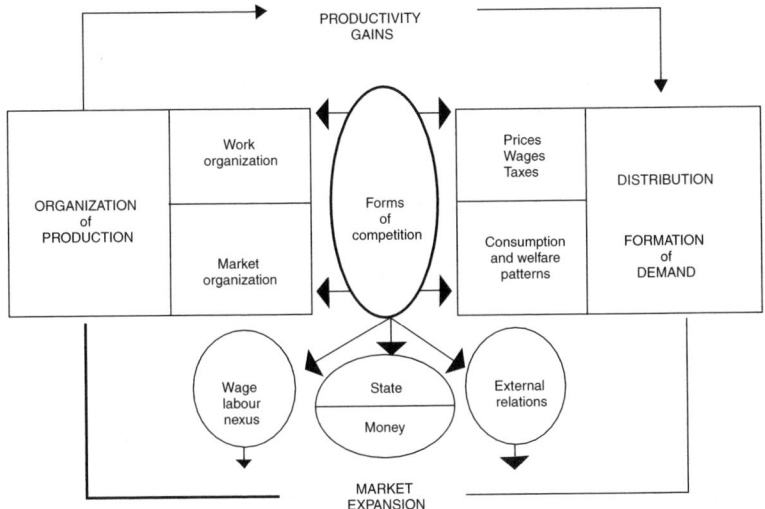

Figure 9.1: Institutional changes in the post-Fordist era: on the centrality of the forms of competition

have transformed the system of international relations of the open world economy. The general changes that we emphasize did, in effect, put an end to the above mechanisms of catching up that linked the growth paths of the various economies. The process of convergence, as we outlined above, came to a halt in the 1980s and 1990s (see, for example, Fagerberg and Verspagen, 1998, Petit, 1999a). In order to understand growth in this new interdependent world, it is necessary to assess the nature and role of the extended international linkages that economies have developed over the past few decades. A thorough analysis of this can help to identify the intermediations and externalities that determine the growth path of the national economy.

On the Forms of Internationalization in a New Growth Regime

The form that internationalization is currently taking can only be understood in terms of the pre-eminent role of the dynamics of the form of competition. We have therefore to consider to what extent specific international relations lead to a better knowledge and provision of products. We already suggested in assessing the mechanisms of the earlier catching-up processes that internationalization includes the issues of technology transfer and access to finance.

We need to add to these two factors a third institutional space which governs the international flows of goods and services, e.g. the regulations on trade and the basic intermediations of the large service networks, such as distribution, transport and communication.[9] These three components help to represent the structural form of international relations, if we take a comprehensive view of these sets of rules and institutions. This includes not only how they intervene, but also to whom they are particularly addressed.

Finally, the forms of internationalization will be defined by three components: the first refers to the 'governing' of international transactions in goods and services; the second to the prevailing regime of technology transfer; and the third to the access to international sources of finance. Table 9.1 summarizes some characteristics of this three-fold structural form. It shows the interdependencies between the various components and suggests that there is a complex relationship. Nevertheless, this recapitulation helps to clarify some of the common traits and differences and to stress how the various types of capitalism can experience synergies and complementarities as they develop their economic relations.

The properties of the forms of international relations, which are limited in our perspective to economic issues (and therefore abstract from the more important geo-strategic issues), are similar to those of the forms of competition. The kind of rules and governing bodies that these forms represent can be considered as a sub-space of the general forms of competition. It is necessary to appreciate two characteristics of these 'rules' to fully understand the impact of these forms of international relations. The first characteristic is the geographical level at which the rules apply, in other words whether it is local, national, regional or global. The second is the kind of agents to which they apply: whether they are individuals, households, small and medium enterprises, or large multinational firms. There is not a strict correspondence between the institutions under consideration and the geographical level or the kind of agents, and obviously the operating conditions of the set of rules and the governance of the bodies will differ. The understanding of the different modes of operation is crucial for our purpose.

To illustrate the two dimensions, we can refer to the cases of some markets where these dimensions are clearly identified.

An important case in this respect is the product markets, which are more or less governed at a global level by a set of rather autonomous international institutions and open international market-places. The

Table 9.1: The structural forms of international relations

	Field of transactions	Channels and means	Characteristics
Component 1	International flows of goods and services, as well as the logistics allowing international transactions	Commercial laws, trade agreements, regulations on health and safety, regulation of large intermediation networks, institutions of expertise and certification	Degree of globalization of markets, existence of specific international regime, relative extent of price and non-price competitiveness, bundling of goods and services, linkages and network externalities, differentiated rules for MNEs and SMEs
Component 2	International transfers of technologies of production or consumption, cross-fertilization of information and knowledge	Media, scientific publications, meetings and travels, tele-communications flows, professional culture and norms	International level of diffusion, existence of specific international regime (intellectual property rights), knowledge barriers, importance of tacit knowledge
Component 3	International financial flows	Currency regulations, monetary laws, banking regulations, ethics, practices and conventions in financial market places	Convertibility regime, degree of liberalization of financial flows, interaction with foreign national systems of financing, quality and international influence of national financial centres

notion of the international regime as developed by Krasner (1983) precisely describes this kind of situation It stresses that some markets have developed their own set of rules and conventions on an international basis, and therefore they operate directly at an international level. A standard example is the oil and primary products markets. The 'market' for intellectual property rights is also an example of what could become an international regime. Such an assessment, however, remains highly conditional, as it may underestimate the many reasons that could lead nation states or regions to keep some active role in the operation of such strategic 'markets'. Nevertheless, this last example shows how, for some markets, the geographical level of governance is at stake.

Another good example is the health and safety regulations, which are key issues in the organization of some product markets. The present conflict between supra-regional, national and intra-regional levels in the monitoring of beef markets in Europe is raising issues which, on two grounds, may concern many other product markets.

The first concerns problems of health and environment in the consumption of these products, and the risks that consumers, as individuals and collectively, are prepared to take in the face of uncertainty. The second concerns the effects of the production of these products on health and the environment and the extent to which the consumers, again either separately or as a group, are concerned for distant production sites and producers. All of this involves a consideration of risk-taking and ethical standards. This, at first glance, seems to concern only the first dimension of trade regulation (in Table 9.1), but, nevertheless, it also impinges on the preferences and tastes of consumers. These 'fundamentals' can be thought of as the 'technologies' of consumption or of production. This terminology leaves open the real possibility for the fundamentals to evolve, which is likely to occur. Therefore, the topic also concerns the second dimension of technology transfer that has been distinguished to assess the forms of internationalization. (see Table 9.1). As this argument can easily be extended to matters of finance, we conclude that the geographical level of the application of 'rules' and the governance of bodies is an essential issue for fully understanding all the dimensions of internationalization.

The same could be said for the kinds of agents to which these rules should apply. Examples will be taken this time from the financial world. Clearly many fiscal issues on capital movements (ranging from direct investment to portfolio investment) are aimed at monitoring the actions of a set of large multinationals and not at SMEs. These fiscal measures can even be differentiated according to the size of the capital flow. Similarly, the organization of patent systems (which is crucial for the still highly differentiated systems of intellectual property rights) is a strong weapon with which to discriminate against SMEs or, instead, help them *vis-à-vis* the large MNEs. The latter undertake most of the expenditure in R&D and, therefore, control most of the supply of patents. It should be noted that the patent systems in most countries are long-established institutions and are therefore highly national-specific. Having retained the three-dimensional form of internationalization and stressed the key differentiating factors that constitute the level and type of economic units to which they apply, we are now in a position to see how these forms relate to what we termed above as the 'new phase of internationalization'.

Clearly more agents have, in this new phase, access to international transactions. Consequently, we may consider that the extension of all these intangible transactions is an enabling factor for these agents. However, we cannot conclude that this move has extended uniformly to all the geographical levels of applications. Access is likely to be either very volatile or very specific. It is interesting to get a better view of the processes by which these extensions of international transactions are developing. In other words, we need to consider what are the characteristics of the fabric of connections that these broadening of market links imply? As many authors have stressed (see, for example, Altvater and Mahnkopf, 1996, and Thrift, 1998), 'global' markets, i.e. markets at some stage of internationalization, have become progressively more disembedded, in the sense of becoming more disassociated from their social base,[10] or more distanced, in Giddens's (1991) sense of the term. They have become structured through time and over space by a new set of devices, procedures, intermediations and technologies. Obviously, the intangible transactions we referred to earlier play a major role in the development of this fabric. But this fabric is subject to uncertainty that either may be occurring during a transitionary period or may be a more permanent phenomenon. A few important facts suggest that it is the latter. These include the fact that large MNEs find it necessary to concentrate on their areas of competence; that success may be quickly followed by failure for a particular enterprise; that the governance of shareholders imposes a binding discipline across the board for all activities; and that companies are engaging worldwide in many mergers and acquisitions. All these suggest fierce competition, which is full of uncertainty precisely at the time when information and knowledge abound. The problem of this 'reflexive capitalism' (to extend Giddens's notion to the context of growth regimes – see Lash and Urry, 1994) is basically that its organizational principles, which should help to take advantage of this greater access to information and knowledge in order to set up long-term strategies, are unclear. At no time has it been more obvious that market relations up to now have been strongly embedded in national social structures. We should view this disembedding process (and not in the absolute sense that the word globalization sometimes conveys) as a counterpart of the growth in influence of the hundreds of MNEs which, according to UNCTAD (1999), are the key international actors, with 25 per cent of world production and over 80 per cent of FDI.

Table 9.1 shows some of the links and issues that we have just discussed concerning the forms of internationalization. It suggests that the first dimension of these internationalization forms is now more influenced by the other two than has been the case in the past. These other two are the capacity to transfer technology and finance, both of which have become widely developed in the new phase of internationalization.

These transfers of technology and finance are linked to imports, as well as exports, and are concerned with the activities of both production and consumption. They involve the transfer of resources that economic agents may use in their production or consumption decisions. The question then arises as to the effect that the increase in these transfers is likely to have on the growth dynamics of countries. It may lead to the development of synergies and positive externalities, which would encourage the endogenous growth of countries. But it may also have counterproductive effects by increasing uncertainty, leading in turn to an inefficient degree of concentration and standardization. Countries, in the last two decades, have tried to rise to this challenge by strengthening their regional links, hoping that it would favour idiosyncratic dynamics.

To What Extent are Regional Levels Relevant for Policies to Increase Growth?

We shall now return to the argument that globalization is largely a regional phenomenon as far as production processes are concerned. We shall see whether the specific changes of the present internationalization phase, which we identified in the preceding section, are compatible with, or even reinforce, the opportunity for consistent intervention at regional levels.

Trade flows expanded more rapidly after a number of regional groups were established (such as the EU, ALENA in North America, MERCOSUR in South America ASEAN in South East Asia, and APEC in the Pacific Rim[11]). All these arrangements boosted intra-regional trade flows: in South East Asia they grew from one-fifth to one-third of trade flows between 1983 and 1993, in South America, from one-tenth to one-quarter. This phenomenon is also apparent in Europe and North America, although it is less pronounced.[12] Trade flows within Europe and North America were also accompanied by a marked development of intra-industry trade, i.e. trade within the same product group. By the mid-1990s, intra-industry trade represented between 60 and 70 per cent of trade flows in most EU countries (approximately 80 per cent in the UK and France and 50 per cent in Greece and Portugal, see OECD, 1996b, Table 1.8). Such intra-industry trade emphasizes the strong dynamics of product differentiation and integration. The levels of intra-industry trade, which were rather low in South East Asia until the end of the 1980s, developed rapidly in the 1990s to reach over 40 per cent total trade by the end of the decade.

Part of this intra-industry trade is undertaken between branches of the same firm. Depending on the sector, intra-firm flows can be very high. In the pharmaceutical, computer, semiconductor, and motor vehicle sectors they are as high as 70 per cent, while in other sectors, such as clothing and steel, they are as low as 7 per cent. The international division of production and distribution (imported goods may not be processed when they are exported) is all the more important with hi-tech products. These are also the sectors most eager to enter into technological cooperation at the worldwide level. As we have already noted, the great majority of technological alliances encompass non-EU partners (and most of the time the alliances are either with the US or Japanese firms). Most advanced hi-tech firms are effectively part of an international network and thus have accords with the world leaders in the industry (see Dunning, 1997). Looking at internationalization of R&D gives a similar picture, as for hi-tech industries, it is not limited to the regional level, but tends to be global from the very start.

There has been a long debate concerning the internationalization of R&D. R&D activities of multinational firms have for the most part, until the late 1980s, been undertaken in the multinationals' home countries (Patel and Pavitt, 1991). R&D activities are central to the activities which identify a firm, and any 'delocalization' to affiliate companies or any collaboration with competitors is thus surprising. However, the economics of R&D are complex, and imply highly strategic behaviour of large firms in particular.

Significant internationalization of R&D took place in the 1990s, but with large differences among countries. R&D expenditures by foreign affiliates in OECD countries in 1994 ranged from 2 per cent of total

R&D in Japan to 68 per cent in Ireland. Significant proportions are found in the UK (35 per cent), Germany (17 per cent), and France (15 per cent) (see Hatzichronoglou, 1998). Innovation systems are consequently being transformed with new external links that go beyond regional levels and are country-specific (see Patel and Pavitt, 1998; Cantwell and Harding, 1998). In such contexts, regional policies can help firms of the member countries to catch up with the technological frontier.

There may be more room for manoeuvre at the regional level in other sectors and/or with small and medium enterprises. Policies to coordinate the use and adaptation of technologies at the European level might reap the benefit of network externalities.

Data on the means to transfer technology or to innovate as given by the European Community Innovation Survey are interesting in this respect. They stress, for instance, the importance of the purchase of equipment as the most frequent source of technology inflows. They also show communication/services from other enterprises as the major source of technology outflows (see Table 9.2). This last is also an important source of technology inflows, which emphasizes the crucial role of intermediation played by other enterprises (including service firms). The consultancy services are as important as the hiring of skilled personnel (see Table 9.2). The data also stress sizeable differences between European countries, all of which underlines the fact that the purchase of equipment generally remains the primary source of technology transfer. This mechanism refers to the old model of catching up and we can either consider that the changes required to be made to the traditional model have been overestimated or, more likely, that changes take time to be completed (compared with the rate of change of the internationalization of R&D). The increasing role of other firms and services in technology transfer may therefore become as important as the purchase of equipment in technology transfer.

All this suggests that regional industrial policy could well influence the regime of technology transfer in all member countries, at least for SMEs and non-high-tech sectors. The form of intervention and the effect of such a policy may not be that clear. It is likely to be an indirect form of intervention, channelling information and knowledge in a coordinated way, rather than the traditional direct financial incentives to invest (which, moreover, are severely limited by free trade agreements). The effect of such network externalities on growth dynamics is even more uncertain. Even if the management of knowledge is highly valued in the business world, its effective impact on

Table 9.2: Relative importance of channels of technology transfer

	Italy	Germany	Belgium	UK	Netherlands	Denmark	Norway	France
Ranking of in-flows								
Use of others' inventions	5	6	4	4	6	5	4	4
R&D contracted out	6	5	4	6	3	6	6	1
Consultancy services	3	3	6	5	3	3	2	5
Purchase of other enterprises	8	7	7	7	7	7	7	6
Purchase of equipment	1	2	1	1	2	1	1	2
Communication/services from other enterprises	4	1	2	3	1	2	3	
Hiring skilled personnel	2	3	3	2	5	4	5	3
Other	7	8	8	8	8	8	8	
Ranking of out-flows								
Use of others' inventions	6	5	4	2	3	3	2	2
R&D contracted out	5	6	5	6	4	6	5	5
Consultancy services	4	3	3	4	2	4	3	4
Purchase of other enterprises	8	7	7	7	7	7	6	7
Purchase of equipment	1	4	6	5	6	2	8	3
Communication/services from other enterprises	3	1	2	1	1	1	1	1
Hiring skilled personnel	2	2	1	3	5	5	4	6
Other	7	8	8	8	8	8	7	

Source: Bosworth and Stoneman (1996); CIS data.

productivity and growth is difficult to measure. Taking into account the new forms of competition in product markets, and the increased role of non-price competitiveness, we can estimate that the impact is likely to be very important in those products that are differentiated according to the specific needs and tastes of the users and consumers. We can see from Table 9.3 of the European Community Innovation Survey that clients and customers are the second major source of innovation (following just behind the internal resources of the enterprise). This suggests that intervention in consumption technology (e.g. consumption patterns) could be the main channel for a policy to stimulate growth at a regional level. If member countries in a region have enough in common about the way they view the quality of life and the environment and they are ready to set guidelines for its preservation and improvement (a comprehensive view of what we called the technologies of consumption), then a structural policy could well be the means to increase growth and welfare at the regional level. Structural policy includes managing knowledge, norms, regulations and all the logistics of investigation and certification that go with it. An objective which could not be obtained in the present state of internationalization by small and medium-sized countries could thus be reached at regional level. The prerequisite of such a policy is a certain communality of basic choices and values which may not exist sufficiently (there is a critical mass problem here), or may require time to gather momentum. The political or democratic deficiencies that plague the development of regions give rise to some pessimism as to whether or not a successful outcome can ever be achieved.

A clear advantage that remains with regions, however, is due to the limitations of international institutions to deal with such large issues. Even an institution such as the recently created WTO cannot cope with the many contradictions that rapidly arise. Regional governance may remain the unavoidable first step towards a broader governance at world level.

We have scarcely mentioned so far the questions raised by access to international finance. The globalization of financial markets has for a long time been the pre-eminent aspect of globalization. In effect, financial markets, with their own prudential rules, have appeared to become totally divorced from their home base. This is not entirely true – even the most automated financial markets require a lot of tacit knowledge and personal contacts, which are strongly influenced by the host country. Furthermore, financial markets may themselves be segmented in various 'secondary' markets responding to various criteria, either in the fields of investment or in regarding ethical choices of investors. But it is chiefly with the banking systems that such differentiation can occur, according to the nature of the project to be financed or to the personality of the investor. Venture capital is a case in point. How various financial systems will adapt in order to finance more risky innovative businesses is interesting, as it is on the margin of both market-based and bank-based systems. Countries have resorted to various forms of intermediaries, which are supported by the facility of exit towards financial markets or by the caution of some affiliates of the banks. The diversity of solutions developed in Europe is striking (see the EVCA European Venture Capital Association annual report on the origins of investors and the conditions of exit of capital risk). It suggests that some coordination of the schemes facilitating their regional diffusion would have been beneficial for the region as a whole.

But once again the success of such structural policy depends on the capacity of member countries to share some common values at the regional level on which to base some positive discrimination in favour of those firms or consumers lacking the capacity to take advantage of the new context.

Conclusions

We have in this chapter argued that the developed economies are entering a new phase of internationalization rather than a final era of globalization. This new phase is characterized by the extension of intangible transactions, which enlarges the scope of economic agents. This enables firms, especially SMEs, and individuals to develop strategies at worldwide levels. The question was therefore to see how such transformations contributed to the growth of nations. It was noted that the present phase is also part of a large change in the dynamics of institutions in developed economies. Transformations of the forms of competition have come to dominate the evolution of the wage labour nexus that dominated the 'golden years of (industrial) capitalism'. In such an environment, the new phase of internationalization could be seen as part of this reshuffling of the forms of competition. The dynamics of the set of rules and institutions presiding over the forms of internationalization of each country has been categorized into three components, namely (i) the governance of trade flows, (ii) the regime of technology transfer, and (iii) the regime of access to international finance. In the new forms of competition, the regime of technology

Table 9.3: Sources of information for innovation

Source	Italy	Germany	Belgium	UK	Netherlands	Denmark	Norway	France	All countries
					Ranking of sources				
Within the enterprise	1	7	1	1	2	2	2	1	1
Within the group enterprises	10	12	6	9	9	9	10	7	14
Suppliers of material and components	4	4	4	3	3	3	4	5	5
Suppliers of equipment	3	6	3	5	4	4	3	4	3
Clients or customers	2	1	2	2	1	1	1	3	2
Competitors	6	4	7	4	6	5	7	9	6
Consultancy firms	9	11	14	13	12	14	13	14	9
University higher education	12	9	11	1	11	12	12	13	11
Government laboratories	13	12	13	14	1	11	11	12	13
Technical institutes	14	14	12	12	14	1	9	11	12
Patent disclosures	11	1	1	11	13	13	14	1	1
Conferences, journals	7	8	7	8	7	7	6	6	7
Fairs, exhibitions	5	2	5	6	5	6	5	2	4
Total (by country)	10	1	4	5	5	2	8	12	

Source: Bosworth and Stoneman (1996); CIS data

transfer and the regime of access to international finance strongly influence worldwide trade flows. We have shown the dimensions of information and knowledge management that these regimes of technology transfer represent. These seem a possible means of entry for structural policies aimed at favouring economic growth in developing synergies and positive externalities.

The conditions for such policies are rather stringent because in some cases the flows of information and knowledge are determined at the global level. For the sectors and the firms (mainly SMEs) where some monitoring would be effective, policies at a regional level may be appropriate. The magnitude of their impact largely depends on whether or not these policies are tied to some welfare-enhancing objectives on the users' side. It follows that such structural regional policies can only have macroeconomic effects if member countries agree widely enough on some common welfare and quality-of-life objectives.

Notes

1. Zysman (1995), for instance, considers that the role taken by South East Asian countries in trade (they grew from 6 per cent to 20 per cent of world trade between 1975 and 1995) and FDI flows is sufficient to constitute a new phase of internationalization.
2. See the survey on this issue presented in the second European report on Scientific and Technologic Indicators (European Commission, 1997, Chapter 11).
3. An average distribution of alliances in Europe is, according to the European Report on STI, 10 per cent purely national, 15 per cent intra-European and 75 per cent involving non-European firms.
4. According to KPMG Corporate Finance, M&A amounted to US$544 billion in 1998 and had reached US$608 billion in the first nine months of 1999, of which US$430 billion was in trans-border M&A by European firms.
5. See OECD (1999, Section 9.1).
6. According to the European Report on STI, Chapter 12. The percentage of course increases for smaller countries.
7. Studies on these effects, according to the European Report on STI (1997), are given on the web site http://www.academia.darmstadt.gmd.de/sweden
8. The area 'specialized business services' already mentioned is a mixture of many types of services, ranging from communication services, construction services, computer and information services, insurance and financial services, royalties and licence fees to other business services, such as renting, management consulting, marketing and engineering or recreational services.
9. Obviously any one of these three large service networks could have been singled out, as we did with the financial services. We simply assume that constraints on these three sectors would be less binding or closely linked

with a regulatory or legal issue and are therefore closely related to the component on tradeability.

10. The large numbers of mergers and acquisitions has further increased this feeling by cutting off the old multinationals from their initial national roots.
11. Such arrangements are all very different in nature. In Europe, governments are very active in promoting economic integration, while in South East Asia firms shoulder this responsibility.
12. Interestingly, Switzerland, a non-EU member, is one of the rare developed countries that did not increase its trade flows with its neighbouring countries (see Freudenberg, Gaulier and Unal-Kesenci, 1998).

References

Altvater, E. and Mahnkopf, B. (1996) *Grenzen der Globalisierung: Okonomie, Politik, Okologie in der Welkgesellschaft*, Munster, Westsfaliches Sampfboot.

Amable, B., Barre, R. and Boyer, R. (1997) Les systèmes d'innovation à l'ére de la globalisation, Paris, Economica.

Archibugi, D. and Michie, J. (1995) 'The Globalisation of Technology: a New Taxonomy', *Cambridge Journal of Economics*, 19, p. 121–140.

Archibugi, D. and Michie, J. (eds) (1997) Technological globalisation or national systems of innovation? in *Technology, Globalisation and Economic Performance*, Cambridge, Cambridge University Press.

Bairoch, P. and Kozul-Wright, R. (1998) 'Globalization myths: Some historical reflections on integration, industrialisation and growth in the world Economy' in R. Kozul-Wright and R. Rowthorn (eds) *Transnational Corporations and the Global Economy*, Basingstoke, Macmillan – now Palgrave, pp. 37–68.

Borrus, M. and Zysman, J. (1997) 'The Rise of Wintelism as the Future of Industrial Competition'. *Industry and Innovation*, volume 4, Number 2, December.

Bosworth, D. and Stoneman, P. (1996) *Technology, Transfer; Information Flows and Collaboration: an Analysis of the CIS*, Luxembourg, Eurostat.

Boyer, R. and Drache, D. (eds) (1996) *States against Markets. The Limits of Globalisation*, London, Routledge.

Cantwell, J. and Harding, R. (1998) 'The Internationalisation of German Companies' R&D *National Institute Economic Review*

Chesnais, F. (1997) *La mondialisation du capital*. Alternatives économiques. Paris, Syros.

Dunning, J. (ed.) (1997) *Governments, Globalization and International Businesses*, London, Oxford University Press.

European Commission (1997) 'Second European Report on S&T Indicators', DGXII, Brussels.

Fagerberg, J. and Verspagen, B. (1999) 'Modern Capitalism in the 1970s and 1980s', in M. Setterfield (ed.) *Growth, Employment and Inflation*, London, Macmillan – now Palgrave.

Fontagne, L., Freudenberg, M. and Peridy, N. (1997) "Intra Industry Trade and the Single Market: Quality Matters" *CEPR, Discussion Paper*, n°1953

Freudenberg, M., Gaulier, G. and Unal-Kesenci, D. (1998) "La régionalisation du commerce international", *Economie Internationale*, N°74,2°trimestre,

Giddens, A. (1991) *Modernity and Self Identity*, Cambridge, Polity Press.

Hatzichronoglou, T. (1998) 'L'internationalisation de la R-D industrielle: structure et tendances', DSTI/OCDE, 15–16 juin, Paris

Hecker, D. (1999) "High Technology Empoyment: a Broader View" *Monthly Labor Review*, June

Hirst, P. and Thompson, G. (1996) *Globalisation in Question*, Cambridge, Polity Press.

Kleinknecht, A. and Wengel, J. (1998) 'The Myth of Economic Globalisation', *Cambridge Journal of Economics*, 22:637–47.

Kozul Wright, R. and Rowthorn, R. (eds) (1998) *Transnational Corporations and the Global Economy*, Basingstoke, Macmillan – now Palgrave.

Krasner, S. D. (ed) (1983) *International Regimes*, Ithaca, Cornell University Press.

Lash, S. and Urry, J. (1994) *Economies of Signs and Space*, London, Sage Publications.

Lloyd, P. J. (1992) 'L'impact des accords commerciaux régionaux sur les échanges mondiaux', *Revue Economique de l'OCDE*, n°18, printemps.

Narula, R. (1996) *Multinational Investment and Economic Structure*, London, Routledge.

OECD (1996a) 'Technology, Productivity and Job Creation', vol 2, analytical report, Paris.

OECD (1996b) 'Globalisation of industry: overview and sector reports', Paris.

OECD (1999) 'Science, Technology and Industry Scoreboard: Benchmarking Knowledge-based Economies', Paris.

O'Shea, J. and Madigan, C. (1997) *Dangerous Company. The Consulting Powerhouses and the Businesses they Save and Ruin*, London, Nicholas Brealey.

Patel, P. (1995) 'Localized Production of Technology for Global Markets', *Cambridge Journal of Economics*, 19:141–153.

Patel, P. and Pavitt, K. (1991) 'Large Firms in the Production of the World's Technology: An Important Case of Non-Globalisation', *Journal of International Business Studies*, 22:1–21.

Patel, P. and Pavitt, K. (1998) 'National Systems of Innovation under Strain: the Internationalisation of Corporate R&D', paper presented at the conference Technologie et Connaissance dans la Mondialisation. Poitiers, 9–11 septembre.

Petit, P. (1998) 'Transnational service corporations in the process of globalisation' in R. Kozul-Wright and R. Rowthorn (eds) *Transnational Corporations and the Global Economy*, Basingstoke, Macmillan – now Palgrave.

Petit, P. (1999a) 'Integration and convergence in the European Union' in M. Setterfield (ed.) *Growth, Employment and Inflation*, Macmillan Press

Petit, P. (1999b) Structural Forms and Growth Regimes of the Post Fordist Era. *Review of Social Economy*, vol LVII, N°2, June

Petit, P. and Setterfield, M. (1999) 'Comprehensive Industrial Policies and the Contemporary Co-ordination Nexus', in Groenewegen, J. and Elsner W. *New Challenges to Industrial Policy*. Boston , Dordrecht, London, Kluwer Academic Publishers, Recent Economic Thoughts series, 1999

Reich, R. B. (1991) *The Work of Nations*, New York, Vintage Books.

Richardson, P. (1997) 'Mondialisation et interdépendance'. *Revue Economique de l'OCDE*, n°28, 1997/1.

Storper, M. (1997) *The Regional World: Territorial Development in a Global Economy*, The Guilford Press,

Strange, S. (1996) *The Retreat of the State*, Cambridge, Cambridge University Press.

Thrift, N. (1998) Virtual Capitalism: the Globalisation of Reflexive Business Knowledge. Working paper, University of Bristol, Dpt of Geography

Zysman, J. (1995) 'National Roots of a Global Economy', *Revue d'Economie Industrielle*, n°71, 1°trim.

10

The Keynesian Micro-Foundations of the Business Cycle: Some Implications of Globalization

Paul Ormerod

Introduction

In this chapter, we develop a microeconomic model of short-term output growth based upon interacting, heterogeneous individual agents operating under uncertainty according to Keynesian principles. Agents are heterogeneous and follow simple non-rational rules of behaviour which take into account each other's behaviour. The model is deliberately parsimonious, and the agents do not exhibit learning behaviour. It is not necessary to invoke any form of exogenous shock in the model, and the cycle is purely endogenous, essentially arising from the existence of heterogeneous agents operating under uncertainty.

Nevertheless, simulations of the model show that it offers an empirical account of the properties of the US business cycle that is decidedly superior to that of Real Business Cycle models. The aggregate output growth series that emerges from their activities has time-series properties that, on a standard range of criteria, are very similar to the cyclical properties of post-war US GNP growth.

An important feature of the model is that the firms are different in terms of size, with the size distribution being based upon American evidence. Other things being equal the model implies that the greater the degree of concentration of size, the greater is the amplitude of the cycle. This further implies that, in so far as globalization produces an increase in concentration, it will be associated with a greater degree of output variability over the course of the cycle. This implication would be offset if globalization reduced the degree of uncertainty which agents felt they faced. Even calibrated on US post-war data, the model suggests that occasional long and/or deep recessions are an inherent feature of the economy. A simulation of the model over a period of 1000 years suggests that a recession in which the cumulative fall in output is more than 5 per cent takes place on average approximately every 50 years.

The next section of this chapter sets out the economic basis of the model, followed by a description of the simulation properties of the model, particularly with respect to comparisons with actual American output data. We then go on to consider the implications, with particular reference to globalization.

The Microeconomic Model of Interacting Keynesian Agents

All the agents in our model are companies, which is very much in keeping with Keynes's view that the primary source of fluctuations over the course of the business cycle is the corporate sector. The model is populated by heterogeneous individual companies operating under uncertainty. The firms are of different size, and reflect the relative size distribution of the 500 largest companies in the USA. Each individual firm decides its own rate of growth of output and its own rate of change of sentiment about the future. The model evolves in discrete time steps, and in each of these steps (periods) the majority of agents update their previous decisions on output and sentiment. A key feature of the model is that firms interact with each other by taking account of the decisions of other companies in their own decisions on the output and sentiment variables.

The key question that every firm must decide during any particular period is the rate of growth of the output that it will produce in the next period. Once this decision has been made, the firm is stuck with it. When the company arrives in this next period, it is allowed to decide a different growth rate for the following period, but not to revise the previous decision on this period's growth.

Obviously, this is somewhat artificial, but it is not completely unreasonable. For in the very short run, there are often substantial costs involved in altering previous decisions about how much to produce. Contracts have been placed with suppliers, the workforce has been alerted as to how much effort will be needed, indeed employees may have been either taken on or sacked depending upon the circumstances, the marketing programme will be committed, and so on. In these circumstances, agents act according to a straightforward rule in order to decide how quickly output should either be expanded or contracted in the next period. They are very short-sighted, and look no further ahead than this. In other words, they are satisficers and not maximizers.

One factor that weighs in a company's decision on how much to alter the amount produced in the next period is the rate of growth at which output is actually changing during the current period. There are costs and difficulties of altering the amount that a firm is producing by large amounts, whether up or down. So a certain amount of inertia is built into the system. But, in addition and more importantly, in deciding the rate at which its own output is to change in the next period, each firm pays great attention to the general level of sentiment, the degree of optimism or pessimism about the future, and how this is changing. This is very much in the spirit of Keynes, who set great store on the role of expectations and the general level of confidence in determining the outcome of the economy, both in the short run and, through decisions on investment, in the longer term.

In terms of the formal model, we let $X_i(t)$ be the growth rate of output of agent i at time t, and $\bar{X}(t)$ the overall growth of output of the population at time t, weighted according to the sizes of the agents (with weights equal to $w_i(t)/W(t)$, where w_i is the size of each agent and $W(t)$ is the size of the total economy). In other words, $\bar{X}(t)$ is simply the weighted sum of the individual $X_i(t)$ values. The degree of optimism or pessimism about output growth in the future held by the ith agent at time t is given by $Y_i^s(t)$, and the (weighted) aggregate of these individual decisions by $\bar{Y}^s(t)$. We use the superscript 's' to stand for 'sentiment', to emphasize that it is not the conventional concept of expectations. The $Y_i^s(t)$ should be thought of as expressing sentiment (optimism/pessimism) about change in the future, rather than being based in some sense on 'optimal' forecasts of the rate of growth of output at some specific point in the future. Keynes himself was deeply sceptical about the latter approach, arguing that 'human decisions . . . cannot depend on strict mathematical expectation, since the basis for marking such calculations does not exist' (Keynes, 1936, pp. 162–3).

In each time period, any firm decides its rate of growth of output, $X_i(t)$. The growth rate of output of agent i in this period is based on a combination of the firm's output growth in the previous period, and the aggregate sentiment in the previous period about future output growth, i.e.

$$(1 - \alpha) X_i(t - 1) + \alpha \bar{Y}^s(t - 1) \qquad (10.1)$$

This represents the rate of growth in the absence of any circumstances that are particular to agent i. The interaction between individual agents takes place through the $\bar{Y}^s$ variable, so that the sentiment of other agents about the rate of growth of output in the future affects the decision on the rate of growth of output taken by agent i.

An implication of Equation (10.1) is that firms feel that there are constraints that operate on their output decisions. It is the aggregate state of sentiment, which could be deduced from newspapers such as the *Financial Times* or *Wall Street Journal*, which is a determinant of any revision to the growth of output of the ith agent. In other words, companies feel that, for example, demand may be a limiting factor on them in the future, and that one way of trying to judge the likely state of demand is via aggregate sentiments about growth in the future. The general level of business optimism or pessimism about the future is inescapably linked with uncertainty, which in turn leads to the important property of the model that the individual agents each take different decisions at any point in time.

Given the existence of uncertainty about the future and the fact that the agents are heterogeneous, each agent may interpret any given level or change in overall sentiment about the future differently. In other words, each agent may draw more or less optimistic conclusions from any given value of the sentiment variable, $\bar{Y}^s$ $(t-1)$.

We do not require that any individual agent is consistently more or less optimistic than any other over time with respect to these interpretations, *but simply that at each point in time, because of uncertainty, agents differ*. In terms of the sentiment variable, $\bar{Y}^s$, there may also be a secondary source of uncertainty. Despite the large amount of information about the sentiment variable available in the financial media, there is no single, published measure of the sentiment variable at any point in time, so firms may be uncertain, and hence differ in their interpretations, about the level of the sentiment variable in the previous period.

In short, *uncertainty means that each heterogeneous agent operates in a different way to every other agent*. There is uncertainty at any point in time about the precise level of business sentiment about the future. And there is uncertainty about what any perceived level of sentiment means for decisions by any particular firm about what its rate of growth of output should be in the period immediately ahead.

This is introduced formally into the model by modifying Equation (10.1). The growth rate of agent i is set according to:

$$X_i(t) = (1 - \alpha) X_i(t - 1) + \alpha [\, \bar{Y}^s(t - 1) + \varepsilon_i(t)] \qquad (10.2)$$

where $\varepsilon_i(t)$ is a random variable with mean zero and variance v_1.

It is important to note, even at the risk of over-emphasizing the point, that in each time period companies do *not* share the same ε. The variable ε is *not* a degree of uncertainty that is common to all firms, but each firm in each period has its own ε. In other words, ε must *not* be regarded as a common, exogenous shock that all firms experience.

The sentiment of the ith agent about the rate of growth of output in the future is derived using similar principles, which can be discussed more briefly. In the absence of circumstances particular to agent i, its sentiment is a simple function of the ith agent's sentiment in the previous period, and of the aggregate rate of growth of output in the previous period:

$$(1 - \beta)\ \bar{Y}^s\ (t - 1) - \beta\ \bar{X}\ (t - 1) \qquad (10.3)$$

This differs from Equation (10.1) in that there is a minus sign in front of the aggregate variable, $\bar{X}$. Other things being equal, the faster that aggregate output grows, the more pessimistic sentiments become about future output growth. This follows from Keynes's *own* definition of the business cycle, or what he called the trade cycle in Chapter 22 of the *General Theory*:

> By a *cyclical* movement we mean that as the system progresses in, e.g. the upward direction, the forces propelling it upwards at first gather force and have a cumulative effect on one another but gradually lose their strength until at a certain point they tend to be replaced by forces operating in the opposite direction; which in turn gather force for a time and accentuate one another, until they too, having reached their maximum development, wane and give place to their opposite.
>
> (Keynes, 1936, pp. 313–14.)

A mathematical approximation to this description is, of course, that of a simple oscillator, and hence the negative sign on $\bar{X}\ (t - 1)$ in Equation (10.3).

Interaction between agents takes place in Equation (10.3) through the $\bar{X}$ term. The decisions of all other agents on the rate of growth of output influences the sentiment of the ith agent about the rate of growth in the future. Heterogeneity of agents is again introduced, by allowing agents to differ at any point in time on their interpretations of what any given value of $\bar{X}$ actually implies. The sentiment formed about the rate of growth of output of agent i in the current period is therefore given by

$$Y_i^s(t) = (1 - \beta)\, Y_i^s\,(t-1) - \beta\,[\bar{X}\,(t-1) + \eta_i\,(t)] \qquad (10.4)$$

where $\eta_i(t)$ is a random variable with mean zero and variance v_2.

Again, it is important to note that in each period each firm has its own value for η, and this latter variable does *not* have a value which is common across all firms.

In summary, our model comprises Equations (10.2) and (10.4):

$$X_i(t) = (1 - \alpha)\, X_i(t-1) + \alpha\,[\bar{Y}^s\,(t-1) + \varepsilon_i(t)] \qquad (10.2)$$

$$Y_i^s(t) = (1 - \beta)\, Y_i^s(t-1) - \beta\,[\bar{X}\,(t-1) + \eta_i(t)] \qquad (10.4)$$

The key economic content of the model is the assumption that agents are heterogeneous, which given the existence of uncertainty leads to them behaving differently. This can be seen as follows. Suppose we removed this aspect of the model, and worked instead with Equations (10.1) and (10.3). Setting the sum of the weights used on individual agents equal to 1, these can be rewritten as a simple pair of difference equations in $\bar{X}$ and $\bar{Y}^s$:

$$\bar{X}\,(t) = (1 - \alpha)\,\bar{X}\,(t-1) + \alpha\,\bar{Y}^s\,(t-1) \qquad (10.5a)$$

$$\bar{Y}^s\,(t) = -\beta\,\bar{X}\,(t-1) + (1 - \beta)\,\bar{Y}^s\,(t-1) \qquad (10.5b)$$

The dynamics of this system of equations can be analysed quite readily by forming a matrix of its parameters and calculating the eigenvalues. For most economically meaningful pairs of values of a and β (i.e. $0 < \alpha < 1$ and $0 < \beta < 1$), the eigenvalues are complex but with real parts that lie between 0 and 1. Therefore the system of equations given by (10.5a) and (10.5b) gives rise in general to damped oscillations. It is the existence of uncertainty and the consequent introduction of the terms $\varepsilon_i(t)$ and $\eta_i(t)$ into Equations (10.2) and (10.4) which gives to the model a pattern of behaviour that is quite distinct from this.

Despite its simplicity, the model does capture many of the aspects of economic behaviour usually associated with Keynesianism and, as we shall see, its solutions have properties that are very similar to those of actual business cycle data, without having to invoke exogenous shocks of any kind.

Model Simulations and Business Cycle Data

In this section, we report the properties of simulations of our model with those of the actual data series on quarterly US real GNP growth over the period 1947Q2 through 1997Q3. These are discussed in more detail in Ormerod and Campbell (1998). The simulations are made over 200 periods, to give data series of similar length to the actual US output growth. The results we present are, in general, summaries of a total number of 1000 simulations, each carried out over 200 periods.

Our interest is in cyclical fluctuations in growth, and so the model solutions are compared with actual growth net of its mean value, using seasonally adjusted data. It would be very easy to introduce a seasonal element to our model, but this would not add in any meaningful way to its economic content. In the first instance, we discuss the ranges over which both the aggregate output growth and the output growth of individual agents typically move, and examine the typical correlations between the rates of growth of output of individual agents over time. We then move on to discuss the time-series properties of the aggregate output growth variable.

Table 10.1 sets out the summary statistics for actual growth and for the average of the output growth variable, $\bar{X}$, in 1000 simulations. There are two aspects of the simulations that concern the results for individual agents. The first of these points can be dealt with briefly. The aggregate output growth variable in the simulations moves within a typical range of around –0.03 to +0.03. The range for the typical individual agent is larger, but not dramatically so, being from –0.09 to +0.09, which seems realistic. Secondly, the model is set up with each of the agents representing a company and taking decisions on short-term output growth, so in its present form the relative volatility of various economy-wide aggregates such as consumption and investment is not available.

Table 10.1: Summary statistics of real US GNP growth (net of its mean) and the average of 1000 model simulations

	Real US GNP growth	Simulated growth
Minimum	–0.0317	–0.0291
1st quartile	–0.0066	–0.0074
3rd quartile	0.0063	0.0073
Maximum	0.0321	0.0290
Standard deviation	0.0107	0.0109

However, a widely accepted property of business cycles is that output changes across broadly defined sectors move together over time. In its present basic form, our model does not lend itself to an obvious aggregation of agents into groups representing, say, the car or alcohol producing industries. Any such aggregation would be purely artificial. But with the current model we can examine the cross-correlations in output growth between each of the agents in the population, and these are summarized in Table 10.2.

In other words, there are, almost universally, positive and statistically highly significant correlations between the period-by-period growth of output of individual firms. The correlations are relatively small, but this seems entirely realistic. For example, although firms within the same industrial sector will be affected in similar ways by developments in the aggregate economy, much of their marketing activity is devoted to struggles with their direct competitors over market share, which can and do fluctuate. So correlation of the short-run changes in output between firms in the same sector need not be high.

Real business cycle models have been criticized strongly in the recent literature for their inability to replicate key qualitative features of cyclical movements of the actual data. Examples of such criticism are Cogley and Nason (1995), Eichenbaum (1995), Rotemberg and Woodford (1996) and Watson (1993). There are two serious shortcomings of real business cycle models in this context. Both the autocorrelation function and the spectral properties of their simulated data are quite different from those of the actual data (although given that the power spectrum is the Fourier transform pair of the autocorrelation function, it is entirely to be expected that deficiencies in one of these aspects are reflected in the other).

The simulated data from RBC models is *qualitatively* different from the actual US data. The actual data has low order positive autocorrelation, and then negative but insignificant autocorrelation at higher order.

Table 10.2: Summary of cross-correlations between the period-by-period output growth of each of the 500 individual agents

Minimum	–0.08
1st quartile	0.19
Median	0.24
Mean	0.24
3rd quartile	0.29
Maximum	0.51

Simulations of RBC models, as noted for example by Cogley and Nason (1995) produce data that is either complete white noise or is negatively autocorrelated at almost every lag. In terms of its spectral properties, actual data has a power spectrum that is concentrated at the frequencies corresponding to those of the business cycle, noted by Cogley and Nason, for example, to be between 2.33 and 7 years per cycle, with maximum power of the spectrum at roughly 3.2 years per cycle. In general, RBC-simulated data has a flat power spectrum, indicating that business cycle components are no more important than components of any other frequency.

Both the ACF and the power spectrum of our simulated data are very similar to that of actual data. The first two autocorrelation coefficients of the actual quarterly data over the 1947–97 period are 0.37 and 0.25 respectively, both of which are significantly different from zero on the usual criteria, given that an approximation to the standard error on the coefficients is $1/\pm n$, where n is the sample size. The third coefficient has a point estimate of 0.01, and the coefficients at four through eight lags are negative but insignificant.

The ACF of the actual data and the average of the ACFs of the simulated data are plotted in Fig. 10.1. The simulated data clearly replicates

Figure 10.1: Autocorrelation function (ACF) of actual and simulated data

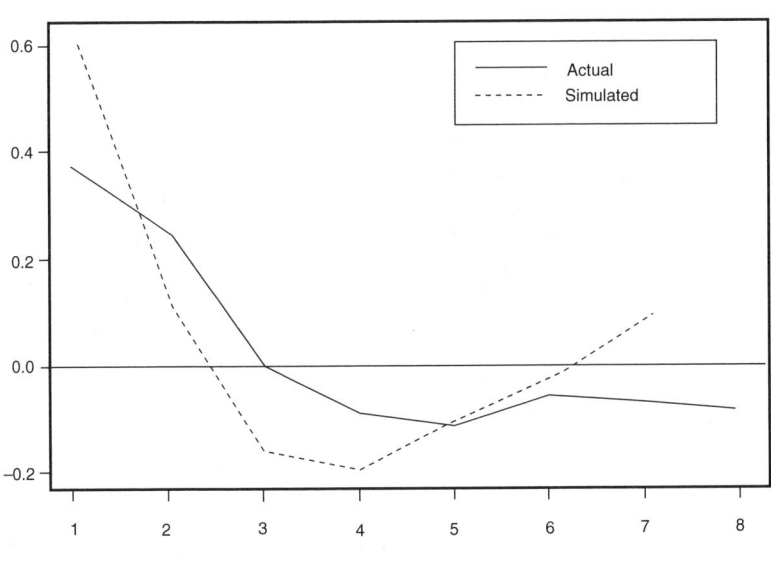

qualitatively the actual data, exhibiting positive low order autocorrelation, and negative autocorrelation at higher lags. Over the first eight lags, the coefficients of the ACF of actual data sum to 0.27, and those of simulated data to 0.29.

The spectrums of both the actual and simulated data are both concentrated at frequencies that correspond to those of the business cycle, with the simulated being somewhat more concentrated than the actual.

The degree of concentration of the data at business cycle frequencies is, however, not strong. An important reason why this is the case was advanced many years ago by Burns and Mitchell (1946). In their classic NBER work on the US business cycle, they argued that 'the sequence of changes is recurrent but not periodic; in duration cycles vary from more than one year to ten or twelve years'. In summary, unlike real business cycle models, our simple model replicates the main qualitative features of actual US output growth. It is deliberately parsimonious in its structure, but nevertheless the calibrations of simulations of the model against actual business cycle data gives the model initial credibility.

Implications for Globalization

An important assumption of the model is that the individual agents have different weights. In other words, the firms are of different sizes. This merely reflects reality in the developed economies, where the very largest firms are very much larger than, say, the 500th largest firm, which itself may well be huge in terms of absolute size.

The implications can be seen when we consider a formal analytical solution of the model. Details of the derivation are given in the Appendix. (Even though such a solution can be derived, it is more convenient, given its complexity, to investigate the quantitative properties of the model by simulation.)

The expression for overall output growth in the model can be reduced to a damped pendulum being driven by a stochastic forcing term:

$$\Delta^2 \bar{X}(t) + (\alpha + \beta) \Delta \bar{X}(t) + 2\alpha\beta \bar{X}(t) = F$$

F consists of terms such as

$$\bar{\varepsilon}(t) = \sum \frac{w_i(t)}{w(t)} \varepsilon_i(t)$$

By the rule of adding random variables, the variance of $\bar{\varepsilon}\,(t)$ is going to be considerably smaller than the variance of $\varepsilon_i(t)$. By the same reasoning, when considering a system with a larger number of smaller agents, the sum is over a greater number of random variables, hence leading to a smaller forcing term variance. Consequently, the amplitude of the cycle will be lower in an economy which has many small firms compared to one which is dominated by a small number of large ones. To the extent that globalization further concentrates the distribution of firm sizes, the model implies that, other things being equal, the amplitude of the business cycle will become larger.

This could in principle be offset if the level of uncertainty facing firms were reduced – in the model, this amounts to reducing the variances of ε and η. Even working with values of these calibrated on the post-war US experience, we can see that in the longer run, long and deep recessions are an integral feature of capitalist economies.

The model was simulated over 4000 periods – 1000 years – and the distribution of both the duration in years and the cumulative size of recessions was examined. A recession is defined in this context as being a year in which the overall rate of growth of output is less than zero. The model is a model of the cycle and not of long-term growth, so it is calibrated against the actual data purely in terms of the cycle, i.e. the actual data has its mean underlying growth rate removed. To obtain the frequency of recessions from the simulated model output, the mean annual growth rate of the US economy since World War II (just under 2 per cent in real per capita terms) is added to all observations.

Figure 10.2 shows the distribution of the duration of recessions. Recessions are rather frequent over the long run, a feature which is certainly reflected in the experience of the capitalist economies over the past 100–150 years.

The cumulative size of the fall in output during a recession is shown in Fig. 10.3. The data are grouped into bands of one percentage point, so the simulations of the model show just over 60 recessions in which the total fall in output was between 0 and 1 per cent, around 50 when the cumulative fall was between 1 and 2 per cent, and so on. Interestingly, there are 19 recessions in which the cumulative fall in output is over 5 per cent, approximately once every 50 years.

To the extent that globalization concentrates the size of firms, and to the extent that there is no offsetting reduction in the overall level of uncertainty that companies face, the distributions of both the duration and size of recessions can be expected to become shifted to the right over time.

Figure 10.2: Distribution of duration of recessions, years. Model simulated over 1000 years

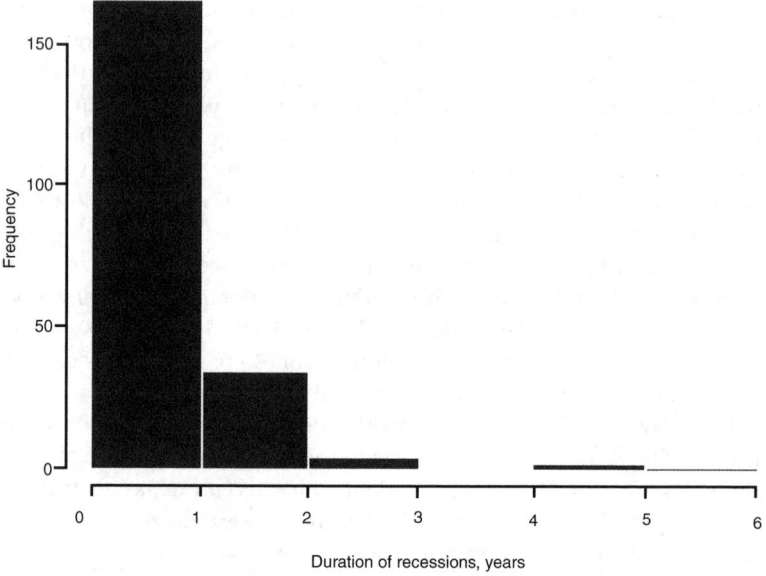

Figure 10.3: Distribution of size of recessions. Model simulated over 1000 years

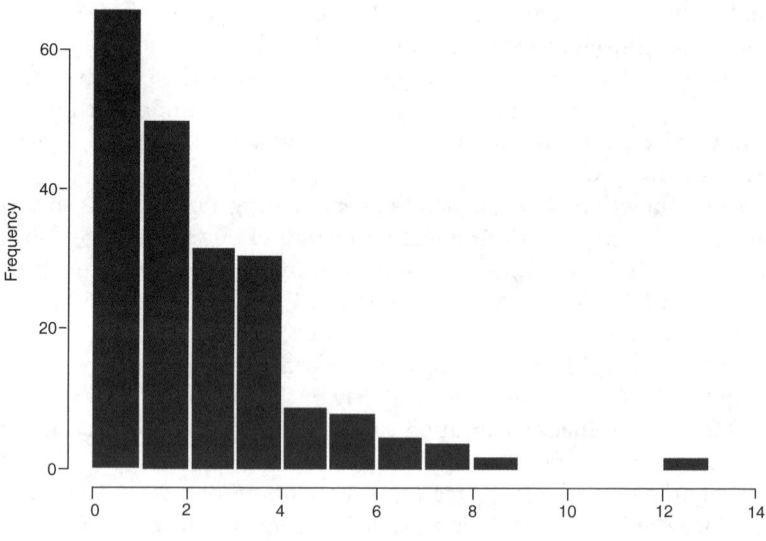

Conclusion

In this chapter, we develop a microeconomic model of short-term output growth based upon interacting, myopic, heterogeneous individual agents operating on Keynesian principles. The individual agents represent firms that differ in size, and are heterogeneous with respect both to decisions on output and to sentiment about future output growth. The decisions on the output growth of each agent are influenced by aggregate sentiment about the growth of output in the future, so that the decisions of others affects directly the behaviour of each agent. The sentiment on future output growth of each agent depends upon the previous value of his or her sentiment, and on the aggregate rate of growth of output. Again, through this latter term the decisions of other agents directly affect the behaviour of each individual agent.

We compare the properties of the output of 1000 simulations of the model over 200 periods with that of the post-war US real quarterly GNP growth over the same number of periods, net of its mean. The model is calibrated so that the output growth variable has the same range of movement as that of the actual data. A widely accepted property of business cycles is that output changes across broadly defined sectors move together over time. In its present basic form, our model does not lend itself to an obvious aggregation of agents into groups representing different sectors. But the correlations between the growth rates of output of the individual agents in our model are generally positive and substantially different from zero, a result which is compatible with this particular stylized fact about business cycles.

The recent literature shows that the simulated data of real business cycle models do not replicate two key features of US short-term growth, namely the existence of significant positive autocorrelation at low order lags and then negative but insignificant autocorrelation at higher order lags, and the concentration of the power spectrum at frequencies which correspond to those of the business cycle.

In contrast to RBC models, our Keynesian model of interacting micro-agents does replicate qualitatively these key features of actual data.

Moreover, our model does not rely in any way on exogenous shocks. The cyclical behaviour which it exhibits in aggregate arises endogenously from the interaction of individual agents at the micro-level.

Our model is obviously a drastic simplification of reality. But the interaction of individual agents operating on Keynesian principles produces, endogenously to the model, a series for aggregate output growth whose qualitative properties are very similar to those of post-war US quarterly GNP growth. An implication of the model is that, if globalization further concentrates the size distribution of firms, the amplitude of the business cycle will increase. This could in principle be offset if policies could be found which reduce the overall level of uncertainty faced by companies.

The model suggests that recessions of considerable duration and size will occur quite naturally under capitalism, and that, other things being equal, these will become more frequent as the process of globalization intensifies.

Acknowledgements

I am grateful to Rod Gibson, particularly for the Appendix, and to Michael Campbell and participants at the conference held at Gonville and Caius College, Cambridge, on 9–11 September 1999 for comments on an earlier draft of this chapter.

Appendix: Derivation of an Analytical Solution of the Model

$$X_i(t+1) = (1-\alpha)X_i(t) + \alpha[\bar{Y}(t) + \varepsilon_i(t)] \qquad (10.1A)$$
$$Y_i(t+1) = (1-\beta)Y_i(t) - \beta X[\bar{Y}(t) + \eta_i(t)] \qquad (10.2A)$$

Let the size of each agent be $w_i(t)$ and the total economy be of size $W(t) = \sum_i w_i(t)$.

Then the growth rate of the whole economy is given by

$$\bar{X}(t) = \sum_i X_i(t)\frac{w_i(t)}{W(t)}$$

Each w_i is dynamically related to the corresponding growth rate by

$$w_i(t+1) = w_i(t)[1 + X_i(t)] \qquad (10.3A)$$

Equation (10.1A) can be partially solved by expressing it as an 'integral' equation

$$X_i(t) = (1-\alpha)^t X_i(0) + \alpha(1-\alpha)^t \sum_{\tau=0}^{t-1}[\bar{Y}(\tau) + \varepsilon_i(\tau)](1-\alpha)^{-(\tau+1)} \qquad (10.4A)$$

The growth rate for the whole economy can now be reached by multiplying Equation (10.4A) through by $\frac{w_i(t)}{W(t)}$ and summing over i:

$$\overline{X}(t) = (1-\alpha)^t \overline{X}(0) + \alpha(1-\alpha)^t \tag{10.5A}$$

$$\times \left[\sum_{\tau=0}^{t-1} \overline{Y}(\tau)(1-\alpha)^{-(\tau+1)} + \sum_{\tau=0}^{t-1} \sum_i \frac{w_i(t)}{W(t)} \varepsilon_i(\tau)(1-\alpha)^{-(\tau+1)} \right]$$

An exactly similar equation exists for $\overline{Y}(t)$.
Dividing through by $(1-\alpha)^t$ and taking differences leads to

$$\Delta\overline{X}(t) + \alpha\overline{X}(t) = \alpha\overline{Y}(t) + \alpha(1-\alpha)^{t+1}\Delta\left[\sum_i \frac{w_i(t)}{W(t)} \sum_{\tau=0}^{t-1} \varepsilon_i(\tau)(1-\alpha)^{-(\tau+1)} \right] \tag{10.6A}$$

Similarly for $\overline{Y}(t)$

$$\Delta\overline{Y}(t) + \beta\overline{Y}(t) = -\beta\overline{X}(t) - \beta(1-\beta)^{t+1}\Delta\left[\sum_i \frac{w_i(t)}{W(t)} \sum_{\tau=0}^{t-1} \eta_i(\tau)(1-\beta)^{-(\tau+1)} \right] \tag{10.7A}$$

Taking differences of Equations (10.6A) and substituting Equations (10.7A) and (10.6A) back in gives

$$\Delta^2\overline{X}(t) + (\alpha+\beta)\Delta\overline{X}(t) + 2\alpha\beta\overline{X}(t) = F \tag{10.8A}$$

The left-hand side represents a damped pendulum, and the right-hand side a forcing term F.
F is quite ugly and of course hides an implicit X_i dependence via w_i.
It is reasonable, at least for short stretches of time, to consider the size of agents to be relatively static, i.e. the weights are independent of time. This allows us to see the essential structure by simplifying the forcing term to

$$F = \alpha\Delta\overline{\varepsilon}(t) + \alpha\beta\left[\overline{\varepsilon}(t)\right] + \overline{\eta}(t)] \tag{10.9A}$$

The bar represents the weighted sum of the components. F is a random variable (although serially correlated). The important point is that if the number of agents in the sum is made larger, then the variance of this forcing term will decrease, tending to zero for an infinite economy.

References

Burns, A. F. and Mitchell, W. C. (1946) *Measuring the Business Cycle*, Washington, DC, National Bureau of Economic Research.
Cogley, T. and Nason, J. M. (1995) 'Output dynamics in real business cycle models', *American Economic Review*, vol. 85, no. 3, pp. 492–51.

Eichenbaum, M. (1995) 'Some comments on the role of econometrics in economic theory', *Economic Journal*, vol.105, no.433, pp.1609–21.

Keynes, J. M. (1936) *The General Theory of Employment, Interest and Money*, London, Macmillan.

Ormerod, P. and Campbell, M. (1998) 'A model of the US business cycle with interacting, non-rational individual agents', mimeo, Volterra Consulting, London.

Rotemberg, J. J. and Woodford, M. (1996) 'Real business cycle analysis and forecastability', *American Economic Review*, vol.86, no.I, pp.71–89.

Watson, M. W. (1993) 'Measures of fit for calibrated models'. *Journal of Political Economy*, vol. 101, no.6, pp.1011–1041.

11
An Historical Perspective on Speculative Bubbles and Financial Crises: Tulipmania and the South Sea Bubble

Michelle Baddeley and John McCombie

Introduction

The rapid pace of globalization over the last decade or so, together with the deregulation of financial markets, has raised concerns about the increasing fragility of the world financial markets. However, as Kindleberger (1996) has shown in his *Manias, Panics and Crashes*, the problems of the instability of financial assets and commodities may be traced back to the seventeenth century. He cites numerous examples of rapid increases in prices being followed by an even quicker collapse. Such an event, when the price of an asset (or commodity) increases rapidly *solely* because investors expect it to happen, is termed a 'speculative bubble'.[1]

In this chapter, we first briefly review the different methodologies that lie behind the various explanations of speculative bubbles. The consequences of which approach is adopted are not innocuous. If speculative bubbles are driven by 'irrational' forces, then this poses serious questions about the efficient markets hypothesis.

In the second part of the chapter, we revisit two of the earliest bubbles, namely Tulipmania and the South Sea Bubble. We have taken a certain liberty in our choice given the theme of the conference is globalization and financial crises. This is because while the South Sea Bubble was part of the first international financial crisis, the same cannot be said of Tulipmania, which affected only Holland. However, there are two reasons for choosing these incidents. The first is to show that speculative manias are nothing new and to consider two fascinating historical examples of financial crises. Secondly, both examples have recently been subject to a major revisionist interpretation. Garber (1989, 1990), in particular, has argued that neither crash can be viewed as the result of mania, herd behaviour, and so on, along Minsky–Kindleberger lines. They can instead be explained simply in terms of a rational response to changing 'fundamentals' and should not be regarded as bubbles at all.[2] We therefore examine these case studies to see whether this argument stands up to scrutiny.

Theoretical Perspectives on Bubbles

There are three types of speculative bubble described in the literature: rational bubbles, contagion bubbles and irrational bubbles. Each of these bubble types is associated with a different conception of rationality and uncertainty. Rational bubbles, such as those described by Blanchard and Watson (1982), emerge in an ergodic world of strong-form rational expectations. In Topol's (1991) model, contagion bubbles are described as existing in an ergodic world of weak-form rational expectations.[3] Alternative models of irrational bubbles and manias, such as those described by Keynes (1936), Minsky (1982) and Kindleberger (1996), are developed assuming non-ergodicity, i.e. assuming that reality is transmutable and changeable. Furthermore, different approaches incorporate a different understanding of the nature of uncertainty: in rational expectations models, risk is assumed to be measurable and the probability estimates of individuals are assumed to coincide with some objective probability distribution. In contrast, in the models of Keynes and Minsky, the future is unknown, unknowable and unmeasurable (Davidson, 1996; Palley, 1993). These different conceptions of uncertainty and measurable risk underpin profoundly different explanations of the genesis and collapse of speculative bubbles.

Rational Bubbles

In the orthodox literature, speculative bubbles emerge when asset prices do not fully reflect fundamental values (which in the case of a share would be the present value of the stream of its future dividends). Rational bubbles are described as emerging in a world of 'strong rational expectations', i.e. a world of perfectly rational, homogenous, finitely-lived economic agents. These economic agents are assumed to form subjective expectations that, on average, coincide with some objective probability distribution (Muth, 1961). This world is ergodic, immutable, fixed and risk is assumed to be measurable. Early rational expectations (RE) theorists believed that asset prices would necessarily reflect only market fundamentals.[4] If agents were perfectly rational and perfectly informed, how could a speculative bubble form in the first place?

Blanchard and Watson (1982)[5] established that rational expectations and speculative bubbles can co-exist – there can be rational deviations of an asset price away from its fundamental value.[6] Rational bubbles are described assuming finitely lived agents or successive generations of new entrants into trading (although mathematical conditions precluded the existence of bubbles in models incorporating an assumption of rational, infinitely lived representative agents).[7] Blanchard and Watson present the efficient market, no-arbitrage condition:

$$R_t = \frac{p_{t+1} - p_t + x_t}{p_t}$$

where r = interest rate, R = return on asset, p = price of asset, and x = dividend. Let us assume

$$E(R_t|\Omega_t) = r$$

where Ω is the common information set. Given that p_{t+1} is the only unknown in period t, it follows that

$$E(p_{t+1}|\Omega_t) - p_t + x_t = rp_t$$

This gives the solution:

$$p_t^* = \sum_{i=0}^{\infty} \theta^{i+1} E(x_{t+1}|\Omega_t)$$
$$\theta = (1 + r)^{-1} < 1$$

where p_t^* is the present value of expected dividends, i.e. the market fundamental value of an asset.

Blanchard and Watson establish the possibility of rational bubbles by showing that this arbitrage condition does not preclude the existence of bubbles because solutions take the general form:

$$p_t = \sum_{i=0}^{\infty} \theta^i E(x_{t+1}|\Omega_t) + c_t = p_t^* + c_t$$
$$E(c_{t+1}|\Omega_t) = \theta^{-1} c_t$$

where c is the bubble term, i.e. the deviation from the fundamental value.

The terminal conditions to be satisfied are:

$$\lim E(c_{t+i} \mid \Omega_t) = + \infty \qquad \text{if } c_t > 0$$

$$\lim E(c_{t+i} \mid \Omega_t) = - \infty \qquad \text{if } c_t < 0^8$$

This implies that there are a number of possible equilibrium paths and the existence of multiple equilibria means that the time-path of an asset price will not necessarily coincide with the path of an asset's fundamental value. Thus, the market price can diverge from the fundamental value without violating the efficient markets condition. For plausible (nominal) interest rates, i.e. when $\theta^{-1} > 1$, this implies that the bubble c must grow over time.[9]

Using the solution above, Blanchard and Watson deny the possibility of deterministic bubbles;[10] they argue that rational bubbles can emerge in a situation where there is a probability for each period of time that the bubble will either remain (with probability π) or crash (with probability $1 - \pi$). Some investors may continue to hold assets whilst the probability that the bubble will remain is greater than zero and thus the bubble proceeds independently of the fundamental value. The probability that a bubble ends will depend on a number of factors, including how long the bubble has lasted and how far the price is from market fundamentals. Therefore, the longer the bubble lasts (i.e. as the probability of a crash in the asset value increases), the faster the market price will have to increase to compensate asset-holders for the risk involved in continuing to hold the asset, in spite of the increased probability of a price collapse.

Critiques of the Rational Expectations Approaches

Blanchard and Watson allow that bubbles can have real effects in precipitating changes not only in the market fundamentals of a given asset but also on other asset prices, e.g. via wealth and substitution effects (Blanchard and Watson, 1982, pp. 301–3). However, in general, the RE approach ignores the complex interactions which characterize most real-world economies. Therefore, in this section we consider some other approaches.

Topol's Model of Contagion Bubbles

Topol (1991) presents a purely theoretical analysis of bubbles, examining the effects of herd behaviour and mimetic contagion. Topol argues that the capacity for rational behaviour is limited and therefore collective views influence asset prices. Thus, the key difference between Topol's model of contagion bubbles and rational bubble models comes in the different assumptions about rationality. The problem with other models of rational and irrational bubbles is that the dynamics in these models are not related to individual characteristics and behaviour. Topol thereby eschews the representative agent hypothesis adopted in the RE literature and demonstrates the role of mimetic contagion in propelling the path of bubbles.

Topol looks at individual investments in cases in which a collective opinion may exist. There is incomplete information so economic agents extend their information by adjusting their prices in response to adjustments in others' prices. The path of asset-prices is determined by an additive-learning process: different investors weight information about others' prices as well as the present value of assets. Via a process of stochastic aggregation, Topol shows that the buy price of an asset, p, will be

$$p = w_B p_B + w_S p_S + w_F P_i$$

where $w_B + w_S + w_F = 1$. p_B is the other buyers' price; p_S is the other sellers' price and P_i is the agent-efficient price which corresponds to the fundamentals and each w reflects the respective weights placed on each of these factors. In contrast to the rational bubbles models, P_i is only one element determining price; other prices will also play a role. In Topol's model, the agent-efficient price corresponds to the rational bubble price (i.e. $P_{it} = V_{it} + B_t$, where V is the fundamental component and B is the bubble component).[11] In a situation of a speculative bubble, there will be excess volatility due to mimetic contagion and/or correlated present values.[12] This process depends upon an assumption of weak-form rationality: that each agent has a different and incomplete information set.[13] Topol shows that if the variance of the agent-efficient price is small, the weights on mimetic contagion are small; thus, the weights are related to uncertainty about fundamentals

The interesting thing about this model is its eclectic nature; the results of the model depend upon assumptions about rationality. If strong-form rational expectations are assumed (i.e. all agents have the same information set and need the same time to infer their model;

thus they all obtain the same 'true' model of the economy), the model converts to the rational bubbles case.

However the model is also consistent with some of the ideas from Keynes: in a situation of incomplete information, it is rational to rely on the information inferred from others' behaviour. Conventions and herd instincts thereby propel action and are more likely to have an effect the greater is the degree of uncertainty. The greater the degree of uncertainty regarding the agent-efficient price, the greater weight will be attached to other agents' prices.[14] Mimetic contagion and limited rational behaviour lead to the social transmission of stock price movements: contagion bubbles develop. However, rational behaviour is limited because prices adjust to present values via reference to an incomplete information set. The key difference then seems to come in that Topol generally assumes an ergodic world. However, Topol does note that mimetic contagion may be strong enough for the ergodicity to fail and, in this case, weak-form rationality no longer applies; the world becomes non-ergodic and the model is transformed into a Keynesian–Minskian model of transmutable reality.[15]

Irrational Bubbles

In contrast to the orthodox RE models, models of irrational bubbles emphasize financial crisis rather than positive speculative bubbles.[16] In Keynesian models, boom phases and depression phases are inextricably linked: the seeds of financial crisis are planted during a euphoric bubble phase.

Keynes's Model

In Keynes's model, uncertainty and limited information play key roles: uncertainty prevents the assignment of precise numerical values to expectations. In particularly uncertain times, when the state of confidence in the economy is very fragile, people will tend to rely on conventional behaviour. They will fall back on the judgement of the rest of the world because the rest of the world is perhaps better informed about the prospects of investments. Thus herd behaviour and crowd psychology will determine the movement of asset prices. Furthermore, because people realize that their estimates of the values of investments are based on precarious foundations, these conventions will be unstable and volatile. Speculative bubbles emerge as professional speculators in asset markets focus on forecasting average opinion of average opinion about the prospective prices of assets. This speculative activity will have a profound effect on entrepreneurial activity because 'there is no sense in building up a new enterprise at a cost greater than that at which an existing one can be purchased' (Keynes, 1936, p.151). Whilst the existence of such asset markets provides much needed liquidity, the market valuation of assets will have no tendency to coincide with the fundamental value of an asset: 'certain classes of investment are governed by the average expectation of those who deal on the Stock Exchange as revealed in the price of shares rather than by the genuine expectations of the professional entrepreneur' (Keynes, 1936, p. 151).

If speculative activity dominates asset markets, there will be substantial negative effects for real activity and output. During a bubble phase, entrepreneurial behaviour is driven by subjective factors such as animal spirits and spontaneous optimism. This subjectively driven level of activity cannot endure because the estimates of the marginal efficiency of capital, which determine investment decisions, are based on precarious and over-optimistic expectations. This over-optimism precipitates a crisis as disillusion sets in at the end of a boom: investors realize that their subjectively-based profit expectations are not justified and errors of pessimism replace errors of optimism and the marginal efficiency of capital collapses. The crisis will be compounded as general instability and uncertainty lead to an increase in the propensity to hoard money via increases in precautionary and speculative demands for money and liquidity traps will develop. The economy will not be self-equilibrating and 'uncontrolled', 'disobedient' business psychology, collapses in the state of confidence, and the state of credit will make the economy resistant to the usual monetary therapies (Keynes, 1936, p. 317).

Minsky's Model of Euphoric Investment and Financial Crisis

Minsky (1982) builds upon Keynes in developing an investment theory of the business cycle, but he focuses more closely on the role of endogenous money and finance in propelling bubbles and crises. Adopting Keynes's insight about the many interdependencies between different markets, Minsky argues that there are 'deviation-amplifying complementarities' in the economy which dominate during expansionary phases and plant the seeds of later financial crisis. Investment is the driving force in the economy and is the key determinant of profits. Investors have access to three sources of finance: hedge finance, speculative finance and Ponzi finance. For hedge finance, the cash flow in exceeds the cash flow out in meeting the financial obligation; for speculative finance the near-term cash flow will exceed the interest cost of debt and the expected future cash flow will exceed outstanding cash commitments. Ponzi finance involves increasing outstanding debt in order to meet current financial obligations and is based on an expectation of future bonanzas; Minsky argues that there is an element of Ponzi finance in many long-term investment projects.

In periods of tranquillity there is a decline in the value of holding money; capital asset prices and investment increase and there is a portfolio shift towards Ponzi and speculative units. The banking system endogenously creates this finance. A speculative bubble phase is generated. But as the proportion of speculative and Ponzi units dominate, the economy becomes increasingly sensitive to interest rate variations. Investment demand increases the demand for finance and interest rates tend to increase as the supply of finance and demand for finance become more inelastic. This leads to more and more rapid rises in short-term interest rates, in turn leading to increases in long-term interest rates.

As short-term interest rates increase, speculative units are transformed into Ponzi units. The rise in long-term interest rates means that the present value of future profits, which justified Ponzi finance schemes in the initial euphoric period, decreases. In the same way, carrying charges accumulate on Ponzi units and short-run cash flow deficits are transformed into permanent cash flow deficits. The rise in interest rates will lead to a fall in investment and as profits are driven by investment, profits will fall. Lowered profit expectations will lead to decreases in the price of capital assets and a decreased ability to fulfil financial commitments. As 'present value reversals' take place (the present value of expected future bonanzas fall), Ponzi units must sell-out assets in order to meet payment commitments. Thus asset prices fall below their cost of production and the financial crisis is under way.

In Minsky's analysis, the speculative bubble phase is merely an irrational, euphoric stage that necessarily precipitates financial crisis. Financial traumas are the inevitable result of the capitalist system: the seeds of crisis are planted in the beginning of the euphoric phase and speculative bubbles are merely the catalysts of inevitable financial crises. The policy implications are profound: supporting Keynes, Minsky argues that conventional monetary policy is not successful in ameliorating crisis. During phases of crisis and deflation, endogenous market processes are inefficient and perverse and capitalist economies need a robust financial structure and strong policies to guide the evolution of finance. Big government and big government deficits will mean that investment is not as sensitive to private sector investment. Unregulated financial decision-making propels unsustainable asset price rises and the central bank must be prepared to act as a lender-of-last-resort and to float off untenable debt structures when financial crises emerge.

Summary of the Theoretical Debate

It is difficult to separate the different theoretical explanations empirically. As shown above, competing theoretical explanations can be devised that are consistent (within the limits of the respective models) with the existence of bubbles. The whole process of bubble generation takes place in a black box (we cannot examine human motivations with any accuracy), and so it is difficult conclusively to resolve empirically which is the more plausible explanation.[17,18] For this reason, it is an interesting exercise to look at the historical experience of bubbles and find out which explanations, broadly speaking, have the most intuitive resonance.

A Reconsideration of Two Early Speculative Bubbles

The first case study we have chosen is the phenomenon of Tulipmania, when the price of tulip bulbs rose spectacularly in Holland over a matter of weeks in the early seventeenth century, only to be followed by an even more spectacular fall. The second example is the South Sea Bubble that occurred in England in the early eighteenth century. As we noted in the Introduction, these case studies are particularly instructive because Garber (1989, 1990) has argued that they cannot be merely viewed as the result of crowd psychology, but merely reflected changes in the fundamental values. As such, he denies that they were even rational bubbles in the sense of Blanchard and Watson (1982).

Tulipmania

Tulipmania was one of the very first speculative bubbles and is still regarded by many as *the* classic speculative bubble. Tulipmania occurred in Holland over three months at the end of 1636 and the beginning of 1637. The traditional view advanced and defended by, most notably, Kindleberger (1996), is that the explosive growth, and the subsequent even faster collapse, of the prices of tulip bulbs conform to a typical speculative bubble or mania, driven to a large extent by irrational forces with inevitable disastrous consequences (Kindleberger, 1996, Chapter 2).

Garber (1989), on the other hand, has forcefully argued a revisionist viewpoint from a naïve neoclassical rational expectations stance. Garber's (1990, p. 35) methodology is based on the heuristic that we should search intensively for market fundamental explanations before 'clutching the "bubble" last resort'. While Kindleberger accepts that for much of the time markets do work and allocate resources efficiently, from a careful study of the historical evidence, he finds compelling the argument that manias and panics do from time to time break out, with dire results. Tulipmania is one such instance. As Kindleberger (1996) puts it, 'the issue provides a classic test as to whether economic theory after an event can invalidate its interpretation by the participants and general historians'. His conclusion is that, at least in this case, it cannot.

The importance of the debate is that if Tulipmania can be shown merely to have reflected changing fundamentals, then perhaps other speculative manias need to be reassessed. There is one major difference, though, that needs to be borne in mind, in that tulip bulbs, almost uniquely, were essentially a consumer good: the bulbs were bought ultimately for their final utility. Most other speculative bubbles have been for financial assets and therefore it has been possible to try to compare how far above market fundamentals the speculative price was driven, by a comparison with, say, the discounted future stream of rationally expected earnings or, in the case of currency, estimates of the equilibrium exchange rate. It is not possible to do this exercise with tulip bulbs and it therefore makes it more difficult to assess their fundamental values.

The approach of Garber, as we shall see, is to compare the rate of decline of prices after the tulip boom with those that other bulbs experienced in the eighteenth century. He concludes that they were very similar and because the latter, he argues, reflects the change in their fundamentals, he infers that this is true of the former.

Tulipmania lasted about three months, beginning in November 1636 and ending in the first week of February 1637. It took place at a time when there was an air of optimism in Holland and substantial investment activity was being undertaken in a number of sectors. The Dutch have an attachment to flowers and bulbs and the tulip was introduced from Turkey in the mid-1500s. By the seventeenth century, the prices of tulip bulbs varied considerably according to their scarcity value. Rare tulip bulbs included the Semper Augustus, Viceroys, Admirals and Generals. These bulbs were expensive, not only because of their rarity, but also because of the spectacular patterns that were caused (unknown at the time) by a virus, in a process known as 'breaking'. The common bulbs were much more modestly priced and there also developed a trade in the offshoots attached to the mother bulb, the so-called 'excrescences'.

It is not clear what was the trigger for the explosion in prices, but the ground was prepared nearly three years earlier, in 1634, with the arrival in the tulip market of outsiders, 'attracted by stories of rising prices for tulip bulbs in Paris and Northern France' (Chancellor, 1999, p. 16). In the course of twelve weeks during 1636/7, the prices of both the rare and the common bulbs tripled or increased by even larger amounts. The rapid increase in prices for a number of rare bulbs has been illustrated graphically by Garber (see Garber, 1989, Figures 3.1 to 3.8, pp. 62–5, and also Table 11.1)[19].

It is important to distinguish between the markets for the very rare bulbs and those that were more common. The prices of both underwent a speculative frenzy, but the participants in each market were very different, if only in terms of their financial assets. With the onset of Tulipmania, people with no knowledge of bulb growing began to trade (Posthumus, 1929). (The role of uninformed outsiders who fuel the increase in prices, entering the market simply because they are unable to resist the prospect of a large capital gain is a common feature of many speculative bubbles.) In previous years, the market had been confined to professional growers, experts and the aristocrats. Before

Table 11.1: Increases in bulb prices during Tulipmania

Bulb	P_0	P_T	% Increase
Gouda	20	225	1125
Admirael de Man	15	175	1167
Generalissimo	95	900	947
Croonen	20	1200	6000
Switzers	60	1800	3000
Admirael de Man	90	800	888
Scipio	800	2200	275
Vice-Roy	3000	6700	223
Coorenaerts	60	450	750
Audenaerden	70	600	857
Centen	40	350	875
Gheele en Root van Leyeden	100	750	750

Notes: P_0 is initial price; P_T is the terminal price in guilders. No time is explicitly given for the period, but it is safe to assume that it is under a year.
Source: The Dialogues; cited by Posthumus (1929, p. 454)

Tulipmania, the purchase of tulips had taken place in the summer when the bulbs were out of the ground. In 1636, the excitement, as Kindleberger put it, began in September when the bulbs had been planted to bloom the following spring. (The speculation in the more common bulbs followed rapidly.) Moreover, 'the exotic shapes and colours which were thought to be fundamentals were last seen the spring before, since bulbs for propagation were lifted from the ground in June' (Kindleberger, 1996, p. 100). Thus, the rapid rise in prices was when there were no specimens available. Essentially, there was a futures market in tulip bulbs (the 'windhandel'). Sellers undertook to supply a given bulb and weight in the following spring and buyers took the right of delivery. This practice developed in mid-1636, probably based on the already existing futures trade in excrescences and in the words of Posthumus (1929, p. 437): 'In this way the speculative element was increased enormously'.

Because of the lack of a sophisticated credit system, down payment was increasingly made in kind. As the trades increased so the nature of the market changed; private deals gave way to informal meetings in the rooms of inns, called the colleges. (Kindleberger (1996) and Posthumus (1929) note that this was where the ordinary, rather than the exotic bulbs, were traded by the lower classes.)

The tulip speculation collapsed suddenly on 3 February 1637. There is no clear indication what triggered the crash. 'In Haarlem, the centre of the flower trade, rumours circulated that there were no more buyers, and the next day tulips were unsaleable *at any price*. Contracts were not settled, and one default followed another. The professional florists attempted in vain to extract money from defaulting speculators' (Chancellor, 1999, p. 19, emphasis added).

The florists acted rapidly to try to limit the damage, but it was not until 27 April 1637, when the States of Holland accepted the advice from the Court of Holland, that matters began to be resolved. In the meantime, commerce in bulbs was in disarray. The matter then lay in the city governments' hands.

The economic impact of the crisis was limited, first because the great merchants and wealthy aristocrats had refrained from entering the market and, secondly, because many of the contracts were annulled. Nevertheless, there were instances of bankruptcy. Garber (1989) presents some data to show that prices did rebound to some extent over the next few years, as certain bulbs could still command high prices six years after the collapse. No doubt the wealthy aristocrats re-entered the market to buy bulbs for their own consumption.

Tulipmania would seem at first sight to contain all the elements of a classic speculative bubble:

> The trade in futures had degenerated into purest gamble, the seller selling bulbs he did not have against a counter value, mostly money at this period. Each succeeding buyer tried to sell his ware for higher prices; and in the general excitement, one could make a profit – at least on paper – of several thousands of florins in a day. The craze spread rapidly with these high profits. All classes of the population ended by taking part in it – intellectuals, the middle classes, and the labourers.
>
> (Posthumus, 1929, p. 439)

Minsky argues that a speculative craze normally starts by a displacement. This is some exogenous shock (such as a bumper crop or a war) which reduces the opportunity for profits in some areas, but opens them up in others. Certainly, as we have noted, there were booms in other sectors of the economy and these may have been mutually reinforcing and spilled over into the tulip market. Also, the rapid rise of prices over such a short period was accompanied by Minsky's *euphoria* or Adam Smith's *overtrading*, as the contemporary literature bears ample evidence. People entered the market who would not normally have traded there and, as we have noted, those who did usually buy bulbs (e.g. the aristocrats) exited at an early stage of the bubble. Indeed, it can be inferred that the latter, who were familiar with the workings of the bulb market in normal times, recognized that the bubble could never last. The rapid increase was purely for speculative purposes, to resell the bulbs at a later stage to realize a capital gain.

So what is the argument that Tulipmania reflected a change in fundamentals? The first issue that needs to be resolved is why the prices rose so rapidly in the first place. Contrary to our argument above, according to Garber it was because of the increase in final demand for them:

> The price increases prior to February 1637 occurred as the status of a variety became clear; and as its renown increased, so would its price. After all, most new varieties were not considered particularly beautiful. This would explain the steady increase in price of Semper Augustus. Similarly, a shift in fashion toward the appreciation of tulips in general over a shorter period would generate rising prices for all the rare bulbs.

232 What Global Economic Crisis?

But there are a number of flaws in this argument. The Semper Augustus had been around for several years prior to Tulipmania and given the small nature of the market (confined to the wealthy) would have undoubtedly been widely known.[20] So why did it increase by 3000 guilders or so in the space of a few weeks? Also, there is no evidence that tulips, *per se*, suddenly came into fashion in this period. As early as 1624, a Semper Augustus had fetched the sum of 1600 guilders. Moreover, even as Garber himself admits, the rapid growth of the common breeder bulbs, which rose in price some twenty-fold or more in the last stages of the boom, cannot be ascribed to a change in the fundamentals. (Given the likely small number of the rare bulbs, much of the mania must have been in the more common bulbs.) Here Garber concedes that the colleges 'consisted of a collection of people without net worth making ever increasing numbers of million dollar bets with each other with some knowledge that the state would not enforce the contracts'.

Overall, it is hard to believe that the observed increase in prices reflected a massive increase in demand for tulips for consumption purposes and hence reflected a rapid increase in fundamentals.

Garber also looks at the decline in the prices of the bulbs from their peak in 1637 over the next few decades. They all fall over this long period to less than 1 per cent of their initial price. Secondly, he compares prices of rare bulbs in the 1707 auction with their prices in 1722 or 1739. He finds that prices also decline substantially, in this case to less than 3 per cent of their initial value. Garber concludes:

> We now have a pattern in the evolution of the prices of newly developed fashionable tulip bulbs. The first bulbs, unique or in small supply, carry high prices. With time, the price declines rapidly either because of rapid reproduction of the new variety or because of the increasing introduction of new varieties. Anyone who acquired a new bulb would have understood this standard pattern of anticipated capital depreciation, at least by the eighteenth century.

Garber finds that during the eighteenth century the annual depreciation rate was 28.5 per cent. This compares with the fact that the three most costly bulbs of February 1637 declined on average by 32 per cent per annum from the peak of speculation to the years 1642 or 1643: 'Using the eighteenth-century price depreciation rate as a benchmark also followed by expensive bulbs after the mania, we can infer that any price collapse for rare bulbs in 1637 could not have exceeded 16 per cent of peak prices. Thus, the crash of February 1637 for rare bulbs was not of extraordinary magnitude and did not greatly affect the normal time-series pattern of rare bulb prices'.

There is a problem, however, with this argument in that there was a far more dramatic collapse in prices in February 1637, far faster than at an annualized rate of 32 per cent, as they became literally unsaleable within a few days. There is evidence of a rebound effect during the immediate subsequent years, and indeed this would not be surprising given the high prices the rare bulbs were commanding prior to 1636. Thus, what is important is the rate of decline of prices over a period of days or weeks, not over a period of five years. The complete collapse of the bulb market in February, the cessation of trading in the months after February and the need for government intervention to sort out the chaos all point to a crash of unprecedented and unforeseen magnitude.

Furthermore, it is possible, as Kindleberger (1996) and Chancellor (1999) have argued, that the depreciation rates calculated by Garber for the eighteenth century were themselves the results of speculative booms (although presumably without such a dramatic subsequent crash) and that the market for bulbs has always been prone to these.

Garber argues that there were few signs of the general distress in the immediate aftermath of the crisis that is symptomatic of a speculative boom. However, he himself provides plausible reasons for this, in addition to those we have already mentioned. It was due to the fact that no significant agricultural resources were devoted to the production of the expensive bulbs and the common bulbs were already in the ground. Consequently, the effect of the crash was merely a transfer of wealth, and in many cases not even this occurred. Speculative bids were often made for bulbs the seller did not have, with money the buyer could not supply. However, Kindleberger argues that, with due respect to Garber, there is evidence of a general slowing down of the Dutch economy in the early 1640s, although followed by a recovery.

It is very difficult to agree with Garber's argument that there was no speculative boom in 1637, in the sense of a buying mania. The fact that the city and government authorities had to step in to rescue the position after the collapse suggests that the events in 1637 were abnormal. Overall, Tulipmania appears to fit the pattern of a classic irrational speculative mania. As Posthumus (1929, p. 449) puts it:

> As soon as the movement was started, it began to show the features of speculation of non-professional people of small means. They had no

control, no knowledge of the market beyond the very limited circle in which they moved, and no discrimination, believing all the rumours and fancies with the credulity of the simple-minded. This fluctuation would do very well as an example of the 'psychological' theory of business cycles. The heated imagination went on and on; the craze spread, till at last doubt began to arise; and as soon as this uneasiness was expressed, the whole tower of prices collapsed in one or two days, everyone now disbelieving in any future possibilities.

The South Sea Bubble of 1720

The end of the seventeenth century saw what might be called the first financial revolution, with the introduction of the joint-stock company and other innovative financial instruments. In 1710, there was the successful flotation of the first insurance company, the Sun Fire. It was against this background that Blunt's South Sea Company was established, as a means to privatize national debt by converting illiquid government debt into a far more liquid form in the shape of shares in a joint-stock company. In 1710, the South Sea Company took over government stock of more than £10 million, which it converted into its own shares. In exchange, it received government interest and other trading privileges, but the latter were in fact of negligible value. In 1719 it took over a further £1.7 million of government debt. This was the year when John Law's Mississippi Company took over the entire French debt and thus there were obvious similarities between the two schemes. Investors flooded into the Rue Quicampoix – the French stock exchange – from all over Europe and the enthusiasm for purchasing shares was contagious and spread to Britain. (Moreover, it has been suggested that there was an international aspect to the collapse of the value of the shares of the South Sea Company. It was partly caused by Dutch investors cashing in to take their profits in order to take advantage of booming conditions on the Continent.) In 1720 the South Sea Company extended the scheme and undertook to take over the whole of the British debt of over £30 million, in exchange for paying the government £7.5 million.[21]

The scheme succeeded only too well. The shares were at £120 in January 1720. With the passing of the refunding act, they jumped to between £200 to £300 in March. The first major subscription on 28 April was at the rate of £375 worth of debt for every £100 worth of stock. It has been estimated that for the holders to actually make a loss on the deal (i.e. to be worse off than if they had actually retained their government annuities) the price would have had to fall below £150. As the market price was between £335 and £343, this was a very attractive deal, especially in the expectation of further substantial rises. A second money subscription the very next day was for a price of £400. As it became clear most of the debt would be acquired, the price rose to about £700.

The method Blunt and the other directors of the South Sea Company chose to ensure the price rise continued was to keep the market liquid, which they did by giving loans on the surety of the existing stock. This was then funnelled back into the Company through the purchase of further issues of new or existing stock and thereby driving up the market price even further. 'In order to pay out of profits, the South Sea Company needed to raise more capital and to have the price of its stock moving continuously upward. And it needed both increases at an accelerating rate, as in a chain letter or a Ponzi scheme' (Kindlberger 1996, p. 71). The shares peaked just after the third money subscription of 17 June at £950. They fell to £775 on 31 August and then collapsed to about £290 on 1 October 1720. £103 million was wiped off a total share value of £164 million. In mid-October they were trading at about £200 and a low was reached in December of about £150.

Prior to, and conditional on, the passing of the refunding act through parliament, the South Sea Company paid substantial bribes to members of parliament, and influential friends of the king. These were in what would be now termed stock options and so the recipients also had a vested interested in seeing the price of shares rise rapidly. However, Garber argues that such practices were not uncommon in those days for a company whose profitability could be seriously adversely affected by parliament.[22]

On the tailcoats of the South Sea Company, there was the rapid growth of a number of new joint-stock companies that became known as the 'bubble companies'. Some were genuine, but others were aimed at gullible investors with what can be only be described as absurd objectives. Only four of the 190 bubble companies founded in 1790 survived.[23] The existence of these bubble companies (and the rapid growth of their share prices) demonstrated graphically the speculative mania that was sweeping Exchange Alley at this time.

It is not clear why the South Sea Bubble crashed, but one suggestion is that the Company, concerned at the rapid growth of the bubble companies inveigled parliament to pass a bill requiring them to keep within the terms of their original charters. Cash that had been poured out of the Company in the form of loans and designed for the Second Money Subscription, the directors saw disappearing into other speculative ventures. Since the threat of prosecution did not have the desired effect, writs for prosecution were issued against three companies who had breached the terms of their charters. Ironically, the end result was that this did not improve the position of the South Sea Company, but, on the contrary, may have actually triggered the collapse of the bubble. The value of the bubble companies fell spectacularly. This led to investors who had purchased bubble company shares on credit having to sell their South Sea Company shares to cover their debts. Moreover, as we noted above, there was an international aspect to the crash. Overseas investors, especially the Dutch, were attracted by the new bubble companies appearing on the continent and sold their South Sea Company stock. Here we have one of the first international causes of a speculative collapse. Chancellor (1999, p. 83), nevertheless, argues that 'one of these factors proved decisive: by late summer the company had exhausted all available means of sustaining momentum in its share price, and without momentum, decline was inevitable'.

Was the South Sea Bubble a Speculative Bubble?

Can the rapid rise in the prices of the stock of the South Sea Company in 1720, and their subsequent fall in the same year, be justified in terms of changes in its fundamentals or was it largely the result of speculative forces? Indeed, the conventional wisdom, going back to Adam Smith, if not earlier, is not only was it was a classic case of speculative mania but also was fuelled by corruption – a 'mere fraud', in Smith's words (1978, p. 519).

In order to determine the answer to this question, we have to return to the question of what precisely is meant by a bubble. Garber (1990) argues that there are three situations in which the observed buying frenzy could actually be considered not to reflect a bubble. It should be recalled that Garber seems to regard bubbles, by definition, as irrational. If the share prices track the change in fundamentals, then there is no bubble. He does not make the distinction between rational and irrational bubbles discussed above. In the following discussion we shall follow Garber and not, for the moment, distinguish between rational and irrational bubbles but regard both as speculative bubbles.

The first situation is that if the Company promised great rewards that had no likelihood of being forthcoming, then it would be a case of fraud or a swindle. However, if the new investors believed these fraudulent claims, they would be acting on what they believed to be the fundamentals and this therefore would be rational. 'This is a situation of asymmetric information in which one player has an incentive to dissemble' (Garber, 1990). Of course, if evidence were widely available that it was fraudulent, and investors chose to ignore this in the hope of getting out before the market crashed, then it would be a speculative bubble.

Secondly, and related to this, if the company did use proceeds from the issue of shares to pay inflated dividends (the Ponzi scheme), but the investors were acting on their perception of the market fundamentals, then the increase in prices could not be regarded as a speculative bubble. But this presupposes again that these dividends were actually perceived as reflecting market fundamentals.

With regard to these two points, there is plenty of evidence that many saw that the rapid price rises could not go on forever. Chancellor (1999, p. 63, 65) notes the warnings issued by the influential Defoe in *The Mist* and by the parliamentarian Hutcheson in a series of anti-South Sea pamphlets. Hutcheson not only pointed out that the government was only committed to a 5 per cent interest and the prospects for commercial trade were not good, but he wrote 'certain it is that the Loss at last must rest some-where'. Both Chancellor (1999, p. 69) and Carswell (1993, p. 99) quote an anonymous pamphleteer: 'The additional rise of this stock above the true capital will only be imaginary; one added to one, by any rules of vulgar arithmetic will never make three and a half; consequently, all the fictitious value must be a loss to some persons or another, first or last. The only way to prevent it to oneself must be to sell out betimes and so let the Devil take the hindmost'.

Of course, it is a matter of conjecture how widely read these pieces of advice were. Carswell (1993) states that the last one 'was not disregarded', suggesting it was certainly accessible, but it could not stop the speculative rise. One significant reason was the deliberate creation of 'moral hazard' by Blunt. The bribes in the form of stocks given to members of parliament noted above were deliberately made common knowledge and this reassured the speculators. Surely parliament would never let the South Sea Company go under with so many important vested interests? Even the king was involved. Hence investors could (and did) in fact disregard the poor 'fundamentals' of the company. Whether it was rational for them to do so is a moot point.

Kindleberger notes that Blunt and the other directors systematically cashed in their capital gains prior to the collapse to buy other more tangible assets such as estates. There is evidence that Blunt certainly used his insider's knowledge in his own financial affairs.

The third situation, according to Garber, where the rapid rise in prices cannot be seen as speculative, is where it reflects the long-term future potential earnings of the Company. Even if these were not realized, and there was an eventual crash, this should not be regarded as a speculative bubble, so long as the outlook seemed realistic at the start. After all, the nature of the venture capital market is some new companies may rapidly earn high profits relative to their initial capitalization, whereas others will collapse. However, there is no convincing evidence that this explanation fits the South Sea Bubble.

Garber (1990) concludes that at the peak of the bubble 'the share values exceeded net assets by five times or more'. However, a share price of about £150 would have represented roughly the break-even price for those initially wishing to convert their government debt into the Company's shares and this was approximately the post-bubble price. What expectations of future earnings could have justified the rapid rise in prices beyond this figure? Garber argues that it was the result of the anticipation of commercial expansion associated with the fund of credit, along the lines that John Law explicitly anticipated for the Mississippi Company. In Garber's interpretation, the liquidity crisis terminated the Company before it had a chance to prove itself: 'Nevertheless, the episode is readily understandable as a case of speculators working on the basis of the best economic analysis available and pushing prices along by their changing view of market fundamentals'. It is, however, difficult to find much justification for this view.

First, it is important to draw an important distinction between the commercial trading aims of the Mississippi Company, John Law's introduction of financial innovations and the machinations of his counterpart in the South Sea Company, Blunt.[24,25] John Law is universally seen as one of the most outstanding financiers of the century with an intellect on a par with Newton. Not only did the Mississippi Company have excellent prospects in overseas trade but also Law was a visionary who strived for nothing less than to engineer an economic boom in depressed France. Blunt is generally regarded in a far less favourable light; namely, as merely a clever opportunist, driven by the prospect of personal gain. Law, in his memoirs complained bitterly that 'I improved the [Mississippi] company's resources, but the South Sea Company did not propose to make its dividends out of its income or the profits of its trade, but simply gave back its proprietors part of the principal yearly'. There is no doubt that Law had genuine schemes to use the flow of income generated by the government's interest payments to fund large commercial schemes. Even his buying the right to collect all the French government's indirect taxes was sound – Law genuinely believed he could collect them more efficiently than the government.

It is difficult to find a description of a serious entrepreneurial activity that the South Sea Company proposed that might, even in the long run, have raised the fundamental price much above £150. Carswell (1993, p. 241) explicitly considers this question. He notes that the Mississippi Company had 'the prospects of all but unlimited overseas trade' and that Law controlled the levers of the largest European power that was geographically well placed to take advantage of such trade. He argues that the opportunities for any such similar endeavours by the South Sea Company were remote. 'It seems more probable that the asset on which the South Sea promoters relied was the possession of political power. They had ensnared the monarchy, the ministers and a large part of Parliament. Their illusion was that the multiplicity of their shares among the propertied public would give that public such an interest in the new monopoly's survival that it would at last dominate the whole scene and put its promoters beyond reach of any reprisal.'

Whereas one may with some justification regard the increase in the price of shares of the Mississippi Company as reflecting its long-term potential, the reading of historical sources gives no support for a similar interpretation of the South Sea Company.

Conclusions

We have shown above that in the case of neither Tulipmania nor the South Sea Bubble can the rapid increase in prices and their even more sudden collapse represent changing fundamentals. But were these price rises propelled by 'rational expectations' as opposed to 'irrational' speculative bubbles? Unfortunately, there is some confusion over these concepts. The term 'rational' in rational expectations is unfortunate, as it does not imply that non-rational expectations are necessarily irrational, in the conventional sense of the term (i.e. pathological). What it does mean is that agents make use of the full information set that is available to them at a given point in time, and this includes a correct specification of the underlying structure of the economy, subject to white noise. Indeed, the fact that agents make use of all the information available to them in forming expectations is perhaps uncontroversial. Many Keynesians would have no difficulty in accepting the explanation that a major bubble-generating mechanism is investors' expectations that the probable gains in the next period are likely to be large enough relative to the chance of the bubble collapsing to justify the risk of staying in the market. This is, of course, just the rationale underlying the RE model.

But there is a major difference between the Keynesian and the RE approach; the approaches differ in the assumptions made about the information set available to a given individual, the degree of belief associated with this information, and the way expectations are formed. The RE approach of Blanchard and Watson largely circumvents these considerations by postulating Ω_t, the information set, as given and taking the probability of a crash not occurring (π) as exogenous. Implicit in this is that there is some objective basis from which the latter can be generated. It is not coincidental that in an example given by Blanchard and Watson, the factor determining π is independent of the behaviour of the investors, *per se*, and is the probability of whether or not a war continues. However, in practice, the bubble does not collapse because of 'news', but for other less well-defined reasons arising from changes in expectations of the investors themselves. It is here that Topol (1991) represents a notable advance.

For the Keynesian, given a world of uncertainty, the best procedure an investor can adopt is perhaps to assume that the market knows best and to follow the trend or adopt one of Shiller's (1990) 'popular models'. A rule of thumb can be an optimal decision-making process in complex situations. But in these situations the crash may well be determined by intangible factors such as an unpredictable change of sentiment by even a small number of investors. In other words, the determination of π is subject to a whole host of subjective factors and π is likely to very volatile. For example, Newton fully appreciated the speculative nature of the South Sea Bubble and initially sold his shares early enough to make a considerable profit. Nevertheless, he could not resist the temptation to re-enter the market and ended up with a substantial loss. As he ruefully remarked, he could track the motion of the planets but not changes in human sentiments. Consequently, in many ways the theoretical approach of Topol is an improvement on the RE methodology, because it takes into account the behaviour of the market in the formation of an individual's expectations. It is along these lines that a more complete understanding of speculative bubbles and crashes is likely to be found.

Notes

1. It is possible that a speculative bubble may actually alter the fundamentals in such a way as to justify eventually the initial rapid increase in prices. We shall not consider these cases here. A much more common result is that the crash actually worsens the fundamentals and has a negative impact on the economy.

2. We shall see that Garber takes a rather extreme view, denying, in effect, that bubbles result for purely rational reasons and ignoring much of the literature on rational expectations bubbles. In such an approach, the essence of bubbles is lost: it is not clear what is meant as a bubble in an asset price if that price is simply tracking fundamental values.

3. Although Topol does allow that if mimetic contagion is powerful enough the world may no longer be ergodic.

4. Thus, early empirical models focussed on establishing that speculative bubbles did not exist (see Flood & Garber, 1980).

5. See also models of Schleifer and Summers (1990), who argue that uncertainty about the time at which a bubble will break, finitely-lived and risk-averse investors and no full arbitrage, all mean that bubbles may persist for long periods.

6. However, they do not deny that large historical bubbles have elements of irrationality; they just show that the existence of speculative bubbles is not inconsistent with rational expectations. Kindleberger (1996) is critical of Blanchard and Watson (1982) who only analyse rational bubbles, because they argue 'it would be much harder to deal with irrational bubbles'. However, they do admit that bubbles are more likely in markets in which fundamentals are not clear; thus they allow uncertainty a key role.

7. In addition, RE models can only demonstrate the existence of bubbles on assets which are not redeemable at a given price at a given date; i.e. bubbles can exist with perpetuities but not with ordinary bonds.

8. The possibility of negative bubbles is excluded because if there is a negative bubble then this implies that the price may at sometime become negative; but as investments can be off-loaded without cost, their price can never be negative.

9. Blanchard and Watson do not address the implications of negative real interest rates within this model.

10. Blanchard and Watson rule out the possibility of deterministic bubbles ($c_t = c_0 \theta^{-t}$) because they imply that prices increase ad infinitum; deterministic bubbles are implausible because it is not rational to believe that a bubble will last for ever.

11. In describing the evolution of contagion bubbles, for the sake of simplicity, Topol excludes the rational bubble component in the agent efficient price.

12. The bubble collapses and volatility diminishes as soon as the behaviour of different agents becomes uncorrelated.

13. Nonetheless, Topol does assume that the world is ergodic in the sense that the variables, relationships and information are the same for the time interval needed for an agent to infer the model of the economy.

14. Note that many empirical tests even in the rational bubble literature are based on examining the magnitude of the variance, which could be seen as a proxy for uncertainty.

15. There seem to be many parallels with Keynes's ideas; for example, as described by Keynes, in certain times conventions are not needed, but in uncertain times, it is necessary to fall back on the judgement of the rest of the world, which is perhaps better informed.

16. The extent to which Keynes believed in 'irrational' behaviour is unclear. There is a considerable literature analysing the evolution of Keynes's ideas

between *A Treatise on Probability (1921)*, *The General Theory of Employment, Interest and Money* (1936) and 'The general theory of employment' (1937). In this literature, it is argued that Keynes did not believe that economic behaviour was generally, fundamentally, irrational, but just that the presence of Knightian (immeasurable) uncertainty prevents strictly rational behaviour such as that described in RE models.

17. For empirical tests of bubbles see Blanchard & Watson (1982); Shiller (1981); Flood & Hodrick (1990) and Shleifer & Summers (1990).

18. See Shiller (1990) on the use of a questionnaire approach to determine how people form expectations. Shiller finds that most people follow 'popular models', e.g. following the trend, buying after prices have begun to rise and vice versa.

19. However, Kindleberger has a word of caution since, especially, in the case of the Semper Augustus Garber uses straight-line interpolation between the price 1625 and 1637, making the price rise seem far more gradual than it really was. In fact the increase was in Kindleberger's words a 'manic swoop'. However, the figures for the other bulb prices in Garber reflect this latter picture more faithfully.

20. The Dialogues report that there were only two bulbs of Semper Augustus variety (Posthumus, 1929, p. 459).

21. For a detailed discussion of the exact procedures adopted, see Neal (1996).

22. Nevertheless, it enabled the Company to remain free to set its terms of conversion even though Walpole in Parliament forcibly, but ineffectively, opposed what he saw as far too high a conversion rate. Garber presents no other evidence of such massive bribes occurring in other circumstances.

23. Garber (1990, p. 51) argues that 'many of the companies born in the 1720 speculation were quite sound' but does not explain how many is 'many' or how he arrives at this conclusion. Moreover, if they were so sound why did only two per cent survive?

24. It is interesting that John Law is mentioned extensively by Garber, but that Blunt is ignored.

25. As Kindleberger put it (1996, p. 71), 'The Mississippi bubble was not a swindle; the South Sea bubble was.'

References

Blanchard, O. J. and Watson, M. W. (1982) 'Bubbles, rational expectations and financial markets' in P. Wachtel (ed.) *Crises in the Economic and Financial Structure*, Lexington, MA, D.C. Heath, pp. 295–315.

Carswell, J. (1993) *The South Sea Bubble*, Gloucestershire, Alan Sutton (revised edition).

Chancellor, E. (1999) *Devil Take the Hindmost. A History of Financial Speculation*, Basingstoke, Macmillan.

Davidson, P. (1996) 'Reality and Economic Theory', *Journal of Post Keynesian Economics*, vol. 18, pp. 477–508.

Flood, R. P. and Garber, R. J. (1980) *Speculative Bubbles, Speculative Attacks and Policy Switching*, Cambridge, MA, MIT Press.

Flood, R. P. and Hodrick, R. J. (1990) 'On Testing for Speculative Bubbles', *Journal of Economic Perspectives*, vol 4. pp. 85–101.

Garber, P. M. (1989), 'Tulipmania', *Journal of Political Economy*, vol. 97, pp. 535–60.

Garber, P. M. (1990) 'Famous First Bubbles', *Journal of Economic Perspectives*, vol. 4, pp. 35–53.

Keynes, J. M. (1921) *A Treatise on Probability*, London, Macmillan.

Keynes, J. M. (1936) *The General Theory of Employment, Interest and Money*, London, Macmillan.

Keynes, J. M. (1937) 'The General Theory of Employment', *Quarterly Journal of Economics*, vol. 51, pp. 209–23.

Kindleberger, C. P. (1996) *Manias, Panics and Crashes*, 3rd edn, New York, John Wiley and Sons.

Minsky, H. P. (1982) *Inflation, Recession and Economic Policy*, Brighton, Wheatsheaf.

Muth, J. F. (1961) 'Rational Expectations and the Theory of Price Movements', *Econometrica*, vol. 29, pp. 315–35.

Neal, L. D. (1996) 'How the South Sea bubble was blown up and burst: A new look at old data' in E. N. White (ed.) *Stock Market Crashes and Speculative Manias*, Cheltenham, Edward Elgar, pp. 154–77.

Palley, T. I. (1993) 'Uncertainty, Expectations and the Future: If We Don't Know the Answers, What are the Questions'? *Journal of Post Keynesian Economics*, vol. 16, pp. 3–18.

Posthumus, N. W. (1929) 'The Tulipmania in Holland in the Years 1636 and 1637', *Journal of Economic and Business History*, vol. 1, pp. 434–66.

Shleifer, A. and Summers, L. H. (1990) 'The Noise Trade Approach to Finance', *Journal of Economic Perspectives*, vol. 4, pp. 19–33.

Shiller, R. J. (1981) 'Do Stock Prices Move Too Much to be Justified by Subsequent Movements in Dividends', *American Economic Review*, 71(3):421–36.

Shiller, R. J. (1990) 'Speculative Prices and Popular Models', *Journal of Economic Perspectives*, vol. 4, pp. 55–65.

Smith, A. (1978) *Lectures on Jurisprudence*, ed. by R. L. Meek, D. D. Raphael and P. G. Stein, Oxford, Clarendon Press.

Topol, R. (1991) 'Bubbles and Volatility of Stock Prices: Effect of Mimetic Contagion', *Economic Journal*, vol. 101, pp. 786–800.

12
John Cornwall: An Appreciation

Mark Setterfield

Introduction

A Festschrift serves to celebrate both an individual and the legacy of their work. In so doing, the contributions to Setterfield (1999) exude a sense of three of John Cornwall's defining qualities as an economist. First, Cornwall has made a variety of important and lasting contributions to economics, spanning theory, application and methodology. Second, Cornwall's contributions *take economics seriously*, i.e. they forego idle (and as it is currently practised, frequently cynical) game playing in favour of explicit and unyielding recognition of the social significance of economics and what this should mean to those who practise the discipline. Cornwall's work has always been motivated by a desire to better the societies in which we live, or, as he puts it himself in reference to the work of those he most admires, 'to do some good'. Finally, Cornwall's care and attention as an advisor, as an 'invisible hand', always guiding but never interfering, has inspired his students in the arts of the scholar-teacher. It is his unique combination of these qualities that have endeared John Cornwall to so many of his colleagues and students.

Cornwall's contributions to economics have been many and diverse. Moreover, the format of his published work has changed over time. In the 1970s, he tired of the 'one idea, one article' structure of the periodicals and turned to publishing books as a means of exploring grander themes.[1] Nevertheless, Cornwall's abiding interest throughout his career has been in macrodynamics. Furthermore, although the object of his inquiry has changed over time and his macrodynamic methodology has evolved, a coherent vision of capitalist macrodynamics emerges from Cornwall's work.[2] This vision is expressed through the interplay of two of the major themes in Cornwall's contributions, namely, that demand matters and that institutions matter.

'Say's Law in Reverse': The Importance of Demand in a Capitalist Economy

Cornwall is a firm adherent of the Keynesian proposition that aggregate demand does not adjust passively to accommodate given levels of aggregate supply over any time horizon. Rather, his work suggests that it is aggregate supply that adjusts to accommodate aggregate demand, so that we have, as it were, 'Say's Law in reverse', and aggregate demand is established as the leading element in the determination of the level of economic activity. This is true both in the short and long runs, owing to the capacity of aggregate demand to influence the utilization of productive resources at any point in time, and (via induced technical progress and so forth) the very development of these resources over time. These ideas have a long pedigree in Cornwall's thought. They appear in his first book (Cornwall, 1972) and date back to his time in Cambridge during the 1960s, where he expressed his dissatisfaction with the prevailing tendency to treat Harrod's natural rate of growth as being independent of the actual rate of growth (Harcourt and Monadjemi, 1999, pp. 12–13). His continued emphasis of these themes offers a marked contrast with orthodox macroeconomics, in which the supply-determined nature of long run growth is taken for granted and, thanks to developments such as real business cycle theory, even the capacity of demand to explain deviations from this supply-determined growth path is treated as questionable.

Conflict, Uncertainty and Institutions

The failure of the price mechanism to create a system that is self-regulating about a supply-determined level of economic activity (or growth path) is central to Cornwall's macrodynamic vision. However, it is not obvious that the price mechanism as idealized by neoclassical economics is even capable of creating a system that is self-regulating in the broader sense of its being structurally stable, i.e. capable of reproducing itself (at *any* level of activity) in a more or less orderly fashion over time. In the first place, the price mechanism cannot coordinate expectations. Uncertainty is an endemic and pervasive feature of economic life, and 'animal spirits' – which involve far more than mere computation and calculation based on price signals – have an important influence on behaviour.[3] Second, the price mechanism cannot (by definition) coordinate incompatible aims and interests that are expressed outside the sphere of market exchange – for example, at the point of production. Hence the potential for socio-economic conflict is endemic and pervasive.

This gives rise to the importance of *institutions* in structuring activity in capitalist economies, and in so doing, playing three vital roles. The first is an enabling function: institutions provide a basis for action in an uncertain world. They do this by specifying procedures ('in situation *x*, do *y*') on which action can be based regardless of the inability of decision-makers to compute optimal behaviours. As a result, institutions play a second, cognitive role. There are many situations in which decision-makers must attempt to form expectations, even if the environment is one of uncertainty. Institutions help by providing a source of information regarding the likely future behaviour of others. Finally, institutions play a conciliatory role, regularizing relations between parties whose interests are mutually exclusive. Relatively enduring institutions can thus ameliorate (although never, of course, eliminate) uncertainty and conflict and their debilitating effects on economic activity creating, in the process, relatively orderly (i.e. structurally stable) episodes in capitalist performance.

Institutions are only *relatively* enduring, however. They can and, of course do, change over time. While it is important to consider an economy's basic structure as an enduring institutional construct, then, we must also bear in mind the propensity of this structure to periodically change over time. Capitalism is subject to inherently transformational growth and development, and important qualitative differences between different episodes of capitalism can be expected.

Path Dependence and Evolutionary Keynesianism

Demand and institutional factors do not function independently for Cornwall. Indeed, their interdependence gives rise to a third major theme in his work – the notion that capitalism is subject to nonequilibrium and non-equilibrating change arising from path-dependent macrodynamics. This theme emerges from consideration of the fact that institutions influence aggregate demand – especially, for Cornwall, through their impact on the viability of reflationary macroeconomic policies – while, at the same time, demand influences institutions. Hence demand-determined macroeconomic performance affects the production and reproduction of the institutional infrastructure within which it is embedded. In other words, there exists a two-way or joint interaction between aggregate demand and institutions. This joint interaction is not perceived as mechanically self-equilibrating. Instead, the vision that emerges is genuinely dynamic (i.e. rooted in history and historical time), consisting of a conception of the economy as a continually unfolding, path-dependent process rather than something that is in or inexorably tending towards a terminal (and path independent) state of rest. This process comprises the recurring, joint interaction of demand-determined outcomes and economic structure (and in particular, of course, the institutional structure) in an evolutionary sequence characterized by episodes of structural stability (arising from the relatively inert properties of institutions) punctuated by occasional (but potentially dramatic), performance-induced structural change. A particularly important claim is that, when applied to the study of the long run, this 'evolutionary Keynesian' framework is characterized by negative feedback: demand and institutional regimes conducive to successful macroeconomic performance are shown to give way to regimes conducive to inferior performance, and vice versa (Cornwall and Cornwall, 2001). Capitalism is, or at least has been to date, subject to alternating periods of better and worse macroeconomic performance, with each episode of good or bad performance being intimately related to the structure and performance of both its predecessor and its successor.

Outstanding Issues: Towards the Further Development and Application of Evolutionary Keynesianism

One of the hallmarks of great scholarship is that its depth and breadth should raise as well as answer important questions. It is not surprising, then, to find that Cornwall's macrodynamic vision as sketched above raises a number of issues that will continue to inspire and challenge economists for some time to come. For example, how can the contemporary macroeconomic performance of the USA relative to other OECD economies be explained within an evolutionary Keynesian framework? Is US performance embedded in an institutional structure that has relaxed the constraints on its macroeconomic policy in such a way that a sustained period of superior macroeconomic performance can be expected? Alternatively, has this institutional structure fostered the emergence of labour-intensive techniques in some sectors of the economy, which realize employment growth at the expense of productivity and (by extension) wage growth? Or is the performance of the USA something of a chimera? Could it be that institutional and hence organizational changes since the end of the Golden Age have so altered the nature of work that conventional measures of employment (based on the possession of a job) systematically understate the hours constraints under which involuntary part-time and temporary workers find themselves, and hence the effective level of unemployment?[4]

Secondly, given the emphasis on negative feedback in Cornwall's evolutionary Keynesianism and the well documented shortcomings of OECD macroeconomic performance since the early 1970s, one is tempted to ask: how bad is bad enough? In other words, what, exactly, does it take to ensure that an episode of inferior performance will give rise to the structural changes necessary for a subsequent episode of superior performance? According to Petit (1999), social solidarity during the crisis matters, but is currently lacking. We now face enhanced divisions between financial and industrial capital, the former's intolerance for inflation dominating the latter's more direct interests in the overall level of economic activity. Meanwhile, new divisions between workers have arisen, both within the workplace (the 'good job/bad job' dichotomy and the emphasis on individual as opposed to collectively determined labour market rewards) and in terms of consumption patterns. These within-group divisions are reinforced by the increasing identification of the 'aristocracy of labour', whose savings are increasingly tied to financial markets, with the interests of financial capital. In sum, the distribution of distress during periods of inferior macroeconomic performance is clearly unequal. For this reason, the ethos of individualism and the concomitant erosion of post-war social solidarity may be an important factor militating against transformational change during the current era.

Finally, and despite the better efforts of John Cornwall, it is tempting to reflect with some despair on the current state of the 'market for economic ideas', the latter having come to represent something of a monopoly, with neoliberalism deemed 'the only game in town'. Even the wealthy financier George Soros has found fault with this state of affairs. Soros argues that neoliberalism has become a new fundamentalism which, like any form of monotheism, represents a threat to the Popperian ideal of an 'open society' (see, for example, Cross and Strachan, 1999). Clearly, then, great importance attaches at this juncture to explicit recognition of the prescriptive functions of an economist, if the hegemony of neoliberalism and the accompanying denial of the existence and/or viability of other economic and social models is to be redressed. This theme, of course, brings us back full circle to the notion of taking economics seriously, of recognizing the social significance of the discipline and its power to affect the lives of others. If this is, indeed, something that is now increasingly important for us to contemplate, then at least we are afforded the advantage of having, in John Cornwall, an exemplary role model.

Acknowledgements

This chapter is based on my opening remarks in the session commemorating the publication of *Growth, Employment and Inflation: Essays in Honour of John Cornwall* (London, Macmillan, 1999). I would like to thank John Cornwall for his comments on an earlier draft of this chapter.

Notes

1. Despite this change in emphasis, Cornwall has continued to publish a series of stimulating articles in journals, frequently in collaboration with his wife Wendy. See, for example, Cornwall and Cornwall, (1994; 1997).
2. Nowhere is this more apparent than in his latest work (Cornwall and Cornwall, 2001).
3. This issue is, of course, related to the importance of demand in Cornwall's work, as discussed earlier.
4. Problems associated with discouraged workers and the under-utilization of the skills (and resulting under-employment) of some workers compound these measurement problems.

References

Cornwall, J. (1972) *Growth and Stability in a Mature Economy*, London, Martin Robertson.

Cornwall, J. and Cornwall, W. (1994) 'Growth theory and economic structure', *Economica*, 61:237–51.

Cornwall, J. and Cornwall, W. (1997) '*The unemployment problem and the legacy of Keynes*', *Journal of Post Keynesian Economics*, 19:525–42.

Cornwall, J. and Cornwall, W. (2001) *Capitalist Development in the Twentieth Century: An Evolutionary–Keynesian Analysis*, Cambridge, Cambridge University Press.

Cross, R. and Strachan D. (1999) 'Soros on "free market equilibria" ' in M. Setterfield (ed.) *Growth, Employment and Inflation: Essays in Honour of John Cornwall*, London, Macmillan, pp. 27–40.

Harcourt, G. C. and Monadjemi, M. (1999) 'The vital contributions of John Cornwall to economic theory and policy: a tribute from two admiring friends on the occasion of his 70th birthday' in M. Setterfield (ed.) *Growth, Employment and Inflation: Essays in Honour of John Cornwall*, London, Macmillan, pp. 10–23.

Petit, P. (1999) 'The reconstruction of full employment: a policy challenge for Europe', CEPREMAP Working Paper, October 1999.

Setterfield, M. (ed.) (1999) *Growth, Employment and Inflation: Essays in Honour of John Cornwall*, London, Macmillan.

Index